GROUNDED

GROUNDED

The Case for Abolishing the United States Air Force

ROBERT M. FARLEY

UNIVERSITY PRESS OF KENTUCKY

Scholarly publisher for the Commonwealth,
serving Bellarmine University, Berea College, Centre College of Kentucky,
Eastern Kentucky University, The Filson Historical Society, Georgetown
College, Kentucky Historical Society, Kentucky State University, Morehead
State University, Murray State University, Northern Kentucky University,
Transylvania University, University of Kentucky, University of Louisville,
and Western Kentucky University.
All rights reserved.

Editorial and Sales Offices: The University Press of Kentucky
663 South Limestone Street, Lexington, Kentucky 40508-4008
www.kentuckypress.com

Library of Congress Cataloging-in-Publication Data

Farley, Robert M.
 Grounded : the case for abolishing the United States Air Force / Robert M.
Farley.
    p cm — (Studies in conflict, diplomacy and peace)
 Includes bibliographical references and index.
 ISBN 978-0-8131-4495-5 (hardcover : alk. paper) — ISBN 978-0-8131-4496-2 (pdf) —
 ISBN 978-0-8131-4497-9 (epub)
  1. United States. Air Force—Reorganization. 2. United States—Military
policy—21st century. 3. Air power—United States 4. United States. Air
Force—History—20th century. I. Title. II. Title: Case for abolishing the United
States Air Force.
 UG633.F35 2014
 358.4'168670973—dc23   2013045094

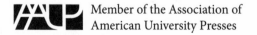

Contents

Illustrations follow page 122

Introduction

In April 2009, Secretary of Defense Robert Gates made clear his plans to cut production of the F-22 Raptor to 187 planes. The Raptor, a stealthy fifth-generation fighter with extraordinary speed and maneuverability, had made no contribution to the wars in Iraq or Afghanistan, despite a price tag of around $150 million.[1]

Advocates argue that the Raptor, designed for high-intensity conflict against peer competitors, will have its day. However, over the past sixty years a disturbing number of expensive United States Air Force (USAF) aircraft have never seen combat. The USAF bought 384 B-36 Peacemaker bombers in the 1940s and 1950s. None ever dropped a bomb in anger, even over Korea. None of the 2032 B-47 Stratojets ever saw action. Twenty-six of the 116 fast, beautiful B-58 Hustlers crashed, but none ever caused any damage to an enemy. Not one of 342 F-106 Delta Darts saw combat in Vietnam or in any other theater.

More modern aircraft have surely done better; the B-1B Lancer and the B-2 Spirit, extraordinarily expensive bombers intended for missions against targets deep in the Soviet Union, now drop bombs on lightly armed insurgents in Afghanistan.[2] Moreover, other services sometimes have the same problem; few of the navy's fleet of ballistic missile submarines have ever launched a missile at a live target. Nevertheless, a clear pattern has emerged in the sixty-five years of air force history. The USAF has built itself around a vision of warfare that does not, despite tremendous investment, meet the defense needs of the United States.

The United States needs airpower, but not an air force. While every military mission requires aircraft, the country does not need an independent military organization dedicated to the employment of airpower. Granting independence to the U.S. Air Force was a mistake in 1947, and maintaining the USAF remains a mistake today. The air force won its independence on theories of the decisive effect of airpower on war but has

1

failed to justify its own existence in war. The U.S. Air Force should be abolished, and its assets divided between the army and the navy.

REVISITING OLD DEBATES

Why waste time on "dead arguments with dead men"?[3] Men may die, but airpower theory endures, the arguments recurring generationally with only mild tweaks. While the experience of World War II decisively discredited the ideas of early airpower prophets such as Italian general Giulio Douhet and American aviator Billy Mitchell, modern advocates declare that "unquestionably Douhet's theories of airpower employment have become more accurate as time has passed."[4] Similarly, the idea of a crisis of American airpower is not new.[5] The practical failure of the long-standing theories behind air warfare should force both strategists and policymakers to revisit the foundations of airpower. Consequently, this book revisits the institutional history of the two independent air forces most associated with airpower theory, the Royal Air Force and the U.S. Air Force.

This book takes a Clausewitzian approach to argue that the current structure of U.S. military institutions has formed a straitjacket around American airpower. The extraordinary effectiveness of military aviation and the revolution that the aircraft has wrought (and rewrought) on military affairs cannot be plausibly denied. However, the promise that airpower can deliver quick, cheap, decisive victories has made military action seem excessively attractive to civilian policymakers. Air force fixation on strategic missions has meant that U.S. tactical airpower has suffered, making American uses of force less effective. Finally, the independent existence of the air force distorts procurement in that the missions the USAF favors receive financial support above and beyond their proven effectiveness.

AIRPOWER THEORY AND THE NATURE OF WAR

In the wake of the Napoleonic Wars, Carl von Clausewitz wrote *On War*, an extensive treatise on the basic principles of armed political conflict between nations. Published posthumously in 1832, *On War* offers numerous insights into the nature of conflict, including the connection between war and politics, the concept of victory in war, and the inevitability of friction, or the "fog of war." Clausewitz argued that war is an extension of politics, and thus that all acts of violence must have political purpose. The ultimate purpose of war is to disarm the enemy, at which point it can no longer continue to fight. Furthermore, uncertainty makes prediction about the outcome of war difficult.[6]

Clausewitz's treatise, enormously influential in the late nineteenth century, remains widely read today. Some have misinterpreted the text as advocating the kind of "total war" theory that held on the Western Front during World War I, where the German, French, and British armies slogged through the trenches for four years. The experience of the Western Front and other World War I battlegrounds seared a generation of military officers and civilian policymakers, who sought ways to avoid such stalemates in the future. Some, such as B. H. Liddell Hart and J. F. C. Fuller, saw promise in the advent of armored mobile warfare. Others sought to outlaw war altogether.[7] Still others argued that aviation held the potential to completely revolutionize warfare, rendering the destruction of enemy armies unnecessary and inefficient.[8]

This book focuses on the last group. Some aviators (such as USAF officers John Boyd and John Warden), have engaged with Clausewitz explicitly, others implicitly.[9] Writ large, however, strategic airpower theory rejects Clausewitz. In effect, airpower advocates aspired to silence Clausewitz in World War I, to render him obsolete in World War II, to ignore him in Korea, to co-opt him in the wake of Vietnam, and to celebrate his demise after the first Gulf War.[10] This response to Clausewitz is both cause and effect of the larger institutional story of Anglo-American airpower, and has not gone unnoticed within the USAF.[11] The rejection of the Clausewitzian approach to war led to the pursuit of a system of airpower organization that could escape the traditional fetters of military conflict. Freed from the need to support land and sea forces, independent air forces might bring about decision in war without needing to destroy enemy armies and navies. Aircraft could attack the enemy center of gravity directly by destroying civilian morale, industrial war-making capability, and leadership infrastructure.

As institutionally manifested in the Royal Air Force and the U.S. Air

Force, airpower theory disregards three of Clausewitz's dicta at its peril. First, airpower theorists have consistently rejected the need for decisive battle against the fielded forces of the enemy.[12] This leaves the decision to terminate war in the hands of a still-armed enemy, which acts according to its own logic. Second, airpower theory puts technology and military theory before politics, disregarding the inevitable political logic of war. The availability of technology and the need for autonomy drive procurement and doctrine, leaving air forces ill suited for the conflicts they actually face. Finally, and perhaps most important, airpower theory has repeatedly failed to take into account the "fog of war," Clausewitz's metaphorical appreciation of the role that complexity and uncertainty play in war. Aviators argue that modern technology can pierce the fog of war, precisely targeting not just critical enemy industry and communications but also the enemy's will to fight.[13] This radically understates the complexity of social and organizational systems, leading to wildly optimistic assessments of the utility of force.

THE CONSEQUENCES OF AIR FORCE INDEPENDENCE

This book tells a fundamentally institutional story of modern airpower. Aviators have insisted that they need independent air forces from which they can fight unfettered by the demands of soldiers and sailors.[14] They have argued that these air forces can win wars decisively and on the cheap.[15] More than any other reason, aviation enthusiasts have argued for the necessity of creating independent air forces in order to free airpower from the constraints created by other services. Airpower advocacy has had an essentially *institutional* object, and institutional victories have led to significant changes in the way nations fight wars. The effort to detach airpower from other forms of military power serves to damage national security in three ways.

First, acting in accordance with the bureaucratic logic of autonomy, aviators tend to prefer airpower missions that grant the greatest independence from other services and that allow the strongest claim on resources. Accordingly, air forces resist missions like close air support and air mobility, which place them at the mercy of ground commanders, preferring missions like strategic bombing, which can be conducted with minimal interference or input from other services.[16] This leaves air forces poorly prepared to support other services when strategic bombing fails or when the political situation demands limited force. For example, the focus of the U.S. Air Force on a nuclear strategic bombing campaign against the Soviet Union left it materially and doctrinally unprepared to fight the air war over Korea or to support U.S. soldiers and Marines against the Viet Cong.[17]

Second, independent air forces have a distorting fiscal effect. Organizations require funding, the development of a permanent bureaucracy, and a position within the constellation of national security institutions. This creates interest groups within government for pursuing the priorities that the departments represent. Consequently, the creation of an independent air force represents an investment of material resources in the concept of airpower. On the fiscal side, this involves not only administrative costs but also the financial commitment generated by creating an organization with its own procurement demands. In the United States, for example, the bureaucratic and lobbying power of the air force earns it a substantial and consistent share of overall military procurement funds, no matter the dictates of politics or technology.

Finally, the most serious effect of creating an independent air force may be political. Just as bureaucratic independence creates a fiscal presence within government, it creates a political interest group focused on parochial airpower interests. Almost all arguments regarding the decisiveness of airpower have suggested that airpower can win victories more quickly, and at lower cost, than other military options. These claims have the political effect of making war seem cheap and easy and consequently may have the effect of making civilians more likely to choose military options.

THE PROPOSAL

Airpower is critical to the national security of the United States, but bureaucratic infighting and historical legacies hamstring the ability of airpower to interact with the rest of the American national security state. These problems will grow as the air force extends its approach to airpower into the space and cyber realms. Consequently, this book argues that the

U.S. Air Force should cease to exist and that USAF assets, including aircraft, weapons, personnel, bases, and missions, should be divided across the remaining services. Four principles should drive this reallocation:

- Principle of organic mission: Each service should, insofar as possible, organically include the assets necessary to undertake its most likely missions. No reorganization can completely eliminate the need for jointness, but the best structures minimize the need for crossing service boundaries in the normal course of events.

- Principle of redundancy: When possible, the potential for redundant capabilities between army and navy air assets should be retained. For critical missions, each service should have the capability to cover the shortfalls of the other.

- Principle of efficiency: As much as possible, reorganization should favor a more efficient distribution of assets and responsibilities, resulting in the elimination of unnecessary maintenance, administration, and other costs.

- Principle of organizational culture: Divisions of responsibility should take into account the necessity for each service to establish and maintain a healthy organizational culture, built around a coherent vision.

This reorganization would create a reborn U.S. Army Air Corps, institutionally committed to the development of airpower but detached from the destructive strategic culture that created the USAF and caused considerable intraservice grief in the 1930s and 1940s. The need to eliminate this culture, based on the idea that airpower is fundamentally different than other forms of military power, is why this book proposes to fold the air force into the army, rather than the other way around. This organization would retain the writ of developing aerospace doctrine, managing aircraft procurement, and training pilots and aircrew, and would also take responsibility for army rotary aviation. The army air corps would preserve insofar as appropriate the principle of centralized command and decentralized execution while more tightly connecting both command and execution to the needs of nonaviation forces.[18]

THE PLAN OF THIS BOOK

The first part of this book sets forth a theory of institutional structure and organizational culture that seeks to explain why independent military organizations exist, how they understand their role in the world, and how airpower fits into modern military thought. Chapter 1 investigates the development of independent military services through history and the phenomenon of interservice conflict. The second chapter probes air force culture, draws explicit and implicit contrasts between airpower advocates and Carl von Clausewitz, and argues that the pursuit of independent air forces tends to create anti-Clausewitzian doctrine and force structure. Chapter 3 explores the legal and moral issues concerning the use of airpower, including a discussion of how "lawfare" increasingly limits the circumstances for appropriate airpower use.

The second part of the book tells the story of the rise and potential fall of the U.S. Air Force, making the case that the Clausewitzian problems associated with an independent air force recur repeatedly throughout U.S. airpower history. Chapter 4 concentrates on the Royal Air Force and the lessons that Americans learned from the British experience, while chapter 5 traces the evolution of American airpower from World War I until the advent of the Cold War. Chapter 6 evaluates the USAF's first four decades of independence, up to and including the 1991 Gulf War. Chapter 7 explores modern American airpower, including the current state of air-ground and air-sea cooperation. Chapter 8 examines the issues associated with the advent of drone warfare. Chapter 9 explores alternatives to the current structure of American military airpower, comparing U.S. institutions to foreign contemporaries and suggesting a series of institutional reforms. I conclude by arguing that the United States can undertake a transformation similar to that of the Canadian Forces, folding the constituent parts of the USAF back into the navy and army.

1

American Airpower
and the Military Services

Bureaucracy may be boring, but it matters for policy. The modern state has grown into a vast collection of bureaucratic institutions, each tasked with certain critical jobs.[1] Inside and outside the state, individuals, interest groups, and bureaucratic organizations strive against one another for influence and resources. In the United States, Congress, the White House, the State Department, the Pentagon, the various organs of the intelligence community, and each of the military services contribute to national security policy. The arrangement of these organizations matters for how the policymaking process plays out.

While the fundamental purpose of foreign policy and military organizations is to disarm enemies, deter aggressors, safeguard commerce, pierce the fog of war, and defend whatever other interests are deemed crucial to national survival and prosperity, each organization sees the world in a particular way, and each tends to seek to maximize its own influence and autonomy.[2] The importance of specific organizations for policy often depends on the personality and background of the executive as well as the relationships between major policymakers. However, the simple fact of an organization's existence can grant it a "seat at the table," through which it can have an impact on policy. Institutional design thus privileges certain foreign policies and forms of war at the expense of others. Organizations working together suffer from what Clausewitz terms "friction," the inability of the component parts to function together seamlessly.[3]

The themes of organizational conflict and airpower culture have played out in the recent history of U.S. airpower cooperation. While airpower parochialism may seem a theme of the distant past (dead arguments by dead men), the organizational structure of the U.S. military continues to support a vision of airpower that creates substantial problems for U.S. war fighting, procurement, and international influence. This chapter introduces the institutions of American airpower, their assets, and their missions. It reviews the logics of air force independence and ends with a discussion of interservice conflict.

AMERICAN AIRPOWER

Airpower provides the foundation for modern American military strength. The national security services of the United States currently operate at least six distinct air forces, with roughly 16,000 aircraft between them. These air forces offer platforms, bases, weapons, and training procedures. Nevertheless, each air force exists within the cultural milieu of its own service, subject to the preferences and priorities of its parent organization.

The present distribution of airpower across military institutions was produced by the National Security Act of 1947, passed in response to postwar changes in the international system and to a revised vision of the role that the United States could play on the international stage.[4] Congress revised this system on several occasions during the Cold War (most notably in 1986, with the Goldwater-Nichols Act), but the basic institutional framework of the U.S. military remains as established in 1947. The U.S. Air Force formally came into being in the National Security Act of 1947, which also created the National Military Establishment (NME, including both the army and the navy). In 1949, the NME became the Department of Defense. The 1947 act also created the National Security Council and the Central Intelligence Agency.

The U.S. Army operates roughly 180 fixed-wing aircraft (mostly dedicated to training and transport), and nearly 5,000 helicopters. These aircraft undertake transport, reconnaissance, close air support, and some interdiction missions. Agreements with the U.S. Air Force limit the bulk of army aviation missions to helicopters, with a few allowances made for fixed-wing service aircraft.

The U.S. Navy (USN) operates over 3,700 aircraft, including 3,000 fixed wing and more than 600 helicopters. USN aviation operates from ships (aircraft carriers and other vessels) and from land bases, and conducts virtually every airpower mission, including air superiority, countersea, interdiction, reconnaissance, counterland, and air transport.

The U.S. Marine Corps (USMC), although formally part of the U.S. Navy, operates its own air force consisting of nearly 600 fixed-wing aircraft and another 600 helicopters. Marine aviation has developed expertise in missions that support fielded infantry, including reconnaissance, air transport, close air support, and battlefield interdiction. The Marine Air Ground Task Force (MAGTF) provides the foundation of USMC aviation capability.

The U.S. Coast Guard, although not part of the Department of Defense, operates about 200 aircraft, including fixed-wing transport and patrol aircraft and a wide variety of helicopters. These aircraft mostly conduct countersea operations, including reconnaissance, rescue, and patrol.

The Central Intelligence Agency operates an unknown number of aircraft, including helicopters, drones, reconnaissance aircraft, and transport aircraft. These aircraft support basic CIA operations (reconnaissance, transport) as well as conduct strategic air campaigns in Pakistan, Yemen, Somalia, and elsewhere. CIA aviation operates in a different legal and political environment than the other U.S. air forces but uses many of the same platforms and conducts many similar missions.

Finally, the U.S. Air Force employs 330,000 personnel and operates roughly 5,600 aircraft, mostly fixed wing. The U.S. Air Force conducts every airpower mission, although it relies on other organizations to undertake the bulk of certain tasks (battlefield transport, countersea operations). The U.S. Air Force also takes responsibility for most American military space assets.

In addition, the various Reserve and National Guard forces associated with the services operate aircraft and personnel. The aircraft associated with these forces fall under the totals of the parent services (Air National Guard and U.S. Air Force, for example), but responsibilities for maintenance and some training remain separate.

This system is best described as the result of evolution rather than intelligent design. When the air force left the army in 1947, the services tried to settle the distribution of air capabilities between them. However, changes in technology, not to mention bureaucratic turf fights, have caused extensive changes over the years, changes often resolved by political power rather than careful analysis. (Chapter 5 details the prehistory of the air force and the process through which it won independence, while chapter 6 examines how the fights for turf and autonomy between the services have played out since 1947.)

THE USES OF AIRPOWER

Aircraft have proven devastating weapons of war, performing many different military missions since their invention. Understanding the missions that aircraft perform is important to appreciating the problems associated with interservice conflict and friction. This section describes the most commonly accepted military uses of aircraft.

Close Air Support

Close air support involves "air action by fixed-wing and rotary-wing aircraft against hostile targets that are in close proximity to friendly forces, and requires detailed integration of each air mission with the fire and movement of those forces."[5] Air units destroy or suppress enemy ground forces, allowing friendly ground units to win engagements.[6] Close air support has been part of virtually every conflict involving aerial units since the First World War. Over time, technological improvements have made close air support more effective but more dangerous.[7] Precision-guided munitions (PGMs) launched by aircraft make the destruction of enemy vehicles and the suppression of enemy strongpoints less difficult. On the other hand, the effectiveness of antiaircraft artillery and surface-to-air missiles (SAMs) have made close air support perilous for many pilots and aircraft. With the development of PGMs launched from standoff ranges (beyond the effective reach of antiaircraft artillery and SAM batteries), modern aircraft can effectively conduct close air support from a distance. The future of close air support may involve fleets of armed and unarmed drones backed up by conventional manned aircraft carrying heavy ordnance.[8]

Interdiction

Interdiction involves the disruption of enemy lines of supply and reinforcement.[9] Modern armies face enormous logistical challenges, and the maintenance of an army in a prolonged engagement requires a continual stream of reinforcement and support. Airpower conducts interdiction by attacking the ability of fielded armies to keep themselves resupplied and reinforced.[10] This can involve direct attacks against supply trains and dumps but also assaults against the infrastructure (roads, bridges, railways) needed to support forces in the field. The borders between close air support and tactical interdiction are often indistinct, and at times concepts like "battlefield air interdiction" have described the overlap and delineated responsibilities.[11] A tactical interdiction campaign can also overlap with a strategic bombing campaign against infrastructure, in that both strike the same target set. Operational intent differs, however, in that the strategic campaign targets civilian and elite opinion, while the interdiction campaign targets fielded forces.

Reconnaissance

Reconnaissance is the oldest mission performed by air units. The earliest use of balloons in war came during the Napoleonic Wars, when balloons were used to identify enemy troop movements and to spot artillery. In every war of consequence since then, air units have been used for reconnaissance purposes. In the modern context, much of the reconnaissance portfolio once conducted by aircraft now belongs to space assets.[12] Nevertheless, many aircraft, including drones, continue to perform reconnaissance over battlefields and other potential areas of concern. Reconnaissance can include large-scale strategic intelligence operations (such as U-2 and SR-71 flights over the Soviet Union) and small-scale tactical operations (drones loitering over a battlefield or searching for terrorists in the wilds of Pakistan).

Air Mobility

In its technical sense, air mobility involves the delivery of troops and supplies from one location to another. Such operations can vary drastically in scale, from the movement of company-level (200-soldier) U.S. Army units in Vietnam to the resupply of entire German divisions on the

Eastern Front in World War II. Modern air mobility can be divided into two types: strategic airlift (the delivery of large concentrations of troops and equipment around the world in a short period of time) and tactical air mobility (helicopters or other aircraft moving small units around the battle space).[13] As the technical capabilities of aircraft have improved, and as small groups of soldiers (Special Forces, for example) have increased in lethality, air mobility has become a more important mission. Similarly, the shift to counterinsurgency wars in preference to conventional set-piece battles emphasizes the relevance of tactical air mobility.

Countersea

Countersea operations cover a variety of different missions that land- or sea-based aircraft perform in the maritime domain.[14] These include attacks against surface ships, antisubmarine warfare, and maritime versions of reconnaissance and air superiority. Since the First World War, air units have played a key role in naval warfare, both in terms of protecting maritime commerce from attack and conducting attacks on enemy surface naval forces. In the Second World War, aircraft played the crucial role in winning major naval engagements in both the Atlantic and Pacific. In the second battle of the Atlantic (the German effort in World War II to starve Britain into submission), aircraft gave a crucial edge to Allied antisubmarine forces.[15] In the Cold War period, the United States built its navy around the concept of aerial countersea missions, flying primarily from large-deck U.S. aircraft carriers.

Strategic Bombing

Strategic bombing takes several different forms. One form, adopted by both sides in World War II, involved direct attacks against concentrations of enemy civilians. These attacks were intended to lower civilian morale and to encourage the populace to withdraw its support for the enemy government.[16] Luftwaffe attacks on London in 1940 and 1941 represent one example of a campaign of this type, while the Royal Air Force (RAF) bombing of Germany and the U.S. Army Air Forces (USAAF) bombing of Japan represent campaigns with similar objectives. The combatants in World War II also engaged in attacks that targeted enemy centers of industry or key economic resources in order to reduce the economic output of the enemy country. Precision daylight bombing by the USAAF against German industry in World War II is the most famous example of an economically targeted strategic air campaign.[17]

Infrastructure-oriented strategic bombing targets key transit and communications nodes in an effort to grind a target economy to a halt without completely destroying its economic capacity. Infrastructure bombing can also aim to reduce civilian morale and interdict enemy forces in the field. Infrastructure attacks have been a major focus of strategic bombing campaigns since the Cold War. The U.S. air campaigns against Iraq in 1991 and Serbia in 1999 and the Israeli campaign against Lebanon in 2006 primarily targeted transportation and communications infrastructure.[18] Precision-guided munitions enhance the effectiveness of such campaigns by making it easier to hit small targets like bridges and roadways.

"Decapitation" targets the enemy leadership in an effort to either kill key individuals or isolate them from power. The idea that certain individuals are crucial to enemy operations motivates a decapitation campaign. Such campaigns depend on precise intelligence about the location of targeted subjects. The United States attempted to decapitate the Iraqi regime in 2003 by killing Saddam Hussein in the opening stages of the war, but failed.[19] The Russian Federation successfully decapitated the Chechen resistance government by killing President Dzhokar Dudayev in 1996, although the resistance persisted for several years.[20]

Air Superiority

Air superiority involves control of the airspace, enabling friendly aircraft to conduct their missions and preventing enemy aircraft from conducting theirs.[21] Air superiority very often involves air-to-air combat but can also include operations against enemy air defense networks and against enemy airbases. Air superiority can be divided into a number of different submissions, including interception, bomber escort, electronic warfare, and SEAD (suppression of enemy air defense) attacks.[22]

The Justifications for Air Force Independence

Air force independence was controversial from the start. The appendix of a British Air Ministry memorandum of June 1921, entitled "Some Arguments for and against a Separate Air Force," detailed seven arguments against independence.[23] In this section, I boil these arguments down to five rationales for air force independence. Some of these rationales speak directly to the idea of an independent air force, while others justify bureaucratic division in a more general sense. The most important rationales for air force independence are that operations in *different media* require different services (the division between earth, air, and water means that we need three services); that service differentiation should depend on the ability to *plan and conduct independent campaigns;* that the need for *redundancy in critical capabilities* should guide division of service responsibilities; that states should *follow the leaders,* looking for international cues regarding how to organize their defense establishments; and that national and organizational *tradition* should inform service divisions. In this section I examine all of these rationales, arguing that none can fully justify the existence of independent air forces.

The Medium Makes the Service

Airpower advocates have long argued that the medium of the air requires a different set of professional and strategic skills than the media of land or sea.[24] There is much to recommend this argument. Military professionals specializing in air operations do indeed require different skills than artillery officers in the army or submarine officers in the navy. Maintenance and procurement of equipment also depend on knowledge of the technical details of flying. Pilots have a better sense of what makes an aircraft or weapon effective than a soldier who has never flown.

However, airpower advocates take this argument too far. First, every modern military service includes a number of jobs that require distinct professional skills. For example, the submariner in the U.S. Navy cannot easily transfer to the surface fleet without considerable training. Armor officers in the army have different skills than infantry or artillery officers. These officers are capable of working in the same service because while their professional and technical skills differ, their military skills are compatible and substantially similar.

Independent armies and navies arose during a period (the age of sail) in which the difference between naval and military professionalism was at its zenith. Skills useful for naval warfare were not useful for land warfare and vice versa. In the modern context, this is less true. The advance of technology has universalized the *military* skill set even as it has led to a profusion of specialized technical professions under the military rubric.[25] Individual military officers will differ widely in terms of their vocational expertise, but they generally share a similar set of *professional military skills*, which involve a mastery of systems of military thinking and analysis. In the terminology of Sam Huntington, professional military officers all share a relationship with the state, with enlisted personnel, and with one other.[26] "Joint" service requirements in the U.S. military after Goldwater-Nichols have reinforced this shared sense of military professionalism.[27]

Mission Autonomy

The most common, and most important, justification for air service independence elevates the concept of mission autonomy. Under this logic, military services derive their independence from the ability to plan and conduct major campaigns according to their own strategic conceptions.[28] The infantry branch of the U.S. Army cannot wage war on its own but requires the close cooperation of armor, artillery, and a variety of other suborganizations in order to do its job. An air force, on the other hand, can conceptualize war independent of the projection of land power, just as a navy can develop a campaign that never touches the shore. At the borders these distinctions break down (an air force requires land bases that require land defense, for example), but the mission justification nevertheless provides some traction on the question of whether a particular military subunit deserves full autonomy.

As later chapters will detail, the logic of mission autonomy was used widely during the interwar period to defend RAF independence and to advocate USAF independence.[29] Strategic bombing does not simply promise to end wars with a minimum of fuss and muss; it allows an air force to plan and conduct a full campaign without more than cursory use of either army or navy assets. Airpower advocates such as Billy Mitchell, Giulio Douhet, and Hugh Trenchard insisted repeatedly on the necessity for independent air forces to plan and wage strategic bombing campaigns in order to win wars.[30] Moreover, they contended that as long as airpower was subjected to the parochial interest of army and naval officers, the doctrine and equipment necessary for truly independent, decisive, war-winning strategic campaigns would not be available.[31]

Justification of service independence in terms of mission creates at least two problems. First, when the independence of an organization depends on its ability to develop its own autonomous capabilities and doctrine, it has little incentive to work with other organizations on missions that may require joint action. Unsurprisingly, airpower advocates focused on strategic bombing (a mission requiring minimal collaboration with land or sea assets) tended to neglect missions that did require cooperation with military and naval organizations. Second, as technology developed in ways that failed to conform to organizational roles, the walls that exist between military organizations tended to become confused. The development of ballistic missiles, for example, left the three U.S. services at a loss as to responsibility.[32] The U.S. military has attempted to address these issues through a series of ad hoc agreements between the services and finally through the legislative hammer of "jointness," an effort to force the military organizations to work more closely with one another in the wake of failures in Iran and Grenada.[33] Jointness became an important objective of U.S. military policy after the Goldwater-Nichols Department of Defense Reorganization Act of 1986.[34]

Organizational Redundancy

Organizational redundancy represents another justification for air force independence. The organizational redundancy argument calls for embedding key capabilities in several different military organizations in order to avoid failure.[35] Military organizations fail often, and for a variety of reasons.[36] Some choose poor equipment, others have destructive internal conflicts, and yet others have made improper doctrinal decisions.[37] Embedding a key war-fighting capability in only a single organization runs the risk of national disaster. Daniel Drezner makes a case for the redundancy argument in the context of terrorism:

> Say a single bureaucracy is tasked with intelligence gathering about threat X. Let's say this bureaucracy represents the best of the best of the best—the A-Team. The A-Team does its job and catches 95% of the emergent threats from X. That's still 5% that

is missed. Now say you have another independent bureaucracy with a similar remit. This agency is staffed by different people with their own set of blind spots. Let's even stipulate that we're talking about the B-team here, and they'll only catch 80% of the emergent threats from X.

If these two bureaucracies are working independently—and this is an important if—then the odds that a threat would go unobserved by both bureaucracies is $.05 * .2 = .01 = 1\%$. So, by adding another bureaucracy, even a less competent one, the chances of an undetected threat getting through are cut from 5% to 1%.[38]

This argument has some evidentiary support. In the Vietnam War, the U.S. Air Force proved inadequate at the tasks of air mobility, close air support, and air superiority. Naval, Marine, and army aviation helped fill this gap.[39] Naval aviation proved more adept at fighting North Vietnamese air assets than its air force counterparts. Marine aviation concentrated on the provision of close air support to Marines engaged in direct combat. Army aviation proved very innovative in bringing the helicopter both to the close air support and air mobility missions.

However, the argument also poses some logical challenges. As justification for an independent air force, the redundancy argument does not discriminate between a single independent air arm and air assets spread across several organizations. In the Korean War, the smaller air assets controlled by the army, navy, and Marine Corps successfully remedied air force inadequacy by concentrating on missions specific to their organizational responsibilities.[40] Moreover, many critical assets do not benefit from any kind of organizational redundancy. The United States has not seen fit to equip its Coast Guard with submarines in order to guard against the failure of the USN. On land, the USMC and the U.S. Army do enjoy some degree of organizational redundancy, but this relationship has not always worked to the benefit of doctrine.[41] Some historians argue, for example, that collaboration with the U.S. Army in Vietnam actively made the USMC worse at its job.[42] Finally, the redundancy argument runs up against a concrete fiscal problem. Each redundant capability increases cost, not simply in the capability itself but also in the administrative and organizational structure needed to maintain the capability. Moreover, every organization created on the behalf of redundancy adds another bureaucratic actor lobbying for funds and for a piece of the wartime action.

Institutional Isomorphism

While the precise division of responsibilities between organizations varies across the world, no observer can miss a considerable degree of similarity in global military establishments. Virtually every country in the world operates according to a similar set of ranks and with similarly sized units. Variation notwithstanding, the world's 182 countries do not have 182 separate and distinct military systems. Rather, military organizations come to resemble each other in form and structure over time. Organizational theorists refer to this phenomenon as institutional isomorphism. Institutional isomorphism happens for two reasons. First, the dangers of the international system can force all states to evolve in a particular direction.[43] In order to survive, states need armies and these armies perform well when they have certain characteristics. This is the neorealist logic for isomorphism: states trying to survive will become functionally similar. An alternative logic for isomorphism is known as "world society." Operating according to a sociological logic, the world society argument suggests that there are templates of "appropriateness" that states take into account when designing their institutions.[44] Why does virtually every state have a navy, including landlocked countries? Because global norms of appropriateness suggest that modern, legitimate nation-states have navies, even if they cannot use them. In the context of this argument, states create independent air forces because other states have independent air forces.

This argument both explains the existence of independent air forces and provides a reason for creating such an organization. If the United Kingdom has an independent air force, airpower advocates in the United States can point to the "successful" example of British military power, arguing that the United States risks being left behind if it lacks such a force. During the Cold War, the Soviet Union and the United States sometimes created "mirror image" institutions out of competitive concern.[45] Similarly, when postcolonial states achieve their independence, they take cues from modern, wealthy, successful states regarding how to structure their military organizations. For example, India and Pakistan adopted military structures substantially similar to that of the United Kingdom because of the heritage of British colonialism.[46] The creation of the Royal Air Force quickly spurred South Africa, Canada, Australia, and New Zealand to create their own independent air forces.[47] Moreover, adopting the international standard can make military cooperation, integration, and procurement much easier for states and can reduce the amount of information that governments need to collect about alternative institutional models. Finally, some research indicates that the push for institutional isomorphism may come directly from military officers who develop expectations about their professional futures from observing similarly placed personnel in other states.[48]

However, there are limits to the virtues of a "follow the leader" strategy. First and foremost, some states, by virtue of their size, wealth, and importance, *are* the leaders. A decision on the part of the United States to abolish its independent air force might incline other countries to consider doing the same. Had the British not granted independence to the Royal Air Force, the Dominion forces would probably not have come into existence in quick succession. Similarly, the French, German, and U.S. air forces might not have won independence when they did. A "follow the leader" strategy can give important clues to small or new states trying to design their military organizations and can provide indicators of success to larger countries concerned about their security. However, emulation for the sake of parity does not always represent the best strategy for cutting-edge military establishments.

Tradition

A final argument justifying the independent air force invokes tradition. Many military organizations enjoy long traditions and appeal to these traditions in an instrumental way. A sense of history explains to new recruits how they fit within the body of the organization. As R. Lee Ermey memorably put it in *Full Metal Jacket*: "Today, you people are no longer maggots. Today, you are Marines. You're part of a brotherhood. From now on until the day you die, wherever you are, every Marine is your brother. Most of you will go to Vietnam. Some of you will not come back. But always remember this: Marines die. That's what we're here for. But the Marine Corps lives forever. And that means *you* live forever."[49]

This perspective suggests that whatever administrative or other gains might be reaped by amalgamation of services would be overwhelmed by the loss of esprit de corps associated with the elimination of an old service.[50] While scholars can imagine perfect constellations of military power for particular times and places, organizations are made of people and their dissolution will have human consequences. Experienced officers may retire, instability may frighten off new recruits and, in general, readiness and capability may suffer. At an extreme the tradition argument may seem to suggest "If it ain't broke, don't fix it," but a reasonable interpretation might be "Even if it's broke, some fixes may make things worse." Whatever the theoretical problems with granting air force independence in 1947, folding the service today into the army and navy would serve little purpose beyond generating chaos.

Although this perspective has some compelling elements, it also has some serious limitations. Military organizations undergo traumatic cultural transformations on a regular basis. For example, the U.S. Army suffered from the diminution of the role of cavalry in the twentieth century, while the U.S. Navy endured the obsolescence of the battleship. More recently, the U.S. Army had to transition from a conscript to an all-volunteer professional force. While none of these crises of identity quite rises to the level of eliminating an entire branch of service, they do suggest that military organizations can survive and thrive after major cultural transitions. More important, taken too far, the logic of service tradition can lead to bad decisions about technology, modernization, and doctrine. The U.S. Army had a long and proud tradition of cavalry warfare in the nineteenth and twentieth centuries, which it abandoned slowly and under considerable pressure.[51] Similarly, in the United Kingdom some officers resisted mechanization because of concerns over losing their horses.[52] The logic of tradition suggests that we should view change with caution, but caution is different than stasis.

INTERSERVICE CONFLICT AND THE DESIGN OF NEW INSTITUTIONS

Military institutions are only occasionally "designed" in the sense of policymakers trying to create an optimal division of military labor. More often, military organizations result from a clash of history and politics.

Like other institutions, military organizations often defy the efforts of policymakers (or even their own leaders) to change or restructure them. It is important not to mistake messy reality for optimal design. Today, as through history, there is no obviously ideal way to organize a nation's military forces.

On the rare occasions that policymakers have the opportunity to design or redesign institutions, they must take into account several realities of organizational behavior. As James Q. Wilson argued in his classic *Bureaucracy*, there is little support for the idea that all organizations want greater resources and more responsibilities. Rather, organizations want autonomy, or "turf." Autonomy involves control of the means through which an organization accomplishes tasks and freedom from the interests and interference of other organizations.[53] Once created, organizations tend to seek greater autonomy, although how they define this often depends on organizational culture.[54] One way in which the air force seeks to maintain its autonomy is through espousal of the principle of "centralized control, decentralized execution," wherein theater air assets come under the control of an air officer who allocates them according to local need.[55] This principle also emerges from the experience of decentralized control in World War II.[56] Organizations will tend to resent and resist intrusions into their specified bureaucratic territory and will rarely hold unbiased interpretations of their own capabilities. Organizations can lobby policymakers and other interested actors (the general public, for example) in pursuit of their preferred ends. Finally, tasks and missions that lie along the borders between organizations almost always suffer from serious coordination problems.[57]

The creation of new bureaucratic organizations invariably leads to conflict over administrative boundaries. The new organization always takes up some responsibilities of older institutions, and the full delineation of new responsibilities involves bureaucratic conflict. The development of independent air forces created particularly difficult problems. Within fifteen years of its invention, the aircraft became a key part of almost every meaningful military mission, both on land and at sea.[58] Aircraft became, if not absolutely necessary, at least very important to such traditional military tasks as reconnaissance, artillery spotting, and frontal assault. Not unlike the rifle, the mortar, or the machine gun, the aircraft became an organic part of basic military tasks. Unlike the tank, the submarine, or the artillery, however, the aircraft then received a service of its own. This made conflict between services over resource allocation, training, and procurement particularly likely.[59] To be sure, civilian policymakers have long understood that they can benefit from interservice conflict and have sometimes welcomed (and even encouraged) services to fight one another. When services attack one another, it provides rationales for cost-conscious budget cutters to kill particular programs.[60] But interservice conflict can take two forms: resource conflicts and mission conflicts. While both help civilian policymakers cut costs, they do not have the same effect on the military's overall strategic preparedness.[61]

The first type of interservice conflict, resource allocation, involves grand strategic emphasis and (as the name implies) resource conflict. Because different services perform different missions, not all contribute equally to certain grand strategic tasks. For example, the ability of the Royal Navy to commit its full strength to the war in Afghanistan is severely limited by geography, just as the ability of the British Army to contribute to the antipiracy fight in Somalia is limited by the unwillingness of the British government to seize and hold pirate havens. Interservice conflict focusing on resources, therefore, is about the prioritization of particular strategic goals. In general, services tend to support resource allocation toward goals that they can contribute to. Services, like any other bureaucratic organization, tend to believe that their own parochial goals fall in line with national security goals. Services develop arguments about strategic orientation and resource allocation that support their own organizational interests. The classic example of a resource conflict involves warship versus army brigade; the units have different capabilities, perform different jobs, and suggest a different focus for national strategic priorities.

These arguments represent a boon for civilians interested in managing strategic affairs and creating a sustainable defense budget. Civilians can borrow arguments from the services in order to politically justify reduced defense expenditures. These arguments insulate civilians from appearing weak on security issues. However, while resource conflicts have the potential to shift a nation's strategic orientation, they typically leave a military organization with a set of tools appropriate to meeting the challenge of those new strategic goals. Interservice conflict on resource allocation provides civilians with a useful tool for managing defense budgets and for keeping the military services in line. For example, in the "Revolt of the Admirals" in the United States, the U.S. Navy supplied civilians with a plethora of data on the shortcomings of the B-36 Peacemaker strategic bomber.[62]

By contrast, interservice conflicts involving mission allocation rarely create positive externalities. Warfare has required the cooperation of different military organizations for as long as professional military organizations have existed. However, in the last century the need for collaboration between air, ground, and sea assets has increased dramatically.[63] The primary driver of such integration has been the expansion of warfare into the third dimension.[64] As argued earlier, aircraft now represent an organic part of most military missions, from ground assault (close air support) and interdiction (exploitation) to antisubmarine warfare and countersea operations. Aircraft are as necessary to the efficient and successful execution of tactical and operational level military tasks as infantry, armor, and artillery. Erecting bureaucratic walls between services makes the development of tacit experiential knowledge difficult and conflict between services on emphasis, doctrine, training, and command structure inevitable.[65] Classic examples of such conflicts involve control over close air support, or control over the aircraft carrier air wings.[66] In both cases the debate regards the proper allocation of authority over an intrinsic aspect of the mission; carriers cannot operate without aircraft, nor can modern infantry brigades operate without air support.

According to historian Steven L. Rearden, "Disputes and disagreements over the respective functions of the Army and Navy did not pose a significant problem until the 20th century."[67] Army and navy officers of the Civil War might disagree with such a sweeping claim, but there is little doubt that the expansion of war into the third dimension, combined with the advocacy of airpower enthusiasts, helped to create bitter divisions within and between the services.[68] An independent air force arose from this battle with a culture inimical to cooperation with the other two services. Giulio Douhet predicted this tension and proposed to resolve it simply by making the air force dominant.[69] As later chapters will detail, this has produced a number of critical interservice conflicts that have had destructive effects on U.S. war fighting, procurement, and strategic thought.

As the complexity of military tasks has grown, organizational borders have developed between professional services. These borders both solve and create problems. Organizations inevitably focus on their preferred mode of operation and try to maximize their autonomy. This makes services very good at certain jobs and not so good at others, especially those jobs that involve collaboration with others. In the United States, the Goldwater-Nichols Act of 1986 tried, with some success, to limit the problems created by organizational boundaries.[70] However, basic institutional borders tell only half the story. Organizational culture, or the way organizations define and understand their missions, also affects how services interact with one another. In the next chapter I review the arguments that airpower advocates have made for independent air forces and also discuss the culture of airpower that permeates the USAF. Giving an air force the freedom and autonomy to pursue its own interests may have some benefits, but it reduces the ability of armies and navies to do their jobs. The question becomes a simple cost-benefit calculation: Does giving an air force independence solve more problems that it creates?

2

Air Force Independence
and Air Force Culture

The U.S. Air Force was born in a cauldron of organizational infighting. As detailed in later chapters, the RAF and USAF fought bitter battles for independence against their parent services. This chapter studies the organizational culture that emerged from that long struggle, especially in the USAF. This culture helped create and sustain the three Clausewitzian misperceptions of airpower theory, misperceptions that persist and continue to distort American national security policy. This chapter begins with a brief discussion of organizational culture, followed by analysis of how airpower theory helps produce three critical misinterpretations (decisive effect, tyranny of technology, and piercing the fog of war) of the Clausewitzian understanding of war. The chapter ends with a discussion of how an independent air force matters for making national security policy.

ORGANIZATIONAL CULTURE

Military organizations are not simply machines that can be wound up, then let loose on some particular problem. Rather, like any other large bureaucracy, they develop procedures for handling particular kinds of problems, and the people within them come to adopt particular attitudes about the world. These attitudes and approaches to problem solving constitute organizational culture.[1] Organizational culture infuses everything that a military organization does, from war planning to procurement lobbying to recruitment to relations with other bureaucracies. Organizational cultures are not static, but they do exhibit long-term continuity. Organizational culture affects how a military bureaucracy thinks about and prepares for the future and also characterizes its response to crises. In short, the behavior of military branches cannot be fully understood without an appreciation of organizational culture.[2]

Military culture stems from multiple sources. National strategic culture, or the lens through which a particular nation understands goals, interests, and threats, affects but does not constitute military culture, through complicated connections dependent on the structure of society.[3] For example, the Austro-Hungarian Army found itself riven with ethnic conflict during World War I, while many Arab armies have suffered from class conflict.[4] Colin Gray divides strategic culture broadly between "continentalist" and "maritime" states, with implications for how each handles its military organizations.[5] Many military organizations have long histories that help constitute their culture and affect their behavior. Other organizations effectively "borrow" culture from historical antecedents or competitors.[6]

Military organizations learn to approach and identify problems in particular, historically situated ways. *Frames* help an organization identify and develop answers to problems in their environment. Organizational frames include what counts as a problem, how problems are represented, the strategies to be used to solve those problems, and the constraints and requirements placed on possible solutions. As those in organizations engage in problem solving, they allocate organizational attention and resources to develop and draw on expertise inside and outside the organization, in general building organizational capacity to solve certain problems but not others.[7] Frames both focus and narrow an organization's attention. The same cultural frame that makes a military organization effective can also blind it to internal and external problems.

INDEPENDENCE AND AIR FORCE CULTURE

How does the U.S. Air Force view war, and how did those views come about? Every military organization, and indeed every bureaucratic organization, has a culture that characterizes its understanding of and approach to its environment. David Johnson describes the role of doctrine and organizational culture as

- prescribing the shared worldview and values as well as the "proper" methods, tools, techniques, and approaches to problem solving within and among the services;
- providing a way in which the services view themselves;
- governing how the services deal with each other and with other governmental and nongovernmental agencies;
- prescribing the questions and the answers that are considered acceptable within the institution or school of thought covered by the paradigm.[8]

The organizational culture of the USAF emerged from larger U.S. military culture but also from its own particular history. The USAF shares some cultural understandings with other U.S. military services (a commitment to civilian supremacy, for example), some with all military organizations (a hierarchical distribution of authority within the organization), and some just with other air forces (a belief in the efficacy of airpower to solve military problems).

The USAF has three distinct and enduring cultural tendencies that create political and military problems for the United States. The first is the belief in the uniquely decisive effect of airpower, which leads to problems with other military organizations. The second is the fascination with aircraft as objects of technology rather than as aspects of national power. Finally, confidence in the essential transparency of war, as opposed to the fog of war, colors the air force understanding of politics and conflict. These tendencies have characterized organized military airpower in the United States since its inception and have helped produce costly mistakes in procurement and war fighting. These tendencies are tightly intertwined with one another: contempt for the fog of war makes strategic airpower sound plausible, the technology fetish is colored by the commitment to strategic bombing and the need to pierce the fog of war, and belief that the fog of war can disappear depends on technological optimism. While not every aviator holds all of these beliefs, the case for the independence of the USAF was built on making these arguments in the strongest possible terms; a rejection of Clausewitz is part of the DNA of the U.S. Air Force.

Independent Decisive Effect

The airpower enthusiasts of the interwar period, including most notably Italian aviator Giulio Douhet, argued that independent airpower, employed against the enemy homeland, could win wars decisively.[9] Not all theorists of airpower shared this vision, but it came to dominate the interwar institutions of airpower because it could offer independence and autonomy.[10] Military analyst Carl Builder argued that the USAF, in contrast to the other services, built itself around this strategic vision.[11] This vision made little allowance for collaboration with other military organizations, and indeed treated their existence as problematic.[12] Because of the decisive potential of airpower, time and attention spent on other military endeavors weakened national capabilities. Builder further argued that the long struggle for independence in the United States and the bitter conflict between the services in the United Kingdom helped exacerbate the cultural tendencies of independence and disdain for alternative forms of military power.[13] In order to win independence, airpower advocates believed that they had to sell aviation in the strongest possible terms, and in the course of making that sale they became captives of their own rhetoric.

The strongest case that airpower advocates could make for independence involved strategic bombing.[14] At its simplest, strategic bombing involves attacking enemy targets from the air in order to inflict harm without facing the fielded military forces of the enemy. The strongest advocates of airpower have argued, in no uncertain terms, that strategic bombing can win wars without the need to disarm the enemy.[15] Airpower can bypass hostile armies and navies in order to strike blows directly against civilians, the economy, and the sinews of the state, bringing wars to a relatively quick and inexpensive close.

The theory of strategic bombing has served as a justification for the independence of both the Royal Air Force and the U.S. Air Force. It has transformed military procurement decisions and changed the course of military campaigns. In the history of airpower thought, strategic bombing theory stands out like a bright shining thread, without which we cannot understand the bureaucratic, procurement, and policy decisions that have affected how nations fight in the air.[16] "Strategic" bombing theory subjects the operational and political levels of warfare to a single technologically driven concept: the idea that long-range bombing can disrupt enemy state, society, and military organizations sufficiently to win decisive victories in war.[17] Historically, strategic bombing theorists have tightly linked this concept to the need for organizationally independent air forces, unfettered by the distractions of ground and naval warfare. Airpower historian Philip Meilinger lists the dictum "Airpower is an inherently strategic force" as one of his ten propositions regarding airpower, along with "Airpower's unique characteristics necessitate that it be centrally controlled by airmen."[18]

The theory of strategic bombing necessarily set airpower advocates at odds with army and navy officers. If airpower, acting independently and without the interference of naval or military elements, can win wars decisively, then countries ought not to waste blood and treasure on tanks and battleships. Historically, navies and armies battled each other bureaucratically for scarce resources, each claiming a greater contribution to "national security."[19] Strategic bombing advocates transformed these debates in a qualitative way by arguing that the other services were useless and counterproductive in securing the safety and political ends of the nation. These claims led inevitably to destructive bureaucratic conflicts between armies, navies, and air forces. These arguments remain relevant today because they produced the institutions that continue to structure our national security debate. Indeed, the belief in the centrality of airpower remains at the heart of airpower doctrine in the modern USAF, epitomized by this passage from the *Basic Aerospace Doctrine of the United States Air Force:* "As the critical element of the interdependent land-naval-aerospace team, aerospace power can be the decisive force in warfare.... Airpower can exploit speed, range, and flexibility better than land and sea forces, and therefore it must be allowed to operate independently of these forces. These characteristics are most fully realized when airpower is controlled centrally but executed decentrally."[20] Similarly, RAND Analyst David Johnson argues that tension over the "equality" of the air force continued to damage army-USAF relations even into the twenty-first century.[21]

USAF culture has never been uniform, with tension long existing between tactical and strategic factions. Nevertheless, the air force has come to understand even tactical efforts to defeat fielded enemy forces in strategic terms. USAF major James Ford has argued that the display of effectiveness of precision-guided munitions in the Gulf War helped build a bridge between tactical and strategic factions, ensuring the centrality of strategic effect in air force culture.[22] Indeed, Cold War aviators John Boyd and John Warden helped create the basis for this bridge by developing the concept of "strategic paralysis." Boyd and Warden separately but directly engaged with Clausewitz in order to develop a new logic of strategic bombing based around precision munitions and direct attacks on enemy centers of gravity.[23] Both argued that airpower campaigns could destroy the capacity of the enemy to resist by inducing strategic paralysis in government and in military organizations.[24] Carefully targeted precision-guided munitions could disrupt communications and other critical infrastructure, leaving an enemy army effectively helpless. The focus returned to defeating the enemy without disarming the enemy, a cultural frame that the aviators of the 1930s would have found familiar and inviting.[25]

Tyranny of Technology

Although technology affects all military affairs, aviators are exceptionally dependent upon the capabilities of their machines. Especially in the early years, aviators also had considerable influence over the development of new technology. In a contest between flying machines, technology might dictate the outcome more often than doctrine or training. The aircraft itself represented a technology that offered the vision of a profound transformation of war. The focus on the transformational effect of technology (as opposed to doctrine, morale, and other aspects of war fighting) played a major role in early airpower theory, as it continues to do today. Philip Meilinger, for example, includes "Technology and airpower are integrally and synergistically related" as one of his propositions.[26]

Evidence of cultural conflict between aviators and other military personnel stretches back to the early days of army aviation. In addition to being criticized for an obsession with flying as a personal pursuit as opposed to as a military project, army aviators were faulted for concentrating on technology at the expense of doctrine and of personnel development.[27]

These critiques had some foundation in truth. At its very early stages, the development of military aviation lay within the realm of the enthusiast. Early experiments with aircraft resulted in numerous fatal accidents, meaning that personnel volunteering for aviation required certain personal characteristics. Moreover, aviation itself stretched the frontier of the possible in the early years of the twentieth century. The novelty of traveling by air, much less fighting in it, generated considerable excitement and enthusiasm. Early airpower advocates can be forgiven for their own engagement in this excitement and enthusiasm and indeed should be admired for the personal risks they undertook in the service of that excitement.

Aviators had their own complaints about the rest of the army. They argued that "ground pounders" had little sense of the transformational impact of airpower and at best saw only the limited effects that aircraft could have on the missions they already wanted to perform.[28] Most important, ground officers had no sense of how airpower, employed independently of ground or naval operations, could have decisive effect. Ground officers simply saw aircraft as a different form of artillery, useful for some purposes but not in themselves decisive.[29] The same sorts of complaints extended to the naval sphere. "Big Gun" admirals focused on the battleship at the expense not only of the aircraft carrier but of the potentially transformative nature of maritime airpower.[30] When Billy Mitchell's bombers sank the obsolete German battleship *Ostfriesland* in a demonstration in 1921, several admirals in attendance wept at the ship's fate.[31]

This affection for technology colors how air force personnel understand their relationship with the service and with military life. Carl Builder writes: "The Air Force is, by far, the most attached of the services to toys. Air Force pilots often identify themselves with an airplane: 'I'm a 141 driver.' 'I flew buffs.' Sometimes this identification goes right down to a particular model of an airplane: 'I fly F-4Cs.' The pride of association is with a machine, even before the institution. One could speculate that, if the machines were, somehow, moved en masse to another institution, the loyalty would be to the airplanes (or missiles)."[32]

Indeed, the affection for particular types of equipment has affected how the air force has reacted to new technological developments. For example, the air force initially resisted the development of the ballistic missile, in part because ICBMs might take the place of strategic bomb-ers in war fighting.[33] When advances in surface-to-air missile technology rendered the B-70 Valkyrie (a supersonic, high-altitude strategic bomber) obsolete, air force personnel argued for its continued procurement on symbolic grounds.[34]

Major General Perry Smith discussed the interrelation between theo-ries of strategic bombing and fixation on technology:

> The coincidence of opinion within the Air Corps on the supreme importance of autonomy can be explained by years of frustrated efforts, the common bond of the joy of aviation, and the crusad-ing attitude of these men. . . . Airpower would defend the nation; air power would guarantee the success of a new international se-curity organization; air power would punish aggression wherever it might manifest itself; air power would save the world. Salva-tion had come; all America and the world needed to do was to maintain and support a strong United States Air Force—a simple, reliable formula.
>
> Objectivity about this weapon was absent within the Air Corps circles for many reasons. Perhaps the foremost reason was the psychological attachment of the airman to his machine. . . . The airman, like the cavalryman of the past, was not known for his modesty, or his objectivity, when it came to the employment of his chosen steed.[35]

The combination of affection for technology and drive for autonomy, rather than a sound appreciation of the relations between military means and political ends, drives much strategic thinking within the air force. To be sure, other elements of the national security bureaucracy share a similar affection for technology, and most organizations desire to retain their autonomy. The air force is almost singular, however, in building its strategic theory around a technological fixation.

The broader impact of this fixation is to detach military means from political ends. Military planning focuses more on the capabilities of par-ticular weapon systems than on national grand strategic goals. Failure (of Operation Rolling Thunder in the Vietnam War, for example) is explained in terms of insufficient commitment of appropriate technology rather than in political or strategic language.

Piercing the Fog of War

Finally, and perhaps most important, technological optimism has also played an important role in convincing the air force to reject the "fog of war." Immediately upon the introduction of fixed-wing aircraft, much of the battlefield that had previously been obscured by distance became visible. Following through on the logic of this increase in the availability of information has helped make the USAF very comfortable with quantitative analysis.[36] Indeed, Michael J. Eula argues that the air force predilection for numbers extends as far back as the work of Giulio Douhet, an Italian airpower theorist who tried to establish with precision the number of bombs needed to destroy city blocks and bring about an enemy surrender.[37] This comfort expanded in World War II, when the USAAF relied on the work of statisticians and economists to most effectively select industrial targets and to determine the most efficient means of destroying those targets. The comfort with analysis continued throughout the Cold War, as the air force retained a close relationship with mathematicians and game theorists developing nuclear weapons–employment strategy.[38] Barry Watts argues, "That American airmen have tended to be overzealous in their enthusiasm for pat formulas and engineering-type calculations seems hard to deny," adding that these tendencies persist across generations, and that this represents a "bedrock error" in U.S. airpower doctrine.[39] Phillip Meilinger goes so far as to argue, "In essence, airpower is targeting, targeting is intelligence, and intelligence is analyzing the effects of air operations."[40]

Of course, both the army and the navy also employ outside analytical organizations to improve their combat effectiveness and institutional efficiency. However, neither the army nor the navy stakes its decisive impact on the ability to discern complex social and economic phenomena. For example, during World War II the best economists available helped identify the German ball bearing facility at Schweinfurt as a target that might cripple the German aircraft industry.[41] The Army Air Forces proceeded to attack the factory at great cost. Later economic analysis suggested the emphasis on ball bearings was misplaced.[42] Mission planners used the best available information, but the complexity of German economy and society daunted their efforts to knock out a critical pillar of the German war machine. Recognizing the fog of war means appreciating that planners will almost never have access to critical precise information about enemy capabilities and motivations.

This comfort with quantitative and game theory analysis has two faces. On the one hand, war fighting and war planning can only benefit from a more rigorous empirical approach. Understanding precisely the costs and benefits not only of war but of specific tactics, operations, and strategic campaigns *during* war is critical to making sensible decisions about war. On the other hand, the air force fascination with analysis suggests a world without the "fog of war," in which consequences of certain actions can be determined with some specificity. For example, John Andreas Olsen argued of latter-day airpower theorist Lieutenant Colonel John Warden: "While Warden argued that air power used offensively could reduce and almost negate friction at the operational level of war, some scholars assert that he was insensitive to Clausewitzian uncertainties. Warden's belief that a modern force could obtain almost perfect information about the enemy's physical capabilities also influenced his preference for focusing on measureable physical effects rather than the intangibles of war."[43]

The idea that uncertainty can effectively be eliminated tends to overstate the predictability of war, which in turn makes war more appealing to risk-averse civilian political leaders. Dismissal of the reality of uncertainty and complexity helps to produce a dangerous confidence in the ability of airpower to disrupt both target societies and enemy military organizations. American aviators in the 1940s argued that the German economy could be brought to its knees by the destruction of vital economic centers; this would sever the links that allowed the "industrial web" to function, with careful analysis determining the weakest link.[44] Indeed, in practice, USAF officers actively sought statistics that would prove the impact of strategic bombing on German industry and dismissed contrary evidence, a phenomenon known as "motivated bias."[45] American aviators similarly argued in the 1990s that target governments could be overturned and enemy military organizations disrupted by attacks on command and control nodes, with careful analysis determining the weakest links.[46] These beliefs betray an unwarranted optimism in the ability of bombs to smash robust complicated social structures.

Mark Clodfelter connects this belief with "progressive" politics of the early twentieth century in the United States, which focused on the ability of the state to solve major societal problems through the application of resources and effort.[47] Unique neither to air forces nor the United States, beliefs of this sort characterize much twentieth-century thinking about the utility of state action. In his book *Seeing Like a State,* James Scott offers a concept he calls "high modernism" in order to explain how states view their populations.[48] In high modernist thinking, states view the social world as essentially understandable and malleable. They attempt to regiment and order their populations and their geographic spaces so that policy can better be formulated and enacted. To be effectively ruled, a population must first be made legible to the modern administrative state. Theories of strategic bombing, conditioned by the belief that the fog of war can be pierced, represent the essence of high modernist thinking. They posit an essentially intelligible target population or organization and propose a relatively programmatic series of steps for influencing and reorganizing that population. The most sophisticated theories of strategic bombing delineate the social, economic, and organizational impact of the destruction of particular targets. Destroy this police station and criminality will ensue. Destroy workers' homes and industrial production will slow. Destroy this factory and the German economy will collapse for lack of ball bearings. Destroy this communication facility and Saddam Hussein will lose control over his military and security services. Sufficiently damage North Vietnamese industry and Hanoi will conclude that further war is too expensive. All of these theories presuppose a social system that is both highly legible and highly susceptible to outside influence.

However, the state can see only certain things. Many social structures and human relationships are essentially invisible to the state, beyond the ability of bureaucracies to catalogue and organize. In active and passive ways, these structures resist high modernist efforts in such areas as urban planning, agricultural reform, and social revolution. Scott shows that many of the best efforts of state leaders have led to authoritarianism and policy disasters, mostly because of incomplete state understandings of its target populations as well as an insufficient ability to mold the population into a legible system.[49]

Experience in the twentieth century, not just in the case of strategic bombing but across the universe of state activity, has demonstrated that states tend to have a vastly overoptimistic sense of both the legibility and malleability of social institutions. In this context, it is hardly surprising that strategic bombing campaigns have failed in particularly destructive ways. Even strategic bombing campaigns that do not depend on deep insight into a target population do demand a very sophisticated understanding of how the enemy thinks about costs and benefits. Strategic bombing campaigns fail because they cannot meet the huge informational demands for success. The campaigns run up against concrete limitations on the reach of the state and the ability of nations to force the world into their preferred shape.

The dismissal of the fog of war has led to overly optimistic assessments of the tractability of military situations. This problem exacerbates, but is separate from, the belief in the decisiveness of airpower. Confidence in the transparency of war allows policymakers to underestimate the risks of military action, whether or not they believe in the decisiveness of airpower. When combined with an overestimation of the effectiveness of airpower, confidence in assessment produces dangerous certainty in uncertain situations.

THE CRISIS OF THE COMMONS

The concept of the "commons" is a good example of how institutional culture matters for how an organization views its mission. The "commons," an old concept in both economics and strategic studies, has recently come to the fore as technology has opened up both space and "cyberspace."[50] The commons are defined by lack of exclusive state legal control. Various states, organizations, and firms can take advantage of the commons for their own purposes, although regulation of the commons often falls to the hegemonic power.[51] Military organizations are the tools that states use to manage and regulate the various commons. Barry Posen has argued that command of the commons is the "military foundation of U.S. hegemony."[52]

Unsurprisingly, service culture characterizes how organizations view management of the commons.[53] The air force understands the commons in the terms set by airpower theory; the air commons is to be dominated so that it can be freely traversed by bombers intent on destroying the property and industry of the enemy.[54] This understanding arises from the work of the early air theorists, which placed control of the commons in strictly zero-sum terms. The air force with supremacy (or at least with the larger number of bombers) can use the commons to destroy the foundations of its opponent's power, whether moral, military, or industrial.[55]

The naval concept of the commons comes from the work of Alfred Thayer Mahan and Julian Corbett.[56] Broadly speaking, nations derive benefit from their ability to use the sea for trade and transport. The key to a successful economy (or imperial project) therefore lies in access to the commons.[57] Cutting off another state's access to the commons could provide the death knell for its imperial and economic aspirations. Nevertheless, in peacetime a safe, regulated commons could provide positive-sum benefits for the community of nations, allowing free, mutually beneficial trade and transit. This understanding of the commons characterizes much modern naval doctrine, including the U.S. Navy's Cooperative Maritime Strategy.[58]

Applied to cyberspace, these different understandings of the commons lead to considerably different policy implications. The air force's conception of cyberspace approaches the commons as a place to be dominated, with offensive capabilities necessary for the deterrence of foes who might attack America's vital Internet infrastructure.[59] The navy, on the other hand, sees the potential for positive-sum interaction in cyberspace while also maintaining capabilities for offensive and defensive action. Alex Vacca argues that this latter interpretation comes much closer to accurately characterizing the emerging properties of cyberspace and has the potential to lead to a more profitable, less paranoid set of policies for cyber regulation and cyber defense.[60] Parallels between the Internet and the maritime sphere as "global commons" are easy and productive to develop. Focusing on defense, resilience, and maintenance makes more sense than concentration on offensive and deterrent capability, especially given the difficulty of appropriately targeting cyber "wrongdoers."[61]

Max Lord has used a similar logic to argue that the air force conception of the commons is inappropriate to space.[62] Extant air force conceptions of space focus on dominance and kinetic military applications rather than on commercial maintenance.[63] In line with Douhet's vision of the air commons, these conceptions include dominance of the offensive and the importance of deterrence.[64] According to Lord, qualities of space such as persistence, location, and multilateral usage make the naval concept of the commons a much more compelling metaphor than the air force conception.[65] Given the relevance of space for commercial application, privileging air force culture over navy could present long-term problems.[66]

The point is not that air force officers and airpower theorists are incapable of thinking successfully about space or cyber policy. Rather, it is that culture frames the way in which an organization approaches particular problems. The air force will likely think about the space and cyber commons in the way it thinks about the air, while the navy will employ a maritime metaphor. The choice of which institution ought to manage the space and cyber commons will consequently lead to different policies and different capabilities with respect to those commons. As the next section discusses, these alternative recommendations find their way into official policy.

Air Force Independence and the National Security State

The implications of a Clausewitzian analysis of USAF independence should be clear. In addition to creating artificial bureaucratic barriers that reduce the efficiency of war fighting, an independent USAF exhibits cultural traits that reduce its contribution to U.S. national security. Confidence in the decisiveness of airpower creates a bureaucratic and procurement reality that leads to a lack of readiness and capability in wars that actually demand the disarming of the enemy. The fascination with technology and equipment helps produce procurement and doctrinal decisions based less on cost-benefit calculation in terms of the national interest and more on parochial organizational desires.[67] Finally, disbelief in the fog of war leads to wildly optimistic assessments of the course of particular wars and military campaigns.

The arguments for air force independence boil down to the idea that the nation's military will not value or be able to project airpower sufficiently in the absence of a capable, proud, independent air force made up of professionals who have devoted themselves to the study of airpower. Without an independent air force, airpower will always be subjected to the parochial interests of services focused on questions other than the decisive transformational impact that airpower can play in war and politics. Army officers will think only of how airpower helps ground assets do their job, while naval officers will think primarily in terms of the defense of naval assets rather than airpower's independent impact. These biases will manifest in procurement and training, where the development of air-oriented capabilities will suffer, overshadowed by other priorities.

However, airpower advocates rarely discuss the negative implications of an independent force. While air force independence may free airpower from debilitating connection with other military objectives, such disconnect carries serious costs. The point of removing airpower from army or navy control is to limit the extent to which training and procurement are focused on the army and navy goals. Naturally, the ability of airpower to conduct missions such as close air support, air mobility, and antisubmarine warfare declines when an independent air force refocuses its attention elsewhere.

If we think of airpower as an organic part of most modern military missions (and in fact airpower does support almost everything that any modern military organization does), then establishing a bureaucratic disconnect between the training, development, and procurement of aviation assets inevitably reduces the effectiveness of airpower support. This flips the logic of air force independence; if airpower requires independence to pursue its own missions, then the ability of aviation to carry out support missions suffers.

Similarly, the existence of an independent air force changes the calculus of civilian leadership with respect to the use of force. While much depends on organizational culture, there are good reasons to suspect that independent air forces make war more likely. Leaders choose between options set forth by their national security bureaucracy. In the American case the venue for conversation is usually the National Security Council, which includes diplomatic representation (the State Department), intelligence advice (CIA, FBI), and civilian and uniformed military advice (secretary of defense, chairman of the Joint Chiefs) and which can include other advisors, such as the service chiefs, on an ad hoc basis.[68] The national security advisor (both the National Security Agency and the National Security Council are creations of the 1947 National Security Act, which also created the CIA and the air force) manages and coordinates these meetings, although presidential management style varies.[69]

The introduction of a new organization (such as the U.S. Air Force) creates another seat at the table with another contribution to the policy debate. While the exact nature of advocacy depends on the situation (relationships between individuals matter; some situations by necessity preclude certain options), an organization tends to argue for policies that will increase its visibility and access to resources.[70] This tendency is mediated by organizational culture; an air force dedicated to strategic nuclear combat might not, for example, volunteer to manage a brushfire war against technologically primitive insurgents. Nevertheless, the constellation of institutions structures the set of options presented to national leaders by the national security bureaucracy. The leaders of independent air forces (not to mention independent navies, independent special forces branches, intelligence organizations, and so forth) try to solve problems with the tools they are familiar with.

To be sure, the availability of multiple points of view in national security decision making is a positive.[71] However, especially when specialists (most civilian presidents) are subjected to complex national security debates, they may find the raw, simple answers offered by air forces inordinately attractive.[72] While there are few studies indicating that air force independence has transformed national security thinking in the United States or the United Kingdom, anecdotal evidence suggests that the allure of easy, decisive victory with minimal casualties has influenced civilian decision making. The possibility that strategic bombing campaigns might defeat Germany and Japan without the need for a bloody invasion certainly appealed to Winston Churchill and Franklin Roosevelt.[73] The U.S. Air Force argued for strong military action against Cuba during the Cuban missile crisis, although President Kennedy rejected the USAF's advice.[74] Lyndon Johnson hoped that Rolling Thunder would forestall the need for greater deployment of ground troops to South Vietnam, a hope abetted by the strong advocacy of the air force.[75] In the Kosovo conflict, the availability and promise of airpower clearly informed the decision of President Bill Clinton to intervene, as he and most other NATO leaders displayed a great reluctance to deploy ground forces.[76] Indeed, David Halberstam argues that the theories of John Warden had a strong influence on the decision of the Clinton administration to pursue an air campaign over Kosovo.[77]

Independent air forces thus affect decisions both to go to war initially and to escalate intensity. In some cases (Kosovo) the influence of the USAF may have been laudable, depending on perspective, but in general the prospect of independent airpower advocacy making war more attractive to civilians should be taken seriously.

The next chapter examines airpower (especially strategic airpower) from a moral and legal perspective, paying close attention to how evolving moral and legal concepts shift the practice and theory of air combat. "Lawfare," a concept coined by Major General Charles Dunlap (retired from the USAF) may further limit the ability of the USAF to conduct operations as it sees fit. Following chapters trace the history of the Royal Air Force and the U.S. Air Force, highlighting episodes in which the three rejections of Clausewitz have characterized the behavior of airpower enthusiasts: rejection of the need to disarm the enemy, rejection of the supremacy of politics over military force, and rejection of the fog of war.

3

Airpower, Morality, and Lawfare

Any critique of airpower and independent air forces must take seriously the argument that airpower constitutes an inhumane, and possibly illegal, approach to fighting war. Surely, the introduction of moral issues to questions of war fighting and international politics is fraught with difficulty. To begin with, moral perspectives (not to mention international law) vary across time and place. Even to the extent that moral considerations matter, there is some question as to how those considerations (especially those focused on the suffering of enemy populations) should weigh in calculations of national interest and military doctrine. However, the destruction of cities (and infrastructure) from the air creates inescapable moral questions. It is important to consider how strategic bombing and airpower advocates have approached these questions and how strategic bombing campaigns have measured up in moral terms. It is equally critical to appreciate how legal considerations have changed the practice of airpower, particularly strategic bombing. This chapter outlines the utilitarian and legal/moral absolutist approaches to thinking about the morality of strategic airpower. It then describes two uses of strategic airpower, contrasting the Allied bombing campaign against the Axis in World War II with the Israeli bombing campaign against Lebanon in 2006. This chapter concludes with an examination of the concept of "lawfare," a term for how law, morality, and public relations serve to constrain American military power.

The utilitarian approach to the morality of strategic airpower asks whether a strategic bombing campaign can deliver victory in war while causing fewer casualties and less destruction to the antagonists than a conventional war.[1] As such, the approach turns on the essentially empirical question of the relative cost of air versus ground campaigns. Over time, many advocates have claimed that strategic airpower represents a more humane approach to war.[2] The bloody stalemate in the trenches of the Western Front loomed large in the minds of early airpower advocates, and the dreadful cost of land war continues to influence modern advocates. While strategic bombing might kill civilians—some directly and some through the collapse of state and economic institutions—surely these few lives would be a small price to pay to avoid the greater bloodshed needed to destroy enemy armies in the field.[3] This thinking features prominently in modern strategic bombing theory, which promises that relatively painless precision attacks on enemy communications and infrastructure can bring enemies to their knees without the necessity of destroying their armies.[4] Strategic bombing saves lives on both sides, and is thus inherently a more moral undertaking than the traditional Clausewitzian approach to winning war by disarming the enemy.[5]

The prospect of killing fewer people and destroying less property in the course of military victory is certainly appealing.[6] However, there are at least two caveats to this appeal. First, the claim that strategic bombing does a favor to the target population (as opposed to conquest and occupation) is rife with potential perversities. Essentially, it suggests that the long-term interests of a target population are better served by a period of intense bombing leading to state collapse or war termination than by a long drawn-out war. Interestingly enough, however, most people would prefer not to be bombed, regardless of how planners in a foreign capital may assess their long-term interests.[7] The utilitarian notion that fewer will die from strategic bombing than from a conventional war sidesteps the moral question rather than confronting it. Some policymakers may have genuine concerns about the suffering of target populations, but many may simply view the utilitarian approach as a way of eliding the horrific costs of war for domestic and international audiences. Moreover, when policymakers face a practical wartime choice between protection of foreign civilians and protection of their own airman, they will often choose the latter.[8] Second, as an empirical matter it is not at all clear that strategic bombing actually is more humane than conventional conflict. World War I was extremely costly, but Germany (the subject of the most intense strategic bombing campaign) suffered more in the Second World

War than the First.[9] The comparison is inexact, because in World War II the Allies conducted both a strategic bombing campaign and a conventional conquest and occupation of Germany. Of course, conventional conquest was necessary because the strategic bombing campaign failed to destroy German war-making capacity. The advent of precision-guided munitions has certainly reduced the need to engage in destructive area bombing, although to have effect such munitions still make life difficult for civilians.[10]

The "absolutist" approach to evaluating strategic airpower depends on the legal structure that emerged to regulate warfare in the twentieth century and on older understandings of the moral requirements of just war. "Absolutist" is something of a misnomer, since laws and moral demands change over time. However, I use it here to highlight the distinction between it and utilitarian arguments and because moral and legal demands depend less than utilitarian ones on an evaluation of the empirical evidence. Even if a strategic bombing campaign proves less costly to both antagonists than a conventional ground war, it remains morally problematic if the rights, lives, and property of noncombatants are systematically and intentionally endangered by combatants. The laws governing modern warfare are difficult to summarize, but in brief they demand the following:

1. Military necessity: Operations or campaigns must contribute to the military defeat of the enemy.

2 Distinction: Belligerents must distinguish between combatants and noncombatants, allowing a certain degree of protection to the latter.

3. Proportionality: The degree of harm caused to noncombatants in the course of pursuing military necessity must be proportional to the military advantage expected.[11]

These three concepts have become part of the fabric of the international law of war during the twentieth century, although they can be derived from older conceptions of just action in war. In practice, these rules lead to the doctrine of double effect, which allows incidental damage to civilians and their property in the course of an attack against military assets.[12] For example, if a government stations a rocket facility in a civilian neighborhood, the enemy can target the facility even though its destruction might kill nearby civilians. However, the prospective damage must be proportional to the military advantage of destroying the target. A combatant cannot, for example, lay waste to a city simply in order to destroy a single small, conventional rocket base.

Work on the laws of war in the first half of the twentieth century returned repeatedly to the question of strategic bombing.[13] Notably, airpower prophet Giulio Douhet argued that modern warfare suspended the distinction between combatants and noncombatants. Because total war in modern industrial states demanded the full resources of the national economy, all components of that economy were culpable and vulnerable, just as if they were fighting at the front. The builder of the artillery piece deserved no more immunity than the soldier who fired it.[14] However, Douhet's argument did not convince the international legal scholars of the time. The Hague Convention of 1923 prohibited terror bombing and the targeting of property of a nonmilitary nature.[15] Although the convention was never formally adopted, it did indicate extant thinking among the major powers in the early interwar period.[16] The Royal Air Force of the interwar period closely followed developments in international law, although most of the senior commanders expected that rules would fall by the wayside soon after the beginning of hostilities.[17] The League of Nations similarly condemned strategic bombing campaigns that targeted civilians and civilian property in 1938, and some of these prohibitions were honored for a time by some of the combatants in World War II.[18]

The compatibility of strategic bombing with the laws of war has varied considerably in both theory and practice since the invention of the airplane. International law on the subject has continued to develop, as has strategic bombing theory. Obviously, the terror bombing proposed by Giulio Douhet and others falls short of the legal and moral requirements of the absolutist framework. More modern interpretations of strategic bombing theory, such as those of John Warden, make a much greater effort to accommodate themselves to the reality of international law and international moral consensus.[19] Indeed, moral and legal questions have dominated the discussion of airpower campaigns such as the 1999 war over Kosovo and Israeli operations against Hezbollah in 2006 and Hamas in 2009.[20]

So Much for Theory: The Practice of Strategic Bombing

Discussion of the legal and moral components of strategic bombing theory can become dry without examples from real-world airpower campaigns. To be sure, all war involves horror, and awful stories could be told about any particular method, venue, or arena of modern warfare. Nevertheless, given the humanitarian claims made by airpower advocates, the physical history of strategic bombing merits attention. This section describes three strategic bombing campaigns. The first two were launched by the Allies in World War II against the Axis. The third campaign was launched by Israel in Lebanon in 2006. These campaigns are not comparable in effect; the damage inflicted by Israel upon Lebanon pales in comparison to the destruction of the Combined Bomber Offensive. However, the differences between the campaigns reflect how understandings of the morality of strategic bombing have changed over the years. As later chapters will provide some operational details of the bomber offensive in World War II, the accounts here concentrate only on the moral and legal issues created by the campaign.

World War II: The Strategic Campaigns against Germany and Japan

During the Second World War, several of the major combatants engaged in campaigns of terror bombing designed to destroy the morale of enemy populations. These terror bombing campaigns directly targeted civilians for incineration in the hopes that the threat of destruction would incline citizens to force their governments to make peace.[21] Germany launched the first terror air raids, attacking Warsaw with heavy bombers on September 25, 1939, and Rotterdam in May 1940. During the latter stages of the Battle of Britain, the Luftwaffe undertook direct bombing raids against London and other British cities. These raids inspired British reprisals although, as noted previously, the British had expected the war to develop in such fashion, and the prospect of attacking German cities had played a large role in British interwar air doctrine. By 1942 the Bomber Command of the Royal Air Force had committed to a major strategic bombing campaign against Germany. This campaign was joined by the U.S. Army Air Forces in late 1942.

The Royal Air Force campaign against Germany was managed by Air Marshal Arthur Harris, commander in chief of Bomber Command from 1942 on, and involved night bombing of urban targets. While the campaign also targeted industry, Harris made clear that the primary objective was destruction of German civilian morale. He argued that any diversion of airpower toward tactical tasks (support of the D-Day invasion, for example), or even to strategic tasks such as destruction of German transport infrastructure was counterproductive to the Allied war effort. Early in the war, Harris offered the British government the only hope it had for defeating Germany.[22] Although German air raids had failed to break British morale, senior RAF commanders believed that German state-society relations were sufficiently distinct from their British counterparts that the bombing might undermine German support for the war.[23] The United States, on the other hand, preferred to characterize its campaign as "daylight precision bombing." Bombing instruments of World War II required daylight for precision, and attacks on industry (especially "critical" industries, such as ball bearings) also required precision. American aviators argued that daylight precision attacks were simultaneously more effective and more moral than the area bombing of their British counterparts.[24] However, attacks in daylight soon incurred unacceptable losses to German air defenses. Moreover, the USAAF overestimated the precision of the attacks and regularly hit civilian areas instead. Eventually, the USAAF suspended daylight precision bombing in favor of RAF-style area attacks.[25] In all, nearly half a million Europeans are thought to have died in Allied bombing raids.[26] Some 81,000 Allied aviators also died in the course of the campaign.[27]

The first strategic raid against Japan came on April 18, 1942. Consisting of sixteen B-25 medium bombers launched from the aircraft carrier USS *Hornet*, the raid did little damage, but presaged the much larger strategic campaigns of 1944 and 1945.[28] Demonstrating that airpower advocates had no monopoly on World War II butchery, the Japanese Army slaughtered up to a quarter million Chinese civilians in the process of searching for the pilots of the B-25s.[29] By late 1944, however, American B-29 Superfortresses were regularly striking Japanese cities from these island bases. Against Japan the United States adopted area bombing, based on the idea that Japanese industry was too dispersed to allow precision bombing and that Japanese cities were uniquely vulnerable to incendiary attacks.

These raids, targeted against Japanese civilian areas, devastated numerous Japanese cities. The USAAF wasted little time with daylight precision bombing, largely because of the belief that Japanese industry was dispersed across residential areas.[30] The most destructive raid took place on March 10, 1945, when 279 B-29s, flying at low altitude, dropped incendiary munitions on Tokyo. The raid caused a firestorm, killing roughly 100,000 Japanese civilians, more than immediately died in either the Hiroshima or Nagasaki atomic attacks.[31] The following is an abridged retelling of an account of the wake of the Tokyo Fire Raid, in which Tsukiyama Minoru and his father sought safety from the fires near a set of elevated train tracks:

Even with the distance between their pillar and the surrounding buildings, the flames crept closer and closer. Soon Minoru and his father were engulfed in a red cloud of sparks. At the base of each pillar squatted seven or eight refugees seeking shelter on the downwind southern side. While huddling in this fashion, Minoru wondered how much the nearby houses were burning and, holding to the pillar, put his head out to get a glimpse. Immediately he was beaten back by a hail of sparks and almost fell. Minoru and his father beat out the red sparks around them— "more like miniature fires themselves"—with their bare hands. There was nothing they could do to stop it when their bicycle and belongings began to burn in the spot they had been abandoned. Much worse, however, the shelter that Minoru's mother and sister had entered was also engulfed in flames. Unable to do anything to assist their loved ones, Minoru and his father slapped with their hands and stomped their feet in a desperate effort to extinguish the fires on and around them.

"If you let your hands or feet be still for even the briefest of moments, your clothes would instantly burst into flame. Small sparks would enter from our collars and sleeves and make their way through our clothes. It was so terribly hot—our clothes singed, and our hands, feet, and faces stung from the burns they received. I could tell at a glance that my father and the others huddled there together were tiring. No one seemed capable of enduring much more."

A boy near Minoru, who looked to be an elementary school first grader, suddenly rolled a few meters forward. Minoru had stamped out sparks that landed on the boy's back several times, but was now far too busy trying to keep from combusting himself. The boy's head covering had caught on fire and Minoru heard him scream: "It's hot! It hurts! Help me!" The child untied his head covering and threw it as far as he could, but after struggling for a few more seconds, his entire body erupted into flames. "It was if he'd been drenched in gasoline. I watched as in a nightmare as his body shook with its last spasms."[32]

U.S. Army Air Forces B-29s attacked dozens of Japanese cities, culminating in the atomic attacks of August 6 and August 9, 1945. Casualty statistics vary, although upwards of 400,000 Japanese civilians may have died in the attacks.[33]

Legal and Moral Evaluation

Legal specialists and scholars of just war have long debated the appropriateness of the Allied strategic bombing campaigns. The campaigns obviously violated many of the commitments made by Allied governments to avoid direct acts against civilians (as opposed to industrial targets) prior to the war. However, given that Germany breached these rules first, and because of the ambiguous applicability of many of the treaties regulating strategic bombing, the legal case remains questionable. Interestingly, the laws of war established after World War II (and even used to condemn German and Japanese behavior during the war) made the area bombing of Germany unequivocally illegal.[34] Few are willing to argue that a similar campaign today would be legal, even among those who defend the propriety of the bombing during the war.[35]

On the moral side, Michael Walzer argues that Britain's inability to strike back at Germany in any other way justifies at least the early part of the RAF campaign. He also argues that later attacks conducted under conditions of Allied military superiority violated the strictures of *jus in bello*.[36] Normally, just war theory prohibits direct attacks on civilians. Indeed, most of the major combatants of World War II foreswore strategic bombing prior to the initiation of hostilities. However, Great Britain attacked German cities in a situation of "supreme emergency," in which drastic measures are permitted in the face of otherwise certain defeat.[37] Supreme emergency does not justify everything, however, as the action taken must have the potential to lead to victory. Given the low success rate of strategic bombing campaigns, direct attacks on cities might not then qualify. However, the British certainly *believed* that attacks on civilians might have devastating effects. In any case, as the war continued the British developed alternative methods of resistance, such as invading France. This made continued direct attacks on civilians less forgivable in *jus in bello* terms. Moral philosopher A. C. Grayling concurs with the argument that area bombing during World War II was immoral, arguing that it would have been appropriate for American and British aviators to refuse to fly such missions. Grayling writes:

> Was area bombing necessary? No.
>
> Was it proportionate? No.
>
> Was it against the humanitarian principles that people have been striving to enunciate as a way of controlling and limiting war? Yes.
>
> Was it against general moral standards of the kind recognized and agreed in Western civilization in the last five centuries, or even 2000 years? Yes.
>
> Was it against what mature national laws provide in the way of outlawing murder, bodily harm, and destruction of property? Yes.
>
> In short and in sum: Was area bombing wrong? Yes.
>
> Very wrong? Yes.[38]

It is worth noting that voices in the United States and the United Kingdom opposed the bombing campaign, even during the war. Vera

Brittain, a British pacifist, wrote and published *Seeds of Chaos: What Mass Bombing Really Means* in 1944. Horrified by the destruction of Hamburg, Brittain argued with considerable accuracy that bombing was unlikely to crush German morale or noticeably shorten the war. Brittain also pointed out examples of frankly eliminationist sentiment in British public life. The book was also published in the United States, where its argument was angrily rejected across the political spectrum.[39]

From a utilitarian point of view, the bombing raids against Germany obviously failed to directly force surrender. Germany was subjected to the destruction associated with invasion and occupation as well as the bombing of its cities. Any utilitarian case must be based on the idea that a German war machine unencumbered by the strategic campaign could have fought off Allied ground forces, or at least substantially extended the duration of the war. A later chapter chronicling the operational history of U.S. airpower evaluates this argument at greater length.

Hezbollah, 2006

The war between Hezbollah and Israel began in July 2006, when a rocket attack and ambush by Hezbollah provoked a massive Israeli retaliatory attack against targets in Lebanon. During the thirty-four-day war, Israel undertook a substantial air campaign, later complemented by a ground campaign, in order to punish Hezbollah and drive the organization back from the Israeli border. During the air campaign, any infrastructure that could support the resupply and reinforcement of Hezbollah came under attack. The campaign was also explicitly designed to create resentment toward Hezbollah on the part of the Lebanese population.[40] To reiterate, the Israeli campaign against Lebanon bears little resemblance to the great city-burning campaigns of the Second World War. Israel made no effort to destroy entire Lebanese cities, instead concentrating on specific targets of (sometimes) dubious legality. Discussion of the 2006 Israeli campaign, however, helps illustrate how understandings of strategic bombing have changed over the years. Most notably, modern strategic airpower campaigns tend to avoid attacks directly intended to kill civilians, instead focusing on infrastructure. Indeed, modern airpower campaigns make substantial and notable efforts to avoid unnecessary civilian casualties. However, every air campaign of the last twenty years has involved substantial attacks on civilian infrastructure. These attacks have carried out both a tactical interdiction mission and a strategic mission. On the one hand, the campaigns have sought to interdict resupply and reinforcement of fielded military forces. In Iraq in 1991 and 2003, air strikes targeted bridges, roadways, electrical plants, and other civilian infrastructure that could enhance Iraqi mobility or communications.[41] The attacks also attempted to drive a wedge between the Ba'athist regime and the Iraqi people, or at least to reduce the ability of the regime to crack down on popular dissent.[42] The air campaign against Serbia in 1999 served similar aims. Serbian targets were chosen for both tactical and strategic value, with the aim of limiting the ability of the Serbian Army to defend Kosovo, but also of creating sufficient economic pain in Serbia to force the leadership to concede.[43]

In 2006 the Israeli Defense Force (IDF) was led by Israeli Air Force (AIF) lieutenant general Dan Halutz. Halutz was the second air force officer to command the IDF and the first in almost fifty years. Historically, the Israeli Air Force (which operates as an arm of the IDF rather than an independent service in the American or British sense) has concentrated on close air support and air superiority missions in support of IDF ground forces, but it has also undertaken numerous successful strategic missions.[44] However, the IAF is also associated with some of the earliest practical applications of "effects-based operations" (EBO), a concept linking airpower to state and organizational failure (a later chapter will discuss EBO in more detail).[45]

The air campaign against Lebanon began on July 12, 2006, and ended when a ceasefire terminated the conflict on August 4. The bulk of the campaign against Hezbollah was carried out by F-15 and F-16 fighter-bombers. These aircraft can carry ordnance loads comparable to World War II heavy bombers and are normally equipped with precision-strike munitions. Helicopters and transport aircraft also played roles. The missions undertaken by the IAF ran the gamut of traditional airpower missions, including close air support, direct attrition strikes on Hezbollah forces (including rocket-launching artillery), air transport and air mobility, reconnaissance, and interdiction. This last loomed largest in a strategic sense. The IDF alleged (with good reason) that Hezbollah was receiving supplies from Iran and Syria before and during the war. Consequently, in order to interdict the flow of supplies, IAF fighter-bombers attacked a wide range of infrastructure targets within Lebanon, including some far from Hezbollah-controlled areas.[46]

The punishment aspect of the bombing created the greatest amount of controversy. On July 24 an IDF radio report suggested that Israel was threatening to destroy buildings in Beirut in response to rocket attacks on Haifa. Although the destruction of buildings by air strike was confirmed by the IDF shortly thereafter, the process of target selection was not made clear.[47] However, the idea that the IAF was engaging in punishment and revenge attacks was supported by several statements from Chief of Staff Halutz, including "There will always be some terrorist to fire a missile. But I believe we'll be able to push them north and reduce the accuracy of their fire. The other side must reach the conclusion that the price it pays for continuing the [rocket] fire is intolerable."[48] The Israeli ambassador to the United States also suggested in some statements that the air strikes were a disproportionate response to Hezbollah rocket attacks, intended to demonstrate Israeli power and credibility.[49]

Attacks on Lebanese infrastructure included the bombing of the Beirut airport, the Beirut-Damascus highway, and numerous other roads and bridges across Lebanon. Bombing was heaviest in the Hezbollah-controlled south, but attacks ranged as far as Lebanon's northern border with Turkey. The cost of infrastructure damage to Lebanon was estimated at $2.8 billion.[50] Although the IDF described the infrastructure attacks primarily in terms of interdiction, it was widely believed at the time that Israel also wanted to inflict pain on the non-Hezbollah-affiliated Lebanese population in an effort to undercut Hezbollah's political appeal.[51] These infrastructure attacks may also have made it more difficult for civilian refugees to escape fighting between Hezbollah and the ground forces of the IDF in southern Lebanon.[52] The IDF also argued that attacks in civilian areas targeted Hezbollah rocket positions and Hezbollah safe houses.[53] Hezbollah did, in fact, regularly fire rockets from and locate military establishments in civilian areas. The IDF also gave advance notice of air strikes in civilian areas.[54]

Legal and Moral Evaluation

To be sure, Hezbollah rocket attacks on Israeli cities and towns did not abide by extant laws of war. Hezbollah attacks, however, were far smaller in scale and in effect than the Israeli air campaign. Hezbollah also tends to view international law with indifference. For these reasons, among others, most of the legal and public attention given the war has focused on Israel, and particularly on the behavior of the IAF during the air campaign. Estimates place Lebanese civilian deaths between 1,000 and 1,200, with a similar number of wounded.[55] In both utilitarian and absolutist terms, the IDF air campaign has generally been found wanting. On the utilitarian side, neither Israeli ground nor air operations could manage to stop Hezbollah from carrying out further rocket attacks against civilian areas in northern Israel. Hezbollah continued to launch rockets until the end of the war. As a military matter, the campaign failed to destroy the Hezbollah organization or to notably reduce its influence in Lebanon.[56] As in many prior cases, people tend not to like being bombed, and tend to blame the people bombing them for their predicament. Israel's reputation for resolve and military capability suffered a serious blow as a result of the failure of the campaign, according to many policymakers.[57] Notably, Dan Halutz received severe criticism within Israel for focusing so much on the strategic air campaign, allegedly to the detriment of the ground campaign. On the absolutist side, the allegations of "punishment" bombing ran afoul of several fundamental precepts of the international laws governing war. Israel also suffered considerable criticism on grounds of proportionality and the doctrine of double effect.[58] In particular, attacks on Beirut neighborhoods (allegedly to strike Hezbollah safe houses) and Lebanese infrastructure came in for heavy criticism.[59]

One aspect of the Israeli campaign deserves more attention. The military planners of World War II, by and large, did not have to worry about a lack of targets. When Germany and Japan ran out of large cities, the bombers simply targeted smaller cities. Similarly, many cities suffered repeated bombing attacks, undoing repairs to previous damage. Modern strategic campaigns, however, depend on a specific and limited set of targets chosen for political and military reasons. These include targets associated with infrastructure, communications, and the symbolic power of the target regime. Many strategic campaigns lasting longer than expected run into problems of target scarcity. Everything worth bombing has, after a few days, been bombed. Like any other bureaucracy, however, military organizations wish to maximize public perception of their value.

Air forces want to continue to "contribute" even after meeting their initial objectives. This desire to "contribute" modifies strategic, operational, and tactical goals, as described in this editorial from *Warship: International Fleet Review:*[60]

> An air campaign starts with a target set, which might be in-formed by adequate intelligence and consists of targets, which are related to the casus belli and susceptible to accurate target-ing. The promise of so-called surgical strikes against legitimate targets makes the use of force acceptable to policy-makers and opinion-formers on the left and the right of politics. However, as the air campaign progresses the intelligence becomes poorer and the targeting more challenging, even for precision weapons (which are only "precision" in terms of means of delivery but are otherwise just as indiscriminate in such circumstances as any other munition). Therefore, inevitably there is "collateral" dam-age. At the same time the intelligence becomes less reliable and the targets become more and more remote from the original set. Eventually the campaign ceases altogether to be intelligence-led and becomes capability-led: Rather than search out those tar-gets which contribute to the campaign, the planners seek des-perately for the targets which are susceptible to their available technology.[60]

The decision of the U.S. Army Air Forces to shift from precision day-light to night area bombing supports this view, as does the history of the Kosovo campaign.[61] While these bureaucratic incentives exist for every military organization, the wide-ranging claims of airpower advocates make them particularly destructive among air forces. Whether made by Hugh Trenchard, Giulio Douhet, or John Warden, claims about the deci-siveness of airpower earn resources for independent air forces, and these air forces feel pressured to create results commensurate with these claims. This tendency becomes especially problematic when wars outlast civil-ian expectations. Air forces feel compelled to do "something" to break a deadlock, which often results in an expansion of the target set. Expanding a target set often requires brushing off the demands of international law.

LAWFARE

The Israeli experience with Hezbollah serves as a useful introduction to the concept of lawfare. A controversial term, lawfare refers to the ability of actors to use international law to limit and mitigate military disadvantage.[62] Organizations like Hezbollah or the Taliban, engaging in conflict with Israel or the United States, attempt to leverage international law in order to force their opponents to forego the opportunities presented by military supremacy. Combined with an effective public relations campaign and abetted by the activity of a wide swath of human rights–oriented NGOs (Wikileaks, Human Rights Watch, Amnesty International), lawfare allows guerrilla organizations or "rogue" states to level the playing field with their more objectively capable opponents.[63]

Although the lawfare concept can apply to sea or ground operations (Somali pirates are sometimes accused of conducting lawfare), commentators argue that it most fittingly applies to air warfare.[64] Advanced Western militaries normally enjoy tremendous advantages over nongovernmental organizations and "rogue" developing countries in airpower, making it imperative for such organizations to close the gap. Without sophisticated surface-to-air weapons, the most effective way to limit the advantages granted by airpower is to force Western countries to limit that airpower themselves.

Lawfare seeks to limit the effectiveness of airpower by creating and publicizing situations in which air strikes kill or injure civilians. In so doing, it forces the airpower organization to take greater care in targeting and to forego potentially effective strikes. Lawfare exploits popular misunderstandings of the laws of wars, conflating accidental civilians deaths with direct targeting of civilians. For example, the organization Wikileaks published an edited video of U.S. Army helicopter operations in Iraq titled *Collateral Murder,* which showed a helicopter gunship attacking a mixed group of civilians and insurgents.[65] Although the attack may not have violated any law, the video created international outrage.

The effectiveness of lawfare is uncertain, but concern about the effect of air strikes on international opinion has likely constrained NATO use of airpower in Afghanistan, U.S. use of airpower in Iraq, and Israeli use of airpower against Hezbollah and Hamas. These constraints have hardly been absolute, as airpower has played an important role in all of these campaigns. Nevertheless, some evidence indicates that civilian policymakers and military officers take the threat of lawfare seriously and modify their behavior according to its constraints.[66] For example, during the command tenure of General Stanley McChrystal, NATO air strikes in Afghanistan declined dramatically in response to heavy domestic and international criticism.[67]

Placing the onus of lawfare on airpower may be unfair; Major General Charles Dunlap, for example, has argued that ground forces break the law and commit atrocities at a rate as great as or greater than air forces.[68] However, if airpower does represent "America's asymmetric advantage," then the focus of lawfare will disproportionately affect air capabilities.[69] Moreover, whether or not lawfare is a nefarious tactic, its practice may nevertheless place severe constraints on the ability of air forces to make war. For example, in response to the U.S. drone campaigns in Yemen, Somalia, and Afghanistan, efforts are afoot to develop legal and normative tools for regulating and limiting the military use of drone warfare.[70]

How Aviators Think about Law and Morality

What do contemporary aviators think about the legality and morality of their actions? As USAF officers Jeffrey Gingras and Tomislav Ruby argue, "The Armed Forces should promote morality in warfare, consistent with our cultural norms and national strategy of advancing democracy and the rule of law. Air operations can be conducted on the strategic and operational level under just war principles while minimizing casualties on both sides and bringing a swift end to conflicts."[71] In a 2000 research paper, Gingras and Ruby argued that while an air campaign can meet the requirements of lawful and just war, "the USAF may have to institutionalize changes to achieve this goal."[72] In particular, Gingras and Ruby engage with John Warden's "Five Rings" model of a strategic air campaign (discussed in more detail in chapter 7), evaluating the morality of decisive attack across the theoretical construct.

Gingras and Ruby argue that direct attacks against enemy military targets, in particular fielded forces, represent the most moral use of airpower.[73] Such attacks minimize risk to civilian lives and civilian property and reduce the threat of disruption of civilian life. Even precision-guided munitions, which can strike targets with great accuracy, suffer from gaps in intelligence. Moreover, even the most precise weapons go awry. While attacks concentrated on fielded forces still run risk of collateral damage, the tendency of civilian populations to move away from high-intensity battlegrounds reduces the probability. Indeed, Gingras and Ruby note the happy coincidence that attacks on fielded Iraqi forces in the Gulf War "stood out as the most decisive in the outcome of the entire conflict." Gingras and Ruby also point out that attacks against Serbian infrastructure during Operation Allied Forces disrupted commerce throughout southeastern Europe, putting the property and livelihoods of civilians at risk.[74]

Gingras and Ruby hardly represent the last word on the morality of aerial bombing, although their argument bears special attention because of the focus on Warden and the engagement with modern airpower practice. Airpower theorist and historian Phillip Meilinger has argued that the problem is less with airpower than with Clausewitz:

> Part of the problem is that military planners are harnessed to an archaic Clausewitzian view of war that emphasizes the destruction of the enemy's armed forces. As a consequence, targeting is viewed in legal terms as referring largely to military forces and those things directly supporting them. For example, if a factory is attacked because it is making military equipment, that factory is a legitimate military target. If, however, the factory makes civilian shoes but is attacked because it is owned by the enemy dictator's brother and striking it increases pressure on the dictator to make peace, most lawyers would argue that striking the target is illegal. Such a view stems from an outdated vision of warfare. Airpower makes coercive strategies increasingly possible and successful— and "successful means incurring less loss of life and damage to both sides. The law must catch up to airpower's increasingly effective coercive capacity.[75]

Recently, the Air Force General Counsel founded a blog concentrating on the legal issues facing the USAF.[76] This suggests that the USAF takes these moral and legal concerns seriously. Indeed, there is considerable evidence that states take not only international law but also international opinion seriously when considering the impact of air campaigns. During the Korean War, both army and civilian authorities worried that a full strategic campaign against North Korea would backfire in world opinion by recalling the horrors of Dresden and Tokyo.[77] In Vietnam, similar concerns about Rolling Thunder and Linebacker II (in relation to both domestic and international audiences) constrained U.S. behavior. And as Dunlap himself has argued, international opinion seems particularly sensitive to civilian deaths caused by airpower.[78]

There is risk in overpersonalizing questions of morality and strategic bombing. For one, men like Arthur Harris and Curtis LeMay genuinely believed that destroying cities would bring World War II to a close faster and less destructively than the conquest and occupation of Germany and Japan. LeMay took great personal risk to make this case. Many, and perhaps most, of the aviators on all sides of World War II, not to mention the Vietnam, Kosovo, and Lebanon conflicts, believed much the same. Participants in early strategic bombing campaigns also believed in reciprocity; the bombs they were dropping were justified by the similar actions of the enemy. This acknowledgment does not absolve commanders and aviators of the responsibility for their actions, but it does make it easier to understand how and why they flew their missions and dropped their bombs.

Still, strategic air campaigns have undergone great change over the past hundred years, in large part because of changes in how we understand the morality and legality of armed conflict. Whereas direct attacks against civilians were once deemed an acceptable tactic of war, modern international law places strict limits on how military operations can put civilians at risk. Nevertheless, virtually every conception of strategic bombing involves direct attacks on civilians or on the infrastructure that modern civilian life requires. Consequently, strategic bombing always hurts civilians, even when bombs are targeted away from civilian homes and delivered with precision. The crucial concept for policymakers to grasp is that strategic bombing does not represent a morally, legally clean way of fighting war. Some forms of strategic bombing are certainly better than others on this score, but all bombing campaigns leave policymakers with "dirty hands." This means that strategic bombing is not in a moral sense different from other kinds of uses of force: ground invasions and shore bombardments, for example, also kill civilians and destroy property. Only strategic airpower advocates, however, make moral cleanliness a central aspect of their arguments about the use of force. As perceptions of law, morality, and armed force continue to evolve, the practice of airpower will necessarily also change.

4

The Struggle for the RAF and the Roots of American Airpower

The stories of the Royal Air Force and the U.S. Air Force are inextricable from one another. This and the next chapter weave these stories together, highlighting how in each service the quest for independence drove theorization of strategic bombing, and how strategic bombing theory provided the foundation for independence. Space does not allow a full detailed history of either the British or the American airpower experience. Excellent works already exist on the air services of both nations, and this book does not seek to compete with the best work that historians have to offer. The institutional histories of the RAF and the USAF offered here are episodic accounts of how organizational interest and organizational culture have affected, and in some sense afflicted, war fighting in the United Kingdom and the United States. Episodes and campaigns appear based on the roles that they played in institution building and in the development of strategic bombing theory.

The analysis in these chapters is motivated by the three Clausewitzian problems with airpower identified earlier. To recap, these include the tendencies of airpower theorists and practitioners to (1) reject the need for disarming the enemy as a means of military victory; (2) detach military issues from political context; and (3) reject the idea that the "fog of war" creates uncertainties that cannot effectively be remedied. The episodes and campaigns discussed work through illustrative examples of these tendencies as well as examine how the institutional battles that led to air force independence in each country helped generate these problems. In particular, these chapters will consistently revisit the contrast between strategic and tactical airpower, which sits at the crux of most debates over the promise and limitations of airpower.

AIRPOWER IN GREAT BRITAIN: THE FOUNDING OF THE WORLD'S FIRST INDEPENDENT AIR FORCE

In July 2011, Minister of Defence Liam Fox spoke to a crowd of defense analysts at RUSI, the Royal United Services Institute: "From its very establishment as an independent service in 1918, the RAF has recognised that despite standing alone as a profession, the utility of air power rests in achieving effect not only in the air, but integrating into other domains and contributing decisive effect to campaigns on the land and the sea. The concept of joint operations is in the very DNA of the RAF." While the minister's comments were understandable in context, participants in the birth of the RAF might remember the event in considerably more fractious terms.[1] Indeed, the early history of the RAF was characterized by bitter, vitriolic bureaucratic infighting between the new air force and the other two services. This infighting affected the course of the Second World War and continues to resonate today. The RAF's position as the world's first air force makes its story uniquely useful for the study of how and why air forces come into existence. Advocates and opponents of independence alike often invoke the experience of the RAF in arguing their cases. The arguments made by proponents and opponents of the RAF are readily available and refreshingly direct. Most important for this study, the debate over the RAF directly prefigured the debate over the USAF.

PREHISTORY OF THE RAF

The Royal Flying Corps (RFC) of the United Kingdom was created in April 1912 and spent its prewar existence mainly as a recreational society for flying enthusiasts.[2] Initially the corps included both army and navy elements, although the navy separated its fliers into the Royal Naval Air Service (RNAS) in July 1914.[3] Two thousand strong at the beginning of World War I, the RFC expanded dramatically as it undertook the responsibility of serving the needs of the British Army in France. These needs included, most notably, reconnaissance, but also some primitive air superiority and close air support missions. The number of aircraft, aviators, and missions increased dramatically over the course of the war, however. By the middle of the war, fleets of biplanes fought each other over every battle on the Western Front, also making appearances in the other theaters of action.[4]

By 1918 the RFC and the RNAS had expanded almost a hundredfold from their prewar sizes. The sophistication, endurance, and reliability of available aircraft had also increased immensely. However, the expansion of aviation in the British military encountered severe teething problems. Insufficient resources were dedicated to industrial production and technological development.[5] Competition between the army and the navy prevented the achievement of certain economies of scale, leading to increases in price and delays in delivery. Early bureaucratic efforts to remedy these problems included a Joint War Air Committee and an Air Board, although both lacked the power to enforce cooperation between the services. British fliers in World War I suffered from dreadful casualty rates, reaching 50 percent for the duration of the war.[6]

Direct attacks on Germany did not play a large role in the early performance of the Royal Flying Corps or the Royal Naval Air Service. However, in 1915 Germany began to launch a series of bombing raids against the United Kingdom, including London. Early raids were conducted by zeppelins and did relatively little damage.[7] The RFC and the RNAS eventually developed aircraft capable of intercepting and pursuing German zeppelins, which led the Germans to discontinue more risky airship raids. However, by 1917 Germany had developed the Gotha G.IV long-range bomber, which was capable of attacking British targets at sufficient speed and altitude to avoid interception. Gotha raids over Britain began in May 1917, with the first raid killing 95 people, including 18 soldiers. A raid over London on June 13 killed 162 and wounded 432.[8] Gotha raids would continue into mid-1918 before British interceptor tactics improved sufficiently to make the attacks too costly. In the last Gotha raid, seven of thirty-eight bombers were destroyed, a loss rate that made it impossible to continue attacks.

Nevertheless, the success of the early Gotha raids electrified British airpower advocates. The ability of the British Army to manage its air assets had come under considerable criticism from pilots and air enthusiasts. In particular, early airpower advocates believed that British Army officers lacked sufficient vision regarding the potential impact of concerted strategic attacks against Germany. Rather than use airpower piecemeal in tactical support of land forces, these early advocates argued for a service that could formulate and direct a strategic campaign against Germany and bring the war to a close.[9] The development of a new service could also help remedy inefficiencies in the employment of aircraft on the Western Front. Prefiguring the concept of "centralized control, decentralized execution," aviators argued that aircraft from less active sectors could deploy in the service of overall air objectives, rather than according to the whim of local ground commanders. Civilians also expressed concern about competition and lack of coordination between the RFC and the RNAS. Indeed, the elimination of interservice competition provided one justification for amalgamating the air assets of the British Army and Royal Navy into a single organization, as resource distribution (especially in terms of engines) was not well managed.[10]

THE SMUTS REPORT

In the wake of several serious Gotha raids, General Jan Christiaan Smuts produced a report on the future of airpower for the British cabinet. Smuts, a former Boer commander who would eventually become prime minister of South Africa, had risen to prominence as a soldier and politician in postconquest South Africa.[11] In the early years of World War I Smuts helped lead the conquest of German South West Africa (now Namibia) and German East Africa. Based on the strength of these victories as well as his prominence in colonial circles, Smuts was invited to join the Imperial War Cabinet in 1917. By this time, Lloyd George had begun to grow skeptical of the advice of his generals and admirals.[12] The army appeared unable to break through on the Western Front and could offer little more than attrition as a strategy for victory. The Battle of Jutland had not notably altered the situation at sea, and German submarines were taking an ever-greater toll on Allied shipping. George sought to shake up British military strategy and wrest control of the war from his generals.[13] Smuts would provide a way forward. Smuts argued that a sufficient commitment to airpower could prove decisive in the Great War.[14] On August 17, 1917,

Smuts would submit a report on the importance of airpower in winning the war and the correct organizational form that British military aviation should take:

> The Air Service . . . can be used as an independent means of war operations. Nobody that witnessed the attack on London on 11th July could have any doubt on that point. Unlike Artillery, an air fleet can conduct extensive operations far from, and independently of, both army and navy. As far as can at present be foreseen, there is absolutely no limit to the scale of its future independent war use. And the day may not be far off when aerial operations with their devastation of enemy lands and destruction of industrial and populous centres on a vast scale may become the principal operations of war, to which the older forms of military and naval operations may become secondary and subordinate. The magnitude and significance of the transformation now in progress are not easily realized. It requires some imagination to realize that next summer, while our Western front may still be moving forward at a snail's pace in Belgium and France, the air battle front will be far behind the Rhine, and that its continuous and intense pressure against the chief industrial centres of the enemy as well as on his lines of communication may form the determining factor in bringing about peace.[15]

This represented a maximalist understanding of the impact of strategic airpower. Smuts also argued that British military aviation should be united under a single organization, amalgamating the air forces of the army and the Royal Navy: "There remains the question of the new Air Service and the absorption of the R.N.A.S. and R.F.C. into it. Should the Navy and Army retain their own special Air Services in addition to the Air forces which will be controlled by the Air Ministry? This will make the confusion hopeless and render the solution of the Air problem impossible. The maintenance of three Air Services is out of the question, nor indeed does the War Office make any claim to a separate Air Service of its own."[16]

The Smuts Report gave the British strategic class a way to think about winning the war without bleeding Germany dry. Airpower could potentially crush Germany's will and ability to fight without the necessity of defeating the Reichswehr in the field. A Royal Air Force might allow Great Britain to escape the Clausewitzian necessity of disarming the enemy in order to defeat him.

The Smuts Report became the foundational document of the Royal Air Force. The War Cabinet accepted the idea of single air service in late August 1917.[17] Legislation enabling the RAF passed November 1917. On April 1, 1918, the Royal Air Force would come into formal bureaucratic existence through the amalgamation of the RFC and the RNAS. Naval aircraft would fall under RAF control:

> Finally, as regards the actual design and construction of the small aircraft carried in H.M. vessels of war it appears better that these, being essentially aerial vessels or craft, should be designed and constructed for the Navy by the Imperial Air Service. Naval requirements in their design and construction would be fully represented by Naval influence not only in the controlling body but also in the Naval Officers and men seconded temporarily or transferred permanently to the Imperial Air Service. There seems to be no more reason for the Admiralty to design and construct aircraft than for it to design and construct guns.[18]

The RAF was supported by the creation of an Air Ministry, giving the new organization important political representation. Upon its creation the RAF was the largest and most powerful air force in the world, a distinction that it retained for many years.

However, the birth of the RAF was not welcomed warmly on the Western Front. Both Field Marshal Douglas Haig, commander of British Expeditionary Force in France, and Major General Hugh Trenchard, commander of the Royal Flying Corps in France, greeted the idea of the Royal Air Force with skepticism. Trenchard was by no means satisfied with the structure of the RFC and the Royal Naval Air Service. Tasked with sending young pilots to die over the trenches, Trenchard found the evident superiority of German engines and airframes deeply frustrating. He blamed the fractured procurement policy of the Royal Flying Corps and the Royal Naval Air Service for producing and delivering inadequate engines and air frames. A central Air Board, he believed, could do much better. Also, Trenchard was bothered by the division of air command responsibilities in France. During the battle of the Somme, Trenchard requested the assistance of an RNAS squadron that was sitting virtually idle. Although the squadron was eventually delivered, it required a herculean bureaucratic effort to force the navy to cough up its planes.[19]

However, as a commander on the Western Front, Trenchard consistently resisted efforts to divert forces from direct support of offensive and defensive ground operations. This is not to say that Trenchard rejected the idea that bombing German industry might damage the enemy war machine. Rather, he believed that possessing adequate forces to command superiority on the battlefield took precedence over schemes to avoid the German Army by flying over it. In response to the German Gotha raids, Trenchard argued that a ground offensive to seize German airbases in Belgium would be the surest way of eliminating the threat. Failing that, direct air strikes on the German bases could reduce the strength of the raids. Both of these suggestions were decidedly of an operational, rather than a strategic, nature.[20]

Consequently, it is not particularly surprising that Trenchard was skeptical of both the Smuts Report and the scheme to unify the RFC and the RNAS. Trenchard worried that the creation of a unified force would tempt the British government to order a premature offensive against German industry while the fight on the Western Front was not yet won, or even secured. Later, when defending the RAF from the attacks of the army and the navy, Trenchard claimed that his opposition to a unified service was only in the context of the potential for disruption during the fighting on the Western Front. However, at the time Trenchard bitterly opposed the RAF.[21] Trenchard believed that the British government was committed to a bomber offensive against Germany that would distract from the needs of fighting on the Western Front. The RAF arrived at a moment of crisis on the Western Front. The German spring offensive, using innovative infiltration tactics, threatened to break the stalemate in the west and drive France from the war.[22] Consequently, the most immediate demands of the RAF were support of British Army forces in the field. Nevertheless, because of continued

German attacks on Britain, civilians kept pressing for strategic reprisal attacks on Germany.[23]

Within the RAF an organization called the Independent Air Force was created, with Trenchard its somewhat reluctant chief.[24] The Independent Air Force was designed to conduct a strategic campaign against German industry and infrastructure. However, at Trenchard's direction much of the effort of the Independent Air Force was dissipated in support of Allied armies during the major German offensive of 1918. After the failure of that offensive, the Independent Air Force supported Allied ground counterattacks.[25] Nevertheless, the Independent Air Force conducted attacks against dozens of German targets, although with little effect on German industry or the German transport network. The Independent Air Force failed to bring the war to a close, but it did herald the vision of independent, decisive airpower that Smuts, Trenchard, and a growing community of airpower enthusiasts would support.

AFTER THE WAR

The battle over independent airpower did not end with the RAF's birth. The postwar British military establishment saw bitter discord between the RAF and the two elder services as the RAF tried to establish its footing and the other services worked to reclaim their lost capabilities.[26] The British Army was skeptical of the independent value of airpower and wanted to reassume control of air assets. The Royal Navy sought to explore the role of airpower in antisubmarine warfare and carrier-based aviation as well as to regain the assets it had lost to the RAF in 1918.

The RAF would not fight this struggle alone. In the aftermath of World War I, a community of like-minded airpower advocates developed in the United States and Europe.[27] While the actual air campaigns of World War I had followed largely Clausewitzian lines, these advocates believed that the military and naval authorities of the day critically undervalued the potential of airpower. They also believed that airpower could, if properly employed, bring quick and decisive results in the next general war. In the strongest terms, these advocates believed that independent air forces could and would replace the other military services and that direct attacks against enemy cities would characterize the war of the future.[28]

Airpower would render sea power obsolete by threatening the direct destruction of warships and merchantmen and also by rendering pointless the armies that sea power can transport and supply. Having made their case, members of this "epistemic community" of airpower set forth to win independence for their air forces and rebuild those forces along strategic lines.[29]

The attitude of postwar Europe made for fertile ground for the claims of strategic bombing advocates. War on the Western Front was perceived (not entirely correctly) to have been a long stalemate of brutal attrition between the armies of the Allies and the Central Powers, won only when one side essentially ran out of will and soldiers. The British military establishment in particular wanted to avoid this kind of war in the future and was leery about any plans to deploy a substantial land force to the continent.[30] The possibility that strategic bombers might defeat the enemy without resort to a long arduous war of attrition appealed to both soldiers and civilians.

Similarly, the Bolshevik Revolution and the near-miss revolution in Germany helped create the sense that modern society was fragile and unstable.[31] Given the right incentives, civilians might revolt against their governments and force peace on major combatants.[32] The rain of fire upon civilian homes might destroy morale and the will to continue fighting. The destruction of police stations and other visible manifestations of the state might allow enemies of the regime to organize, rebel, and bring their government to its knees.

Giulio Douhet is cited by most authorities as a key early figure in the theorization of airpower. An Italian Army officer who served in Libya and elsewhere, Douhet began arguing before the beginning of World War I that airpower would require an independent service in order to have decisive effect.[33] Douhet argued so strongly for emphasizing airpower during the war that the Italian Army sent him to prison for a year. In 1918 he resigned from the army, and in 1921 he published a seminal work on airpower titled *Command of the Air*. Douhet argued that fleets of strategic bombers operated by independent air forces would dominate future warfare.[34] Victory in war would depend on the ability to destroy enemy industry and enemy civilian morale. Destroying industry would limit the ability of the enemy to utilize its own fleet of strategic bombers, and destroying civilian morale would bring about the collapse of the enemy government.[35] Douhet held armies and navies in great disdain, arguing that they would have effectively no decisive impact on the course of the next war.[36] A defensive military posture, enabled by technological developments such as the machine gun, would give airpower the time and space it needed it order to win victory. In fact, Douhet argued that air defense measures, up to and including the development of fighter aircraft, were a waste of time.[37] Bombers would always get through, and would cause such grievous harm to civilian areas that the war could not continue. Douhet argued that, as a practical military matter, airpower should not be shackled to the two older services, which had antiquated understandings of war and strategy. Douhet's predictions about the future of air warfare proved optimistic, but his ideas slowly became enormously influential. He published two editions of *Command of the Air* in the 1920s, the second more aggressive in its advocacy of airpower than the first. Douhet also took to the pages of Italian aeronautics journals to wage an increasingly acid fight on behalf of airpower.[38]

Other developments in British military theory supported a shift toward strategic bombing. The experience of World War I created major problems for existing British political and military institutions. The evident superiority of the Royal Navy over its German counterpart had not produced military victory, although the effects of the naval blockade did eventually weaken the German government and war machine. Similarly, the British Army did not regard the World War I experience as particularly successful. Although the army managed to hold together without any major mutinies, and eventually helped defeat the Reichswehr, British casualties far surpassed the expectations of 1914.

Historian B. H. Liddell Hart argued that the strategic class of the United Kingdom had failed to take advantage of Britain's true military advantages, which in both a strategic and tactical sense involved an "indirect approach" that sought to avoid direct attacks against enemy strongpoints.[39] On the tactical level, the indirect approach could involve such concepts as blitzkrieg, although German military innovation in World War II owed more to Germany's own experience than to Liddell Hart. On the strategic level, the indirect approach could easily be interpreted as meaning the avoidance of direct attacks on enemy *military* forces in pref erence to attacks on enemy civilians and industry. While Liddell Hart was not a particularly enthusiastic advocate for strategic bombing, his theory helped contribute to the popularity of the concept.[40]

The earliest shots in the battle between the RAF and its sibling services involved symbolic efforts to set the RAF apart from the two elder services, with the RAF seeking to create its own independent identity by designing a new system of ranks.[41] Trenchard himself ceased to be a major general and became air vice marshal, then air marshal. Trenchard was the most important theorist-practitioner of airpower in interwar Britain, but he was not alone; among his most important comrades was John Slessor, a World War I aviator who helped develop and codify the RAF's interwar doctrine.[42] Trenchard and Slessor formed the vanguard of a community of officers dedicated to the task of keeping the Royal Air Force independent.[43] This cause (which would incur bitter fights against the other two services) required a financial case for airpower and eventually a theoretical case for the supremacy of the RAF. Imperial policing would become the former, and strategic bombing the latter.

The first big fight over the future of the RAF would come against the Royal Navy, which wanted its naval air service back.[44] The U.S. Navy and the Imperial Japanese Navy each had an organic naval air arm that controlled training and procurement. Although the Royal Navy had pioneered aircraft carrier aviation and in 1921 possessed more aircraft carriers than any competitor, the aircraft and pilots belonged to the RAF. For its part, the RAF did not have much interest in carrier aviation or in naval aviation more generally. During the war Trenchard had resisted the commitment of aircraft to antisubmarine operations. However, naval aviation made up a substantial portion of the RAF, and Trenchard worried that if the Royal Navy seized its aircraft back, the RAF would have been left a shell. A Royal Navy victory might also have emboldened the army to finish the RAF off. Accordingly, Trenchard went on the offensive, adopting the strongest possible rhetoric against the navy. He argued that Royal Navy battleships and aircraft carriers would shortly become so vulnerable to attack from the air that they would no longer constitute a reliable defense for Great Britain. Trenchard cited recent experience in the United States, where General Billy Mitchell's bombers had just sunk the German battleship *Ostfriesland*. He also sparred with the navy over particular operations, such as the response to the Chanak crisis.[45] A Turkish victory over allied Greek forces precipitated this crisis, which threatened to bring British and Turkish troops into direct conflict. Although the crisis passed without fighting, both the navy and the air force claimed a central role in resisting the Turkish advance.[46] In part because of a lack of government interest in another major reorganization, the return of the Royal Naval Air Service was denied, and the RAF remained in control of British naval air assets. The next enemy would be the British Army.

The prospect of another general European war seemed distant in 1920, and an organizational concept formed around large-scale war against a continental power could not form the entirety of the case for independence. The RAF believed that it could win additional resources through contributing to imperial maintenance and "savage warfare."[47] An Air Ministry memorandum from June 1921 argued:

> As an outcome of the war, countries such as Palestine, Mesopotamia, and Persia have increased the commitments of the Army, since in these law is to an abnormal extent dependent on the presence of adequate armed forces; in these countries it may be proved that the Air Service is capable of maintaining order at a small cost as compared with military occupation. If these "policing duties" can be successfully carried out by the utilisation of air power, the enlargement of the Air Force to meet greatly increased responsibilities must follow; it is in such work that the commitments of the Royal Air Force are likely to show their greatest present increase.[48]

The RAF conducted colonial policing operations in Somaliland in 1920, Iraq in 1921, and Afghanistan in 1928. In both Somaliland and Iraq these operations were relatively successful, although in both areas the RAF received the support of ground forces. Indeed, Trenchard resisted the idea of a full military withdrawal from Iraq, in part no doubt because of the contribution that the RAF could continue to make.[49]

The British Army remained skeptical of the independent effect of airpower in savage warfare. As part of a general attack on the utility of the RAF, a War Ministry report responded with an argument that will sound familiar to many modern readers. The ministry report is worth quoting at length, in large part because many of the concerns expressed will recur:

There is general agreement that the moral effect of continued intensive air action on the inhabitants of towns and villages is great. The inhabitants, in order to avoid casualties, are obliged to leave their houses by day and seek cover from view in palm groves and orchards, returning to their houses only after dark. All business is thus suspended and the life of the community rendered intolerable. Night raids carried out in addition to raids by day naturally increase the moral effect.

In the case of nomadic or semi-nomadic tribes, or in fact any tent dwellers, such effect cannot be hoped for. The difficulty of keeping track of their movements, or identifying changing targets, and of disentangling the camps of hostile from those of friendly tribes with which they purposely mingle, renders continued intensive air action unlikely to be either effective or confined to the guilty.

Errors both in intelligence, and in identification of targets from intelligence, must inevitably be relatively frequent, unless the alternative of extreme caution is adopted, which involves the surrender of one of the greatest factors in the moral effect of aircraft, rapidity of action.

The effect of such errors is naturally exasperation, and, even in dealing with the guilty, the opinion expressed that the initial state of terror produced by intensive air action is followed by a sense of exasperation rather than of submission. This is largely due to the fact that in many cases, women and children and the infirm are apt to suffer equally with, or more than, fighting men. Hatred and a desire for revenge are likely to be engendered thereby. . . .

The general consensus of opinion is that in their present stage of development aeroplanes cannot be replied upon as the main weapon of an administration in its task of preserving law and order. . . . Although the moral effect of intensive air action is great, it is transient, and the indiscriminate destruction of life and property which will inevitably result must tend to alienate the sympathies of the inhabitants from the administration.[50]

Although the Royal Air Force made a distinction between strategic campaigns intended to bring a conventional adversary to its knees and campaigns designed to win "savage wars," both types of campaigns fall under modern definitions of strategic bombing. Bombing raids against Iraqi villages had little to do with disarming the enemy and much to do with attempting to destroy the will of the enemy to fight. As the army memorandum points out, the intelligence demands of air operations against guerrillas were prohibitively high, representing an early example of airpower advocates dismissing complexity and the "fog of war." Ironically, the RAF's preoccupation with imperial policing would undercut its readiness for conventional war in 1939.[51]

The fight over independence also involved skirmishes over jobs that the RAF did *not* want to do. Airpower advocates took pains to distinguish between the missions that they could perform and the missions that other branches might conduct. In particular, advocates resented the implication that airpower could be treated as analogous to artillery.

I [Christopher Bullock, principal private secretary to the secretary of state for air] see Lord Cavan [British Army general and chief of the Imperial General Staff] takes the opportunity of comparing the predominant part of the Air with the artillery at the Battle of the Somme. This is what makes me so uneasy—allowing the General Staff to have anything to say on the subject of Air action. They think the Air is only to prepare the way for the Infantry to go forward and annihilate the enemy's infantry and take the country, with all the laborious work and untold casualties and expenditure such a course would entail, whereas we think of the Air in a totally different aspect. I am certain the General Staff will come round to our way of thinking in another five or six years, but they will not for the present. Our view is that the Air will induce the enemy Government, by pressure from the population, to sue for peace, in exactly the same way as starvation by blockading the country would enforce the Government to sue for peace. This is the predominant part of the Air, and not what Lord Cavan says it is.[52]

Part of the resistance to the artillery analogy came from the pursuit of organizational freedom and independence. Artillery, by its nature, acts in concert with other elements of the army, most notably infantry and armor. Treating aircraft as artillery necessarily committed them to use in cooperation with ground elements, which might require aircraft to come under the direct command of British Army officers. The artillery analogy, therefore, ran counter both to the optimistic vision that enthusiasts had for airpower and the organizational interest of the RAF in independence from the British Army.[53]

The skirmishes with the navy and the army over savage warfare and control of assets were important for the RAF to win, but the RAF did not yet set forth a central organizational identity. In order to give the Royal Air Force a reason to be, RAF leadership would return to strategic bombing in its full, modern, anti-industrial form.[54] The Smuts Report had justified independence in part in terms of achieving certain efficiencies, but mostly on the case for strategic bombing.[55] During the First World War, Trenchard had exhibited a considerable degree of skepticism regarding the prospects for independent strategic bombing campaigns. But whatever Trenchard's personal feelings about strategic bombing, the idea of winning wars through quick, decisive bombing campaigns necessarily appealed to the British government and the public at large. As such, strategic bombing represented a weapon in the fight for independence, a weapon that the senior leadership of the RAF found too useful to throw away.[56]

Over the course of the 1920s, Trenchard steadily became more comfortable with both the moral and the operational aspects of strategic bombing. During the air inquiry of 1923, which resulted in the continued inclusion of naval air assets in the Royal Air Force, Trenchard wrote, "It is on the bomber offensive that we must rely for defence. It is on the destruction of enemy industries and, above all, on the lowering of morale of enemy nationals caused by bombing that ultimate victory rests."[57] This represented an embrace of the concept of strategic bombing in Douhetian terms; bomber offensives against enemy cities would win the war by destroying enemy morale and enemy industry. This was a far cry from Trenchard's resistance to a strategic bombing campaign in 1918, but circumstances had changed. Trenchard was now fighting not to win a war but rather to win the material and organizational independence to fight the next war. France provided a convenient hypothetical foe during this period.[58]

Hugh Trenchard, who in World War I had resisted creating the Royal Air Force because it represented a potentially disastrous shift of resources away from the Western Front and who, when given command of the Independent Air Force in 1918, had directed it mainly against the fielded forces of the German Army, by the late 1920s abandoned the Clausewitzian idea that victory required the disarming of the enemy. Like other senior commanders of the RAF, Trenchard argued that while an army or navy needed to defeat its opposite in order to bring about victory, air forces operated under a different set of rules. Air forces could bypass the destruction of their counterparts through continual offensive action and could cripple an enemy war machine through the destruction of industry and civilian morale.[59] A capable air force could win total victory even as the enemy still possessed the means to resist. This represented a logically perfect argument for air force independence—and indeed for the preeminence of the air force among the military services.

Nevertheless, perhaps because of the experience of the Gotha raids, civilian leaders in the United Kingdom raised concerns over the defense of London from enemy attack. Although most early aviators believed that bombers had important advantages over fighters, the RAF still worked on developing an integrated air defense system, including advanced monoplane fighters.[60] Similarly, although the RAF believed that carrier aviation was pointless, the Royal Navy held sufficient clout to force the development of some carrier aircraft, although these aircraft lagged badly behind Japanese and American counterparts.

EVALUATION

In the years shortly before the war, the United Kingdom reorganized and rationalized its air assets. In 1936 the RAF transferred administrative responsibility for the Fleet Air Arm to the Royal Navy, and in 1939 the navy resumed complete control of its own air assets. The shift of assets back to the navy may have resulted from the RAF's greater degree of confidence in its own survival. In 1936 the RAF divided itself into Fighter Command, Bomber Command, and Coastal Command.[61] The first two continued to focus on strategic operations, the former on defense of the realm, and the latter on strategic attacks against enemy homelands. Coastal Command was tasked with maritime defense, including antisubmarine operations. Tactical cooperation suffered in this scheme; the ability of the RAF to conduct close air support over the British Army was found sorely wanting in France and North Africa.[62] Fighter Command's "finest hour" came in defense of the United Kingdom from the Luftwaffe onslaught of 1940, while Coastal Command helped turn the tide against the German U-boat offensive in 1942 and 1943.

In part because of its strategic nature, Fighter Command did relatively well in terms of equipment and doctrine during the interwar period, developing advanced fighter aircraft and sophisticated doctrine for coordinating fighter, antiair, and radar assets. Although the attention paid to fighter aircraft detracted from the development and procurement of bombers, maintaining a defense against the perceived threat of enemy bombers remained a critical strategic task for the RAF. Perhaps more important, the United Kingdom was sufficiently cash strapped that the air force found it more convenient to develop and buy single-engine fighters instead of four-engine bombers.[63]

Coastal Command and the Fleet Air Arm were not so fortunate.[64] Tasked with defense against U-boats, Coastal Command received substandard aircraft and initially had great difficulty coordinating with the Royal Navy.[65] Naval aviation saw little investment, limiting the degree to which the Royal Navy could develop effective carrier doctrine. British carrier aircraft fell a generation or more behind their counterparts in Japan and the United States. The Royal Navy eventually won control over its carrier aircraft, but at such severe cost to procurement and innovation that Royal Navy carrier aviation suffered relative to Japan and the United States.[66]

It bears note that the organization Trenchard nurtured was almost completely unprepared for war in 1939. With the exception of Fighter Command, which performed brilliantly in the early years of the war, the

RAF was deeply constrained by its prewar heritage. Trenchard's vision of a war-winning bomber offensive against Germany dominated, but the need to demonstrate the utility of the RAF in colonial wars made this vision difficult to articulate in doctrinal and technological terms. The RAF entered the war without a usable heavy bomber and without any good doctrine for cooperation with the other two services.[67] This meant that the RAF could make only a limited contribution to the British effort in France and to the defeat of the German U-boat campaign. Fortunately, each of Fighter Command, Bomber Command, and Coastal Command got better over the course of the war; disaster has a way of focusing the mind. But it is no stretch to argue that the idea that provided the foundation of the RAF—that only airmen in an independent air force could adequately prepare the country for air war—fell on its face at the start of World War II. RAF independence left the Royal Navy without a usable carrier air arm, the British Army without an aviation partner, and the organization itself without the tools it needed to win a war on its own.

Institutions matter. The United Kingdom centralized military aviation under one command at the end of World War I. This helped achieve certain economies of scale and bureaucratic efficiencies (the disputes between the RNAS and the RFC really were a mess), but it chained military aviation to the priorities of a single organization. The Royal Air Force was deeply committed to its own survival, and Hugh Trenchard was willing to adopt almost any argument that would ensure autonomy from the two older services. Savage warfare did part of the job, but strategic bombing writ large won the day. Strategic bombing provided a perfect argument for maintaining an organizationally independent air force, unfettered by the needs of the other two services.

In pursuing the logic of strategic bombing, the Royal Air Force rejected the idea that future war would require the defeat of a conventional enemy army in the field. Given the dreadful experience of World War I, Trenchard's sales pitch was all the more attractive. Unfortunately, the RAF failed to work through the logic of how strategic bombing might force an enemy surrender. Trenchard and others allowed their enthusiasm for a particular technology and mode of fighting to overwhelm their sense of how military tools work to create political outcomes. Instead of starting with a justification and finding a tool, Trenchard started with a tool and found a justification.

Some, but not all, countries followed British suit. In Italy, the Regia aeronautica was founded in 1923 as an independent service. The German Luftwaffe was established in 1933, with the French Army of the Air (Armée de l'air) gaining independence in 1934. The Soviet Air Force operated under the umbrella of the Soviet Armed Forces but remained largely subordinate to the Red Army. Japan created two air forces, one part of the army and the other part of the navy. However, the concept of strategic bombing found less ready soil in continental Europe than in the English-speaking world. Although references to Douhet appeared in some French doctrinal documents, the focus of French airpower remained support of ground forces on the continent and in the colonies. Despite Giulio Douhet's international influence, air power theory in Italy similarly focused on the support of ground forces in the field. Soviet interwar aviation made some effort to develop the capacity to carry out strategic campaigns, but again the need to support ground forces in the field took precedence. The most interesting developments came in Germany, where the strategic bombing campaign against the United Kingdom in 1917 and 1918 was largely considered a failure. Although strategic bombing advocates existed in Germany, the Luftwaffe eventually developed a doctrine and force structure that favored multifaceted support of ground forces in the field. This doctrine would serve Germany well in the first two years of World War II.[68]

The air service besides the RAF most interested in strategic bombing did not win its independence in the interwar period. The United States created the Army Air Service, then the Army Air Corps, and finally the Army Air Forces. The next chapter chronicles the road to independence of the U.S. Air Force.

5

From Army Air Service
to Air Force

The U.S. Air Force did not win its freedom until 1947, after fighting the two major conventional wars of the twentieth century. The theoretical debates over airpower during the first half of the twentieth century played out in the United States against the backdrop of an institutional struggle within the U.S. Army and between the army and the navy. In part because of this long history of bureaucratic struggle, the current arrangement of U.S. military aviation remains complicated. The USAF represents only one of four different aircraft fleets in the U.S. military arsenal (the number increases if we include Coast Guard and Air National Guard fleets). The U.S. Army, U.S. Navy, and U.S. Marine Corps all operate their own air forces independently of the USAF.

The battle for U.S. Air Force independence was necessarily influenced by the independence of the Royal Air Force (and other independent air forces) as well as by the air campaigns of both World War I and World War II. However, the quest for air force independence itself affected U.S. doctrine, procurement, and strategy, especially during the Second World War. The U.S. Army Air Forces fought as an organization that wanted independence and tailored its efforts not just to the goal of defeating Germany and Japan but to separating itself from the army.

PREHISTORY OF THE USAF

The history of American airpower began with the creation of the Aeronautical Division of the U.S. Army Signal Corps in 1907.[1] The Signal

Corps, an organization dedicated to maintaining military communication, had dabbled with balloon aviation since the Civil War and seemed the natural choice for the introduction of aircraft. Despite the fact that a pair of U.S. inventors (the Wright brothers) had pioneered heavier-than-air craft and attempted to market them to the U.S. government, the U.S. military was slow to appreciate the possibilities of the aircraft. The Aeronautical Division was very small, including only twenty-three aircraft by 1914.[2] The first use of airpower in anger came in 1916, when Woodrow Wilson authorized the Punitive Expedition against Mexico.[3] As in the United Kingdom, however, the pressure of war and of technological development spurred expansion, and by 1918 the Signal Corps could no longer handle both its aviation and its communication responsibilities. In May 1918, the United States created the Army Air Service (USAAS), although ad hoc organizations had already been developed to manage the air units of the American Expeditionary Force in France. U.S. fliers had trained and flown with British and French units before U.S. entry into the war and continued to do so in the months immediately after. U.S. airpower capabilities were plagued by slow production and a weak aeronautic sector, although by the end of the war the American situation was improving.[4]

U.S. naval aviation began on November 14, 1910, when a Curtiss Co. aircraft was launched from the cruiser USS *Birmingham*.[5] The first naval aviation unit was formed in the summer of 1911, and early work involved the development of seaplanes and of catapult takeoffs from warships. As with all other such services, naval aviation expanded dramatically during World War I, growing from 201 personnel in April 1917 to 37,000 in November 1918. Naval aircraft in the First World War engaged primarily in maritime reconnaissance and antisubmarine warfare.[6]

The Army Air Service remained in control of U.S. Army air assets after the war ended. As was the case with other belligerents, the size of the air service shrank dramatically, dropping from 138,000 personnel in 1918 to 9,500 in 1926.[7] Demobilization bit more deeply in the United States than in the United Kingdom, in part due to the belief that participation in the Great War represented an aberration from American foreign policy. The long, bitter fight for an independent U.S. air force began in earnest during demobilization. The earliest legislative rumblings began in 1919 with proposals by Representative Charles Curry and Senator Harry New to establish a separate Department of Aeronautics.[8] The initial stages of the debate echoed the fight over the creation of the Royal Air Force.[9] Airpower advocates argued that aviation required a separate service in order to realize its potential as a decisive strike force.[10] They also contended that a separate service would reduce redundancy across the U.S. military and consequently save money. Opponents feared inadequate cooperation between ground, air, and sea assets.[11] Both sides invoked the creation of the RAF, advocates calling it a great success, and opponents a tragic failure.[12]

The National Defense Act of 1920, however, kept aviation within the army. Interwar army aviation activities included patrolling the U.S. border with Mexico, monitoring forest fires, carrying out coastal patrols, surveying, emergency relief, and even restoring order during labor disturbances. Airpower advocates also won government support for U.S. civilian aviation, believing both that greater public visibility for aviation would help their cause and that the development of an aviation industry would drive technological innovation and lay the foundation for wartime expansion.[13]

The best-known interwar airpower advocate was Brigadier General Billy Mitchell.[14] As a lieutenant colonel, Mitchell had played a prominent role in preparing the way for U.S. Army air assets in France in the First World War.[15] The war helped connect Mitchell and other U.S. fliers with the broader international aviation community. Mitchell worked closely with French and British aviation officers in assessing the role that American fliers and U.S. industry could play, and by the end of the war he commanded all U.S. Army air units on the Western Front. The relatively unsophisticated state of the American aircraft industry meant that the United States had to borrow foreign designs, which brought Mitchell and others into contact with Giovanni Caproni, aircraft designer and associate of Giulio Douhet.[16] Granting some differences of emphasis, Mitchell largely held to Douhet's maximalist views of the effectiveness of airpower, including Douhet's contempt for the other services. Parts of Douhet's *The Command of the Air* appear in the interwar Air Corps Tactical School curriculum.[17] Lieutenant Colonel Peter Faber discusses the centrality of strategic bombing theory to the pursuit of an independent American air force:

To ensure that American airpower realized its full potential, early air leaders and thinkers such as Mitchell, Patrick, Gorrell, Milling, Sherman, Benjamin "Benny" Foulois, and Henry "Hap" Arnold haltingly developed an ad hoc, four-part strategy designed either to create new roles and missions for the Air Corps or to steal old responsibilities away from the Army and Navy. Specifically, the strategy sought to (1) redefine America as an airpower rather than a maritime nation; (2) demonstrate and publicize the versatility of airpower in peacetime roles; (3) create both a corporate Air Corps identity through political maneuvering and an independent air force through legislation; and (4) perhaps most importantly, develop a unique theory of air warfare—unescorted high-altitude precision daylight bombardment (HAPDB) against the key nodes of an enemy's industrial infrastructure.[18]

Mitchell argued relentlessly for the decisiveness of airpower and made clear his belief that airpower required an independent military organization in order to realize its potential. Mitchell was frustrated with legislative inaction and the opposition of ground-focused army officers such as General John J. Pershing, commander of U.S. forces in Europe in World War I.[19] Rather than giving Mitchell command of army aviation after the war, Pershing had turned army aeronautics over to Major General Charles Menoher, an artillery officer.[20] Such a step intentionally yoked U.S. military aviation to the traditional concerns of ground officers.

In frustration, Mitchell decided to launch a public campaign.[21] As Mitchell's enthusiasm for airpower extended to the maritime domain, in 1921, he helped arrange a demonstration of the effectiveness of aerial bombers against warships at sea. The obsolete German battleship *Ostfriesland* was attacked and sunk by Mitchell's bombers. Naval authorities disputed the realism of the demonstration, arguing that a battleship under way, with operational damage control and firing antiaircraft guns, would have a much better chance of survival.[22] On the other hand, the *Ostfriesland* was not loaded with munitions, the internal explosion of which, under attack, proved a primary cause of battleship loss.[23]

Mitchell continued to press the case of the independent air force after the *Ostfriesland* demonstration. He became vocally critical of U.S. government policy on aviation, of the U.S. Navy, and of his own superiors in the U.S. Army. In the wake of a dirigible crash in 1925, Mitchell castigated government and military authorities in brutal terms.[24] As a serving U.S. Army officer, Mitchell was vulnerable to discipline and was eventually court-martialed and suspended from the army. He left the service shortly thereafter. After Mitchell left the army he remained in the public eye, continuing to argue enthusiastically for an independent air arm.[25] Mitchell became a public martyr to the cause of American airpower, with his struggle eventually featured in *The Court-Martial of Billy Mitchell*, a 1955 film starring Gary Cooper and Rod Steiger.[26]

Mitchell was hardly the only airpower advocate in the United States Army. Among the most notable remaining evangelists were Henry "Hap" Arnold, Claire Chennault, and Benjamin Foulois. Arnold, an early member of the Signal Corps, also argued airpower's case and for an independent air force.[27] Arnold did not suffer Mitchell's fate, instead remaining with the army through World War II, commanding the U.S. Army Air Forces and masterminding the American strategic bombing campaign in Europe. Chennault, a fighter pilot who did not share Mitchell and Arnold's enthusiasm for strategic bombing, served in the Army Air Corps until 1937, when he resigned because of poor health and disagreement with superiors over the relative merits of bomber and pursuit aircraft.[28] Chennault would eventually help found the Flying Tigers, a group of American pilots flying for Nationalist China, and command the China-based Fourteenth Air Force. General Benjamin Foulois, who would lead the Army Air Corps during the 1930s, also supported an independent service and helped lay the foundations for the technological development of World War II heavy bombers such as the B-17, B-24, and B-29.[29] Foulois resigned from the Army Air Corps in 1934, in part because he believed that he could more effectively advocate for airpower outside the army than inside.[30]

In 1926 a temporary compromise in the struggle for independence was reached, allowing the creation of the U.S. Army Air Corps (USAAC), an organization with additional autonomy within the U.S. Army.[31] In 1935, U.S. military aviation took another step toward formal independence with the creation of the General Headquarters Air Force, which controlled the combat operation of all U.S. Army air assets. However, the Army Air Corps continued to manage procurement and doctrine, creating a separation between direct command and the development of capability.

A key institutional difference between the United States and the United Kingdom was that control of air assets in the former remained separate; there was never any serious bureaucratic effort to unite all military aviation under a single umbrella. While the navy played a role in the larger debate over the utility of airpower to the United States, naval aviation remained largely separate from its army counterpart, which used different aircraft and different personnel.[32] Although the most enthusiastic advocates of air force independence argued that airpower could eclipse the navy, the actual struggle for independence remained mostly confined to the U.S. Army. The navy kept a tight hold on its own aviation priorities, including training, procurement, and the formation of doctrine. The navy and army did skirmish over control of coastal defense, with the Army Air Corps arguing that heavy bombers operating from land bases could effectively defend from maritime attack. The navy wanted to ensure unity of command between land- and sea-based aircraft operating over maritime space and thus also wanted the coastal defense mission.[33] The conflict was temporarily resolved by giving the army control of land-based aircraft. The USN invested heavily in aircraft carrier aviation, constructing several large, fast ships and developing carrier employment doctrine. The navy also continued to work on the development of fast, effective carrier-borne aircraft. While naval aviators resented the focus of the navy on dreadnought battleships, they did not trust Mitchell or believe that a unified service would either protect their interests or serve the cause of naval aviation.[34] This would have profound effects on the relative effectiveness of U.S. and British naval aviation in World War II. The U.S. Marine Corps also sought an independent aviation capability.[35] A USMC aviation company was formed in 1915, and Marine fliers supported Marine operations during the war with air superiority, reconnaissance, and close air support missions.

Throughout the interwar period, the leadership of the USAAS and the USAAC remained dedicated to the goal of full service independence and undertook to push U.S. Army aviation in the direction of strategic airpower.[36] Only strategic airpower provided a mission-centric justification for independence; a strategic bombing campaign conducted by an independent air force could win victory in war without the interference or assistance of the army or navy.[37] Although the USAAC suffered from factionalism, with "pursuit" pilots arguing for fighters and bomber pilots arguing for heavier bombers, the bombing faction consistently won. Major General Perry Smith argues that the debate between "pursuit" and "bomber" factions in the Army Air Corps in the 1930s became intractable because the bomber faction was unwilling to admit that pursuit (later fighter) aircraft could catch and disrupt bomber formations. Anything that suggested the vulnerability of heavy bombers was detrimental to the cause. Consequently, the Army Air Corps neglected the development of pursuit aircraft and pursuit tactics in favor of bombers. This led to disaster as the Germans developed effective defensive tactics during World War II. Eventually, the Army Air Forces had to use long-range pursuit aircraft to escort bombers to their targets. But then, as Smith argues: "Instead of making the common mistake of planning to fight the next war with weapons and techniques that had been effective in the last, the Air Corps planners were laying plans to conduct the next war using weapons and techniques that had been proven largely ineffective in the present war. The reason is quite obvious: the planners were not making detailed plans for fighting the next war but rather were planning for a force that could provide the justification for autonomy."[38] Some might argue that the quest for autonomy so dominated Army Air Corps thought that it took precedence over the pursuit of victory.

In contrast to the Royal Air Force, the USAAC's approach to strategic bombing had a specifically economic focus. In part because aviators worried that the idea of area bombing of enemy cities might disturb the American public, the targets discussed in American planning and training involved "critical" economic sectors, the destruction of which would bring the enemy's economy to its knees. As Lieutenant Colonel Donald Wilson argued: "The industrial nation has grown and prospered in proportion to the excellence of its industrial system, but, and here is the irony of the situation, the better this industrial organization for peacetime efficiency the more vulnerable it is to wartime collapse caused by the cutting of one or more of its essential arteries. How this is accomplished is the essence of air strategy in modern warfare."[39]

This represented a clear rejection of the idea that the "fog of war" precluded information dominance and also a rejection of the idea that systems and societies were sufficiently complex to survive without "essential" arteries. American strategic bombing remains fixated with the idea of "critical" targets to the present day.

As war approached in the late 1930s, the Army Air Corps took impressive steps forward on equipment, doctrine, and training. The centerpiece of AAC doctrinal and technical development was the Boeing B-17, a high-altitude heavy bomber designed to carry out strategic bombing missions.[40] The AAC intended the B-17 to operate without fighter support and consequently required a strong defensive armament. Some also expected the B-17 to enjoy service as a maritime bomber, although these hopes did not materialize to any good effect. As the United States prepared to enter World War II, it reorganized its military aviation. In June 1941, the U.S. Army Air Corps became the U.S. Army Air Forces. The USAAF represented a de facto recognition that aviators would receive their own independent service at the cessation of hostilities and provided an administrative foundation for the massive expansion that war would require.[41] The USAAF brought together both functional air command and procurement for the first time, although, as before, naval and marine aviation remained under the control of their respective organizations.

THE EVE OF WAR

At the beginning of the World War II none of the major combatants was well prepared to undertake a strategic air war. Luftwaffe doctrine remained focused on tactical support of the Wehrmacht, while the Royal Air Force had not fully put the ideals of strategic bombing into procurement practice. Only the U.S. Army Air Corps had prepared itself doctrinally and materially for a strategic bombing campaign, and the United States would not enter the war until December 1941.[42] The combatants in World War II did not immediately resort to strategic bombing, although early tactical attacks such as the German bombings of Warsaw and Rotterdam portended a grim future.[43] After the fall of France, the German Luftwaffe launched an air campaign to destroy Great Britain's ability to resist an invasion. The Battle of Britain (or "England Attack," as the

Germans termed the campaign, began in July 1940, with the Luftwaffe initially attempting to establish air superiority over the English Channel and southern England. Eventually, the Luftwaffe moved on to attacking airfields and infrastructure, later expanding its target set to include industry associated with aircraft production. However, the Luftwaffe was poorly equipped for undertaking a full strategic campaign and had weak intelligence regarding British capabilities. In early September, a series of tit-for-tat raids on Berlin and London became a full-fledged urban bombing campaign, targeting industry and infrastructure in London. At one point, German bombers struck London on fifty-seven consecutive nights. However, the campaign failed to severely dent British war production, which continued to increase (albeit at a rate some 5 percent lower than expected) throughout the bombing. Also, the morale of the British public did not falter. In exchange for these limited gains, RAF Fighter Command exacted a terrible toll on the Luftwaffe, which never fully regained its strength.[44]

The American Contribution in the Air

Upon entering the war in December 1941, the U.S. military faced tremendous demands on its airpower assets. Naval aviation dominated the Pacific theater, with carrier aircraft accounting for the destruction of a vast amount of Imperial Japanese Navy vessels. Indeed, carrier aviation would contribute more to the course of the Pacific war than any other single factor, with the possible exception of submarines. In the Atlantic, naval aviators took primary responsibility for the air component of the antisubmarine campaign, although army fliers participated early in the war.[45] U.S. Marine Corps aviators conducted air superiority and close air support missions during the long island-hopping campaign across the Pacific, often flying the F4U Corsair. During several major amphibious assaults, USMC aviators provided both the air cover and the ground support for advancing troops. The Marines insisted on maintaining their aviation capability because of the perceived inadequacy of naval and army close air support.[46]

The tactical needs of the U.S. Army in Europe and the Pacific were the responsibility of the Army Air Corps. In Europe, this included Ninth and Twelfth Air Force support of the campaigns in North Africa and Italy as well as the invasion of France in June 1944.[47] The general attrition of the Luftwaffe (itself a result of the Combined Bomber Offensive) allowed the tactical elements of the Army Air Corps to concentrate on attack and reconnaissance missions, which they conducted with great success. In the Pacific, the Fifth, Seventh, and Thirteenth Air Forces supported USN and U.S. Army operations against Japan.

The core of the U.S. air campaign, however, remained the strategic bombing forces in Europe and the Pacific. The deployment of the VIII Bombing Command to Great Britain gave the United States its first real opportunity to contribute to the war against Germany. Using B-24s and B-17s, VIII Bombing Command launched its first strike on German-controlled Europe on July 4, 1942. By late August 1942 the command was conducting strikes on German targets in France, Belgium, and the Netherlands.[48] Lieutenant Colonel Curtis LeMay led several of these early missions, helping to develop tactics that would improve the performance of USAAF bombers later in the war.[49] By early 1943 the USAAF began to conduct missions against industrial targets in Germany, including aircraft factories, synthetic rubber plants, and oil production and refining infrastructure.

VIII Bomber Command was accompanied by VIII Fighter Command and VIII Support Command, collectively known as the Eighth Air Force.[50] The former provided escort for bombers attacking German targets, while the latter conducted reconnaissance, air transport, and close air support. In addition to the deployment to Great Britain, the Twelfth Air Force conducted operations in the Mediterranean in support of the war against Italy and the invasion of French North Africa. The operations of the Twelfth Air Force were similar to those of the Eighth, with more emphasis on close air support because of the greater incidence of land combat in the Mediterranean theater of operations.

The successor aircraft to the B-17 Flying Fortress and the B-24 Liberator was the B-29 Superfortress, a larger aircraft with a pressurized cabin, a higher bomb load, and a greater range. B-29 delivery was prioritized to the Pacific theater, which fell under the responsibility of the Twentieth Air Force.[51] Teething problems with the aircraft prevented its operational deployment before spring 1944.[52] Initial plans for a strategic bombing campaign against Japan considered using Chinese bases as launching points. In 1944 the USAAF, in combination with the Chinese Army, attempted to turn these plans into a reality in a campaign dubbed Operation Matterhorn.[53] The Allies lacked a land route for resupplying bases in China, so that the B-29s had to fly their own fuel and bombs "over the hump" from India. This limited operational tempo, meaning that the aircraft could have only a restricted effect on Japanese industry and morale. Moreover, the launch of strategic bombers from Chinese bases helped provoke the 1944 "Ichigo" offensive, in which the Japanese Army inflicted a devastating defeat on Chinese forces and captured several major Allied airfields.[54]

A second, much more successful campaign developed as the U.S. Navy and Marine Corps seized Pacific islands from Japanese control. The Mariana Islands, captured in mid-1944, proved suitable bases for the USAAF campaign. Eventually, the vast bulk of the strategic bombing campaign against Japan would come from these bases.[55] Control of these bases came with its own costs, of course, as Japanese defenders exacted a heavy toll on invading U.S. forces. By late 1944, however, B-29s were regularly striking Japanese cities from these island bases. Against Japan the United States adopted area bombing, based on the idea that Japanese industry was too dispersed to allow precision bombing, and that Japanese cities were uniquely vulnerable to incendiary attacks.[56]

Evaluation

Since World War II, military analysts and civilian scholars have expended tremendous effort trying to determine the exact impact of the strategic bombing campaigns against Germany and Japan. Most of this effort involves examination of the economic effects of the bombing campaigns because in neither case did the purported morale effects of strategic bombing meet the claims made by airpower advocates. Attacks against civilians broke the will of neither the Japanese nor the German government to continue fighting, nor did they lead to widespread unrest. To the extent that the attacks had strategic impact, they did reduce industrial output of German and Japanese war material and forced redirection of German and Japanese war efforts toward air defense, although even these effects were limited, and far below what airpower advocates predicted.[57]

The best argument for the success of the Combined Bomber Offensive concentrates, ironically, on the impact it had on German military capabilities. For example, in *A War to Be Won*, Williamson Murray and Alan R. Millett argue that while strategic bombing broke neither German nor Japanese morale, it did force both countries to divert a substantial portion of their defense establishment to air defense.[58] Especially in Europe, assets used in air defense might have had greater effect on the Eastern Front and in other theaters of the war. Moreover, during 1942 and 1943, the Allies had relatively few means at their disposal for bringing war to Germany or for supporting the Russian war effort. Strategic bombing represented the most useful contribution that the United States and the United Kingdom could make during the early portion of the war. However, this impact was purchased at tremendous cost to the United States and the United Kingdom. Some 55,000 British aviators lost their lives during the strategic bombing offensive over Europe, along with 26,000 Americans.[59] John Fahey argues based on cost data on construction, fuel, personnel, and infrastructure that the RAF strategic campaign contributed to British postwar impoverishment.[60] On the American side, some estimates suggest that the cost of developing the B-29 heavy bomber exceeded the costs of the Manhattan Project.[61] As Richard Overy notes, faced with the prospect of these costs, the Soviet Union determined that the easiest way to destroy the Wehrmacht and the Luftwaffe was to concentrate on tactical, rather than strategic, aviation.[62]

However, there is no question that the USAAF dedication to strategic bombing stemmed from a commitment to organizational independence. This commitment led it (and the RAF) to promise huge gains from a combined bomber offensive, gains that were not realized. Fortunately, the Americans, British, and Russians had sufficient advantages to meet their tactical airpower requirements alongside the Combined Bomber Offensive. With regard to the themes of this book, the USAAF clearly exhibited the three Clausewitzian problems identified in this argument. Both the RAF and the USAAF hoped that strategic bombing would win the war without the necessity of invading Europe or Japan, and both forces resisted and resented the diversion of forces to the tasks associated with "disarming" Germany and Japan. The USAAF saw the war as an opportunity to demonstrate the technical and doctrinal viability of its military model, a priority that sometimes conflicted with strategic necessity. Finally, the

British commitment to winning the war by destroying German morale and the American belief that the German economy would collapse if the crucial "link" was found both reveal a contempt for complexity and for the "fog of war."

Evaluation of the Combined Bomber Offensive mattered for the future. As World War II wound down, the USAAF sought to produce an evaluation of the effect of the strategic bombing campaigns in both Europe and the Pacific. The first effort began well before the war had ended and involved the establishment of a Committee of Historians to evaluate the impact of strategic bombing.[63] However, this committee delivered a verdict that did not fully accord with air force institutional interests.[64] A second effort resulted in the United States Strategic Bombing Survey, a large-scale project to determine the military, political, and economic damage inflicted by the USAAF on Germany and Japan. The survey entailed substantial on-the-ground reporting by hundreds of U.S. military and civilian personnel. Ambitious in scope, the survey eventually determined, "Allied air power was decisive in the war in Western Europe. Hindsight inevitably suggests that it might have been employed differently or better in some respects. Nevertheless, it was decisive."[65] The Pacific survey was less conclusive, suggesting that Japan might have surrendered even in the absence of the strategic bombing campaign.[66]

1947 NATIONAL SECURITY ACT: BIRTH OF THE U.S. AIR FORCE

An independent postwar U.S. Air Force was not a foregone conclusion, although many in the Army Air Forces expected such a development. However, commanders of both the army and the air force during the war had operated on the assumption that independence might come in the postwar period.[67] This assumption had helped alleviate some tension within the army, although disagreements over strategic and procurement priorities persisted. As Major General Perry Smith succinctly argued:

> Although there may be some question as to whether, in the thirties, this doctrine was used to justify the Army Air Corps case for autonomy or whether autonomy was a means the Army Air Corps leadership tried to use to [e]nsure that American military air-

power would be heavily weighted in favor of the strategic bombing mission, the evidence indicates that in the 1943–1945 period
the former was the case . . . if strategic bombardment could not
be decisive in warfare, and if victory could be obtained only by
having an army actually meet and defeat the enemy on the battlefield, then it would be difficult to refute the case for maintaining
within the United States Army the Army Air Corps.[68]

As Smith notes, U.S. Army Air Forces' rhetoric became progressively
more dismissive of the possibility that the navy or the army could mean-
ingfully contribute to victory in future war. Although Billy Mitchell had
tried to demonstrate the obsolescence of the dreadnought through the
sinking of *Ostfriesland,* army aviators had largely restrained themselves
in the latter part of the interwar period. During and after World War II,
the gloves came off. Naval aviation became vulnerable; air force generals
debated whether the aircraft carrier was wholly obsolete or if its aircraft
should be subjected, RAF style, to U.S. Air Force command.[69] In late 1943,
General George Marshall proposed a plan that would unite the armed
forces under a single cabinet department and chief of staff.[70] Marshall
worried that an independent air force would leave the army without necessary air support.[71]

The navy, however, rejected the idea of a unified service. Naval command tradition stood too far distant from those of the army and Army
Air Forces. The navy was also concerned that unification would result in
the transfer of naval aviation assets to an autonomous aviation branch.
Lessons on the effect of the RAF on Royal Navy carrier aviation weighed
heavily with the navy. Consequently, the navy proposed an institutionally
independent air force that would sit as coequal to the army and the navy
in the presidential cabinet.[72] Compromise resulted in the 1947 National
Security Act, a transformative moment in the history of U.S. security institutions, giving birth to the U.S. Air Force as well as the Department
of Defense and several other key organs of the postwar national security
state.[73] The air force achieved independence on the same level as the army
and navy and won (briefly) a position in the cabinet, although this was
quickly subordinated under the new secretary of defense. The 1947 National Security Act also created the National Security Council, the Cen-

tral Intelligence Agency, and the Joint Chiefs of Staff. Like the USAF, all of these organizations grew from predecessors that had operated in World War II.

Unlike in the United Kingdom during the early interwar period, there was no serious effort to turn the clock back on USAF independence. However, that independence did not end the bureaucratic infighting. The distribution of all air assets between the services remained to be determined. The 1948 Key West agreement helped specify the relationship between the air assets of the three major services.[74] The USAF would gain control of all strategic air units as well as most tactical and logistic support assets. The army would keep a rump force intended for reconnaissance and medical evacuation, mostly in the form of helicopters but including a few fixed-wing aircraft. The navy would retain its own air arm "to conduct air operations as necessary for the accomplishment of objectives in a naval campaign."[75] The agreement effectively gave the USAF control of the greater portion of U.S. airpower, while leaving the navy and Marine Corps air forces alone.

The peace of 1948 would not endure. In the immediate wake of the 1947 U.S. military reorganization, the USAF argued for the preeminence of strategic bombing in U.S. military doctrine and called for the development and large-scale procurement of the B-36 Peacemaker, a new strategic bomber.[76] The navy, however, continued to have faith in carrier aviation and argued for the construction of new "supercarriers" that would replace the World War II veterans that then made up the fleet.[77] The first supercarrier was supposed to be the USS *United States* (CVA-58), laid down in April 1949. A change in personnel at the Department of Defense, however, led to the quick cancellation of the aircraft carrier. In response, a group of admirals broke into open disagreement with civilian officials about procurement priorities. The admirals also began a low-level propaganda campaign against the B-36.[78] Although the "Revolt of the Admirals" did not involve direct conflict over the organizational responsibilities of either the air force or the navy, it did reveal serious disagreements over the strategic direction of the U.S. military and the value of nuclear weapons.

While the separation of the USAF from its organic association with close air support, air mobility, and other collaborative missions would eventually create problems, the separation did not devastate other areas of military aviation. The navy and the Marine Corps kept their air forces, preserving redundancy in key capabilities. In short, the United States benefited enormously during World War II from delaying service independence for the U.S. Air Force. Had Mitchell prevailed in the early 1920s, the aircraft carriers that won the Pacific war might have flown the same substandard aircraft as their British counterparts—or worse, they might never have been built at all.

THE NUCLEAR TURN

The use of two nuclear weapons against Japan in 1945 necessarily heralded a shift in airpower practice. Early atomic weapons were extremely destructive, but not so much that they could revolutionize the doctrine of strategic bombing. However, developments in nuclear technology (in particular the invention of the hydrogen bomb) necessarily shifted the terms under which strategic bombing would be conceived and conducted. As the certainty of confrontation with the Soviet Union grew, the USAF concentrated on developing bombers that could penetrate Soviet air defenses from both forward and transcontinental bases, then deliver nuclear payloads to Soviet cities and military bases. These bombers were expected to enter Soviet airspace at a high speed and high altitude in order to avoid Soviet defenses.[79] Presumably in response to a Soviet invasion of Western Europe (although several other trigger events were envisioned), the USAF would carry out strikes to destroy Soviet industry and decapitate the Soviet state. As the number and power of nuclear munitions increased, the type of warfare envisioned by the USAF came to resemble less Giulio Douhet's concept of destabilizing and demoralizing bombing raids and more the total destruction of the Soviet state and of Russian society. In case of war, there might be no more Russians left to revolt against their government. The USAF also began to work through the implications of the nascent Soviet heavy bomber force, developing radars and interceptors capable of attacking Soviet forces.[80]

From 1947 on, theoretical work on strategic bombing would come primarily from the U.S. Air Force and its associated organizations, such as the RAND Corporation.[81] RAND was tasked with developing the theoretical foundation for the USAF's postwar force structure. RAND's work fit easily into the air force's vision of warfare, especially in its use of advanced analytical techniques to pierce the fog of war.[82] Researchers at RAND included Albert Wohlstetter, Bernard Brodie, and a host of other luminaries of the world of strategic theory in the 1950s and 1960s.[83] Of course, when RAND analysis ran against air force cultural priorities (as it would early in the missile age), the USAF did not feel bound by RAND recommendations.[84]

The nuclear age was greeted by the development of a new fleet of strategic bombers. The extraordinarily expensive B-29 had a shelf life of about five years.[85] B-29s could neither deliver the most advanced nuclear weapons to the depths of the Soviet Union nor fight off the new class of Soviet interceptors. In 1949, the air force began to replace the B-29 with the B-36 Peacemaker, a huge propeller-driven bomber that could attack the USSR from bases in the United States.[86] However, the big, slow B-36 was also vulnerable to Soviet interceptors. The B-47 Stratojet was a jet-powered medium bomber that lacked the range to penetrate deep within the Soviet Union. Designed to operate from bases around the Soviet periphery, B-47s would deliver tactical and strategic nuclear weapons against available Soviet military and civilian targets in case of general war. In essence, the B-47 was a medium bomber pressed into a strategic role.[87]

The chief lesson of the struggle over U.S. airpower between 1918 and 1947 may well be that aviation advocates do not need an independent service in order to create mischief; they need only a committed belief in the dominance of airpower. The USAAF arguably adopted an even more extreme stance on the effectiveness of strategic bombing than the RAF, although the former fortunately suffered from constraints that the latter did not experience. What did the USAF learn from its battle for independence? Strategic bombing works, if not to win wars then to win bureaucratic battles. The U.S. Air Force won its independence, but the environment it faced in 1950 looked different than what anyone had expected. The USAF was challenged by technological transformations (including the development of nuclear weapons and the advent of the missile age) and by shifts in political tectonics. The newest U.S. military service did not react quickly or well to these shifts. As the generation of pilots who had begun serving in or before World War II moved into retirement, new factional fighting broke out, this time motivated by the tension between tactical and strategic visions of airpower. These tensions did not, however, produce any lasting peace between the air force and its sibling services.

6

American Airpower in
the Era of Limited War

For defensible reasons, the early USAF focused on what it believed was the greatest threat, nuclear war. Unfortunately, the USAF found itself, in Korea and Vietnam, engaged in limited conflicts that it had not prepared for. The experience of operating under these limitations proved transformational for the airpower institutions of the United States and helped clarify the borders between services. The treatments of these campaigns is of necessity cursory in some respect, as the intent is more to demonstrate the repetitive nature of problems associated with independent airpower than to supply an authoritative account of the campaigns in question.

Several organizational problems recurred through this period. First, the air force consistently put strategic imperatives above tactical considerations, leaving it unprepared for the tasks of fighting limited wars. Second, the air force consistently overestimated the impact of its strategic campaigns. Finally, the air force rarely collaborated effectively with its partners in the U.S. Army and the U.S. Navy, although experience tended to remove impediments to cooperation over time in specific wars. These problems correspond with the cultural issues identified in chapter 2 and represent a manifestation of airpower theorists' rejection of Clausewitz.

Korea: The Air Force Tastes Combat

On June 25, 1950, the armed forces of the Democratic People's Republic of Korea (DPRK) escalated a long-running conflict between North and

South Korea by launching a major invasion of the South. The invasion achieved operational surprise against the South Korean military, and Republic of Korea (ROK) forces quickly fell back. U.S. intervention came in July, with the Republic of Korea Army (ROKA) and the U.S. Army establishing a defensible perimeter around the southern port city of Pusan in August. In September U.S. forces carried out an amphibious landing at Incheon, threatening North Korean logistics, and by early October American and South Korean forces had pushed the DPRK back from its initial positions. Chinese intervention in late October tossed the American offensive back, with the two sides settling into an uneasy war of attrition around the 38th parallel by early 1951. Several additional offensives on either side failed to have decisive effect, and the war ended with an armistice in July 1953.

Airpower played a key role in the United Nations response, counteroffensive, and war of attrition.[1] However, the U.S. Air Force was not optimally designed for conventional combat on the Korean Peninsula. The relatively primitive state of the North Korean economy, combined with the willingness of China and the Soviet Union to supply the DPRK with weapons, limited the effectiveness of the strategic bombing campaign.[2] Moreover, the air force had (as was the case with the U.S. intelligence community) severely underestimated the technical capabilities of new Soviet aircraft. Soviet MiG-15s exacted a dreadful toll on USAF B-29s and obsolescent USAF F-80 Shooting Stars. Although USAF strategic bombers, fighter-bombers, and attack aircraft eventually concentrated on interdicting Chinese and North Korean logistics, the ability of the enemy to operate at night and in bad weather limited U.S. effectiveness. Also, cagey use of MiG-15s put U.S. interdiction missions in jeopardy, even after the introduction of the F-86 Sabre.[3]

The air force also faced bureaucratic problems. Strategic Air Command (SAC) chief General Curtis LeMay resisted efforts to commit SAC forces to Korea, believing that a potential Soviet offensive required keeping strategic bombers in reserve. A veteran of the bureaucratic battles associated with the birth of the air force, LeMay also resisted subjecting air force assets to local army control. Tension with both the army and the navy would persist across the conflict, with disagreements developing over the conduct of interdiction, close air support, and strategic bombing.

U.S. Army soldiers repeatedly voiced preference for Marine Corps close air support (CAS) over that provided by the air force. The Strategic Air Command even resented navy and Tactical Air Command success against strategic targets in North Korea, such as the hydroelectric industry.[4]

Evaluation

Despite the problems associated with the USAF in Korea, American airpower was important to the ability of the United States and its allies to win a draw in Korea. The USAF caused tremendous damage to the North Korean economy and significant damage to the Chinese and North Korean militaries, although neither campaign had decisive effect.[5] Major lessons learned included a newfound respect for the capabilities of Soviet equipment and for the difficulty of carrying out interdiction and close air support missions in difficult terrain. All told, while the USAF contributed to the war, it failed to demonstrate that it could deliver independent decisive impact, or that service independence was necessary to the effective conduct of an airpower campaign. However, it is fair to say that the political influence of the air force played little to no role in the decision to go to war, which was made by political and military authorities with little reference to the air force's ability to win wars cheaply and quickly.

PROCUREMENT AND THE ADVENT OF THE MISSILE AGE

The United States continued to invest in strategic bombers after the Korean War. The air force never used either its 384 B-36s or its 2,032 B-47s in any combat capacity, except for a few reconnaissance missions over the Soviet Union.[6] The B-52 Stratofortress effectively combined the capabilities of the B-36 and the B-47, having the range to operate from the United States and the speed and payload to deliver nuclear weapons to targets within the Soviet Union. The B-52 entered service in 1956, quickly replacing the B-36 as the USAF's primary long-range strategic bomber.[7] However, the B-52 proved flexible enough as a platform to survive the shift from high-altitude, high-speed bombing to low-altitude penetration bombing and also found itself a major conventional role in Vietnam, Afghanistan, and both Iraq wars. The B-58 Hustler was less fortunate. A supersonic high-altitude penetration bomber, the B-58 was ill suited to low-level missions. Attempts to fly such missions produced an unacceptable loss rate, leading to the retirement of the bomber by 1970. Like the B-36 and the B-47, none of the 116 B-58s flew a combat mission, although twenty-six aircraft were lost in accidents.[8] A large fleet of KC-135 refueling tankers helped support the bomber force.[9]

The effectiveness of MiG-15 fighters in the Korean War demonstrated the need for more advanced fighter aircraft. Not coincidentally, the 1950s and early 1960s were a period of remarkable innovation in fighter technology. The Century series of U.S. fighters included such important aircraft as the F-100 Super Sabre, the F-101 Voodoo, the F-102 Delta Dagger, the F-104 Starfighter, the F-105 Thunderchief, and the F-106 Delta Dart. These aircraft, along with the F-4 Phantom II, would bear the brunt of the load during the Vietnam War.[10]

Missiles

The advent of the missile age changed the relationship between military power and the strategic bomber. For one, the development of accurate, fast, high-altitude antiaircraft missiles (fired from either interceptor or ground bases) rendered much bomber doctrine obsolete at a single stroke.[11] After the Soviets and the Americans deployed credible surface-to-air (SAM) missile systems, flying bombers at high altitude and speed into enemy territory became suicidal. Strategic bombers were repurposed for low-altitude penetration missions.[12] This development effectively killed two USAF bomber projects, rendering the B-58 Hustler fleet obsolete and leading to the cancellation of the B-70 Valkyrie.[13] The air force took the latter cancellation hard, as the B-70 was a powerful symbol of the concept of the unescorted strategic bomber, near and dear to the Bomber Command veterans of World War II.[14]

The development of the intercontinental ballistic missile (ICBM) transformed the strategic bombing debate, at least from the perspective of delivery. Russia would no longer be destroyed by brave men flying bombers along the nape of the earth through air defenses, but rather by ICBMs launched by buttons pressed in North Dakota. Similarly, fighter jocks could no longer protect Americans by shooting down incoming Soviet bombers before they reached U.S. cities. However, many of the concepts associated with strategic bombing remained the same.

Nuclear-tipped missiles continued to target Soviet cities, as USAF doctrine continued to contemplate the destruction of enemy economic and population centers.

The U.S. Army Air Forces began developing ballistic missile technology in the immediate wake of World War II, as the extent of German work became clear and German scientists became available. The army proper and the navy also began to investigate missile technology.[15] By the 1950s, all three services were working on developing long-range ballistic missiles as well as shorter-range tactical missiles. In November 1956 the Department of Defense transferred responsibility for all long-range land-based ballistic missiles to the USAF, while the navy retained control over its own submarine-launched ballistic missile (SLBM) project.[16] The army retained shorter-range ballistic missiles with nuclear warheads designed for tactical use. In theory, this made the air force responsible for strategic nuclear weapons and the army for tactical, although the air force also retained the ability to deliver nuclear warheads from tactical aircraft. The navy would acquire a strategic nuclear capability with the Polaris SLBM, launched from *George Washington*–class nuclear ballistic missile submarines (SSBNs), and could use tactical nuclear weapons from a variety of surface ships, aircraft carriers, and submarines in the form of aircraft and cruise missiles. In practice, each of the three services had enough nuclear weapons to fight its own nuclear war. Possession of ICBMs, however, confirmed the USAF's status as the "strategic" service, focused less on tactical warfare than on nuclear confrontation with the Soviet Union.[17]

Helicopters

In 1952, the Pace-Finletter Memorandum of Understanding (Frank Pace and Thomas Finletter were secretaries of the army and air force, respectively) restructured the Key West agreement such that the army had access to a greater variety of helicopters and could use them with more flexibility.[18] However, the agreement also placed a hard ceiling on the size and carrying capacity of fixed-wing army aircraft. This prevented the army from developing its own fixed-wing close air support warplane. Nevertheless, frustrated with air force inaction, the army sought an organic air mobility capability as well as some close air support aircraft. Impressed by the effectiveness of French helicopter gunships in the Algerian War, the army invested heavily in rotary aviation.[19] The air force saw army developments as an effort to build a new air force on the sly.[20]

While the army worked on developing new tactics and weapons for its helicopters, the air force lobbied Congress to eliminate the program. General Curtis LeMay offered to demonstrate the effectiveness of fighter aircraft against assault helicopters by holding a duel between the two.[21] This offer missed the point. Helicopters could engage in close air support and enable air mobility without having to shoot down enemy fighter aircraft as long as some provision was made for retaining air superiority. Nevertheless, LeMay identified army aviation as a potential threat to the parochial interest of the USAF, regardless of whether helicopters met a particular tactical need. The price that the USAF demanded for allowing the army to develop assault helicopters was the remaining fleet of army fixed-wing aircraft, including the C-2/C-7 Caribou, a tactical airlifter. The Caribou were turned over to the USAF, then quickly retired at the end of the Vietnam War. The air force then rejected the development of a more modern fixed-wing tactical airlift aircraft, citing dangers from surface-to-air missiles.[22]

Vietnam: Conventional Airpower in the Cold War

The experience of airpower in the Vietnam War illustrates the multiple uses of airpower in a politically limited conflict and of how the organizational interest and culture of the USAF affected war fighting. In short, the disjuncture between the technological and organizational goals of the USAF and the political demands of the Vietnam War produced considerable friction.

The Major Campaigns

In the Vietnam War, the USAF spearheaded one major strategic bombing campaign and two campaigns that linked strategic bombing with other airpower missions. The debate over the effectiveness of air assets in the Vietnam War extended across virtually every facet of airpower and continues today. In 1965, the USAF and the USN launched Rolling Thunder, a campaign targeting a variety of industrial, military, and infrastructural targets in North Vietnam.[23] The Johnson administration intended the campaign to coerce North Vietnam into acquiescing in the independence of South Vietnam and to cease its support of South Vietnamese guerrillas, although the specific way in which it sought to bring about such an outcome differed from month to month.[24] Informed by the work of political scientists and economists such as Thomas Schelling, the campaign was based on the premise that threatening North Vietnamese targets was as important as destroying them.[25] While destroying a target might hurt the Vietnamese, threatening a target might convince them to give up. This represented a conventional interpretation of the emergent thinking on nuclear weapons doctrine. It was also hoped that bombing would cause enough damage to North Vietnamese industry and infrastructure to make resupply of Communist forces in South Vietnam difficult or impossible.[26] The campaign represented coercion rather than denial, making little effort to target or destroy Viet Cong or PAVN (People's Army of Viet Nam) forces in the field.

The Johnson administration pursued Rolling Thunder as the best in a series of bad options. Johnson did not want to commit substantial ground troops to the conflict, hoping that bombing would suffice. To this purpose he found support from the general concept of strategic bombing presented by the air force, which suggested that an air campaign could find and disrupt the key pillars of North Vietnamese economy and society. Civilians as well as the air force believed that the North Vietnamese leadership strongly valued its infant industrial base and would give up the war in the South rather than risk its destruction. Bombing would also display American resolve.[27]

Debates over the effectiveness of Rolling Thunder began almost as soon as the bombs started dropping. The campaign undoubtedly inflicted damage on the North Vietnamese economy and caused some tension within the Worker's Party of Vietnam (VWP).[28] However, by most accounts this campaign failed to achieve its objectives while politically committing the United States to military escalation. However, the exact reasons for the failure remain subject to debate. Without doubt, both civilian and military leaders were at fault. First, the air force and navy found it very difficult to determine the actual degree of damage inflicted by Rolling Thunder or to develop a coherent theory of how that damage could affect North Vietnamese war-making capacity. Second, the air force consistently resisted political limits on the extent of the bombing, rejecting the idea that military force serves political aims. Finally, the attacks failed to disarm North Vietnam, having little demonstrable impact on the ability of the North Vietnamese to continue their military campaign against the South.[29] The USAF and its supporters blamed civilian officials for placing restrictions on bombing targets and payloads and for graduating the campaign.[30] These restrictions gave the North Vietnamese the time and breathing room to absorb the attacks and to improve their defenses. However, these pauses had relatively little effect on the ability of North Vietnam to resupply its allies in the South. In any case, North Vietnam continued the war and did not collapse in the face of bombing.

Later bombing campaigns, including Linebacker I and Linebacker II, supported more confident claims of success. Linebacker I, launched in the May 1972, was geared at stopping a North Vietnamese conventional offensive into South Vietnam. Linebacker included an interdiction campaign, as well as a series of strategic attacks against North Vietnamese infrastructure. By almost all accounts, the attacks were largely successful.[31] North Vietnam suffered serious infrastructure damage, including the loss of bridges along railways between China and Hanoi. The North Vietnamese offensive stalled, and Hanoi resumed peace talks.

Linebacker II, launched in December 1972 to reassure the South Vietnamese government of U.S. support, involved widespread infrastructure attacks by B-52s and other aircraft against North Vietnam.[32] Damage to North Vietnam was severe, although U.S. losses included twenty-four aircraft, twelve of which were B-52s. However, the political effect of the "Christmas Bombings" appeared limited. U.S. negotiators later admitted that North Vietnam made no significant concessions in response to the campaign. Indeed, the international outrage caused by the bombing helped buttress the resolve of the VWP.[33] The campaign did help convince South Vietnam that the United States would continue its support and thus helped solidify the foundation of the 1973 peace accords.[34] In 1975, without U.S. air support, South Vietnam would fall to a conventional North Vietnamese ground offensive.

The Institutional Debates

Disputes between the navy and the air force over targeting and command and control were initially resolved by assigning the services to different geographical sectors rather than by integrating their efforts.[35] Because the U.S. Air Force in the early part of the Cold War interpreted its writ primarily in strategic terms, it did not view air superiority over a combat area or close air support as priorities.[36] When the USAF began to operate over North Vietnam, American pilots found that their aircraft and training were inadequate to dominate the complex Vietnamese air defense system or to manage the demands of close air support and interdiction against a hybrid opponent. Aircraft designed to intercept Soviet bombers instead found themselves dropping bombs on bridges and small trucks, missions for which they were not well suited.[37]

Air combat also proved problematic, as both the navy and the air force suffered unacceptable casualties in air-to-air combat against North Vietnamese MiG interceptors. The air force initially viewed the problem through a technological lens: its aircraft could not detect MiGs approaching from behind and below.[38] Accordingly, the USAF sought technological solutions to this problem, including improving the weapons capabilities of its F-4 Phantom II fighter-bombers. Conversely, the navy believed that its combat aircrews lacked sufficient experience and training in air-to-air combat.[39] Consequently, the navy sought to solve the problem by improving doctrine and pilot training. The navy effort became the Top Gun program, and over time the USN kill ratio increased from 3.7:1 to 13:1. The air force kill ratio did not improve until much later in the war, when it began to train its pilots against dissimilar aircraft.[40] Air force personnel policies also contributed to the problem, as pilots better suited for bombers and transport aircraft found themselves forced into fighter combat.[41] However, the weakness of USAF tactical aptitude during the war helped lay the foundation for the ascendance of the "Fighter Mafia" during the 1970s, which transformed air force procurement priorities and shifted the air force in a much more tactical direction.[42]

Evaluation

The lessons of airpower in Vietnam generally support a Clausewitzian approach to war. Airpower can have dramatic tactical effect on enemy forces in the field, sometimes defeating staged offensives without resort to strong ground forces. Moreover, the destruction of enemy fielded forces has strategic effect. However, airpower intended to avoid the need to disarm the enemy, which is to say airpower targeted directly against civilians and the state, failed to have political effect. The fog of war remained, preventing the United States from fully penetrating either North Vietnamese decision making or the structure of the North Vietnamese economy. Finally, both the air force and the civilian leadership (particularly in the Johnson administration) misunderstood the relationship between political and military aims. Carl von Clausewitz would have had no difficulty understanding the failure of Rolling Thunder or the success of Linebacker I. The air force preferred to focus on the "success" of Linebacker I and Linebacker II, divorced from their political context.[43]

Just as important, Clausewitz could likely explain the combat shortcomings of the air force. Focus on the strategic mission at the cost of tactical preparation left the air force unprepared to fight in Vietnam from both a human and material standpoint. Fighters designed to kill bombers could not easily shift to other, more tactical missions. Ironically, the air force had great difficulty imposing air superiority against an enemy that it massively overmatched in material and technological terms. The air force remained shackled to strategic bombing; it adjusted eventually, but only at tremendous cost.

Post-Vietnam Procurement

The influence of the Fighter Mafia, combined with the obsolescence of Vietnam-era fighter aircraft, led to the development of two fighter aircraft that would become the mainstays of the USAF fleet from the 1970s into the current decade.[44] The experience of Vietnam demonstrated shortcomings in the USAF's design approach and requirements, undoubtedly leading to the production of superior aircraft. The F-15 Eagle, produced by McDonnell Douglas (and later Boeing), is a high-performance heavy fighter capable of conducting both air superiority and strike missions. The F-15 first flew in 1972 and continues to fly in large numbers for the USAF and allied air forces.[45] The F-16 Fighting Falcon (also known as the Viper) is a lighter, cheaper alternative to the F-15.[46] Designed as an air superiority fighter, the F-16 has excelled in all roles, with more than 4,500 aircraft produced to date. The F-16 makes up a large percentage of the frontline fighter force of the USAF as well as of a large number of allied air forces. Together, the F-15 and F-16 have amassed a remarkable record of success.

On the strategic side, attention would shift to the B-1 bomber, a supersonic swept-wing bomber designed to penetrate Soviet airspace at high speed and low altitude. The B-1A, a high-speed variant, was cancelled in favor of the B-1B, which sacrificed speed in pursuit of low cost and a low radar profile. One hundred B-1Bs were eventually procured, with most remaining in service. The follow-up to the B-1B, the B-2 Spirit, moved in an entirely different design direction. Instead of speed, the B-2 concentrated on stealth, allowing it to penetrate enemy airspace and proceed to its target without detection.[47] Post–Cold War austerity would eventually cap B-2 production at twenty-one units, most of which remain in USAF service.

The struggle between the army and the air force over rotary aviation continued. The 1966 Johnson-McConnell agreement (so named after army chief of staff General Harold Johnson and air force chief of staff General John P. McConnell) briefly made peace once again, this time by transferring almost all fixed-wing army aircraft to the USAF and giving the responsibility for almost all combat helicopters to the army.[48] However, this agreement did not end the fight. The army, seeking its own close air support capability, became interested in the AH-56 Cheyenne, a technologically advanced attack helicopter.[49] The air force offered to develop a dedicated close air support aircraft in lieu of the troubled, expensive Cheyenne. Under assurances from the air force and pressure from Congress, the army eventual gave up on Cheyenne.[50]

Without the threat of an advanced army attack helicopter, some within the air force proposed disposing of the dedicated close air support aircraft. However, army influence, congressional pressure, and changes in the balance of power between USAF factions saved the A-10, which joined the air force fleet in the mid-1970s. Armed with a 30-mm cannon (a very large gun for an aircraft its size), the A-10 Thunderbolt II (affectionately known as the Warthog) was expected to hunt and kill Soviet tanks in a general war between NATO and the Warsaw Pact.[51] The aircraft remained generally unpopular in the USAF (pilots preferred to fly fighter aircraft), but its presence in the arsenal led to the development of a community of trained and committed CAS operators. Nevertheless, the air force curtailed procurement in the 1980s, and by some accounts initially resisted deployment of the A-10 in service of Operation Desert Storm.[52] In the early 2000s, the air force again commissioned a study into the possibility of killing the A-10 but backtracked in response to public pressure.[53]

All of these aircraft would carry much-improved ordnance. While guided air munitions had existed in World War II, most ordnance used in Vietnam was "dumb," lacking any terminal guidance to target. During the war, the air force and navy deployed a variety of systems to improve this situation. Early versions of precision-guided munitions relied on small television cameras with transmitters to allow the aircraft to guide the bomb to its target. By the end of the war, laser-guided bombs had sufficiently improved to allow an increase in targeting effectiveness. Later developments included the acquisition of the AGM-65 Maverick, a guided missile that could penetrate Soviet armor and other hard targets.[54] These weapons substantially increased the tactical effectiveness of USAF aircraft against ground targets.

John Boyd and the Late–Cold War Air-Ground Team

The generally acknowledged failure of strategic bombing to win the Vietnam War helped bring about a crisis of confidence in the U.S. Air Force. Significant concerns about the tactical performance of the air force as well as USAF collaboration with the army also left a bad taste.[55] A struggle between tactical and strategic elements developed, with the former eventually breaking the leadership monopoly of the latter.[56] Strategic bombing capabilities would not disappear from U.S. military theory or the U.S. arsenal, but the focus of USAF efforts moved in a tactical direction.[57] Inspired by fighter pilot John Boyd, the Fighter Mafia would for the first time in the history of American airpower push procurement and doctrinal attention toward fighters rather than bombers. The designs pursued by the Fighter Mafia would emphasize air combat superiority over interceptor roles: the former with the expectation of combat against other fighters and the latter in expectation of combat against bombers. Platforms emerging from the heyday of the Fighter Mafia include the above-noted F-15 and F-16, which remain the mainstays of the modern USAF.[58]

However, the focus on tactical and air superiority aircraft created a crisis of identity in the USAF, which had achieved its independence through the espousal of strategic airpower as an independent means for winning wars. Vietnam demonstrated the necessity for increased emphasis on air superiority doctrine and procurement, but air superiority remained fundamentally a supportive rather than war-winning mission.[59]

However, strategic bombing theory would soon experience a renaissance. Partly in response to the work of John Boyd, the effects-based operations (EBO) concept emerged during the 1980s as part of the emergent Revolution in Military Affairs (RMA).[60] The RMA, according to advocates, promised a fundamental reinvention of modern warfare based on information technology, high-power sensors, and precision-guided munitions launched from standoff ranges. In the wake of the Yom Kippur War, in which precision-guided munitions (PGMs) wreaked massive destruction on both Israeli and Arab armies, theorists in the Soviet Union and elsewhere argued that these technological developments would render current military doctrine inadequate and obsolete. Boyd argued that modern weaponry, properly employed, could inflict paralysis on target organizations, effectively destroying their capacity to act. Boyd coined the term "OODA loop," referring to a cyclical observe-orient-decide-act process of organizational activity. Boyd engaged with Clausewitz, arguing that a full appreciation of the OODA loop and the use of modern airpower technology could eliminate the need to disarm the enemy, at least in the traditional sense of the term.[61]

At a theoretical level, these developments helped revive the "operational" level of war, as opposed to the tactical and strategic. While the tactical level focuses on the means with which individual units fight one another, and the strategic level deals with the conduct of large-scale campaigns, the operational level concentrates on how organizations plan for and maintain themselves during extended engagements. As an operational doctrine, EBO expected PGM attacks along the entire depth of enemy formations conducting either offensive or defensive operations.[62] Attacks on enemy front lines, reinforcements, and logistics would become part of the same operation, with the objective to paralyze the enemy military organization and prevent it from conducting its own operations.[63] The radical increase in information processing and communications technol-

ogy, combined with the expansion of intelligence collection and aggrega-
tion capabilities into the upper atmosphere, would render the battle space
more intelligible (and more plastic) than ever before, making the identification of critical targets possible. Theorists in the Soviet Union and the
United States suggested that NATO and Warsaw Pact forces would require reform and reconstruction in order to conduct warfare under these
new technological conditions. However, the inability of the Soviet Union
to compete with the West, and its eventual collapse, helped prevent a full
test of these doctrinal concepts.[64]

By the mid-1980s, the army and the air force had reached a modus
vivendi around the AirLand Battle doctrinal concept.[65] This concept defined the tactical and operational responsibilities of both services in context of war between NATO and the Warsaw Pact. AirLand Battle replaced
Active Defense, the army's first response to the Yom Kippur War. Hear-
kening back to interwar conceptions of operational art, AirLand Battle
envisioned an integrated battle space that would attack Soviet forces in
depth while retaining the capacity for maneuver. AirLand Battle incorpo-
rated some aspects of the Revolution in Military Affairs without adopting
the logic wholesale; it remained fundamentally a doctrine for fixing and
destroying enemy ground forces in battle. However, this destruction often involved paralyzing the organizational sinews of the enemy by striking logistical and communications targets deep behind the front lines.

AirLand Battle was army doctrine, not air force doctrine. Nevertheless, the army developed the doctrine in collaboration with the air force
and with an appreciation of air force boundaries.[66] The most important
issues at stake regarded the line of responsibility between USAF and army
responsibilities, and the ability of the air force to conduct operations in
collaboration but not coordination with ground forces. Within a certain
line (the Fire Support Coordination Line [FSCL]), the army (using artillery, missiles, and aviation assets) would conduct interdiction and close
support, with the air force conducting strikes only in coordination with
ground commanders. Interdiction beyond that line would fall to the
air force. However, both the army and air force recognized that actual
battle conditions would render a restrictive line of control awkward and
counterproductive.[67] To resolve these problems, the army and air force
adopted a set of distinctions between close air support and battlefield

air interdiction (BAI).[68] The willingness of elements of the air force to adopt a positive attitude toward cooperation with the army on CAS and BAI helped resolve tension between the services as well as produce an effective, coherent doctrine for defeating the Red Army. However, critics in the air force resisted this collaboration, believing that AirLand Battle misunderstood Soviet doctrine and that yoking airpower to the concerns of local ground commanders remained a serious mistake.[69] In particular, although BAI inside the FSCL required only coordination with the army, not army control, many aviators worried that BAI represented a backdoor effort to give ground commanders undue influence over air force assets.[70] In practice, the air force would dispose of BAI at the earliest opportunity.

THE GULF WAR AND THE RISE OF NEOCLASSICAL AIRPOWER THEORY

The 1991 Gulf War would provide a test for the new logic of strategic bombing. The Iraqi Army invaded Kuwait in August 1990, conquering the country in a matter of days and provoking the United States and a coalition of allies to build up ground and air forces in Saudi Arabia. The coalition's political emphasis soon shifted from defending Saudi Arabia to ejecting Iraqi forces from Kuwait. As in other wars, airpower advocates argued against army officers committed to ground operations. Early debates revolved around the question of whether a ground campaign would be necessary at all. While Colonel John Warden believed that airpower alone could defeat Iraq, others disagreed.[71] Eventually, a hybrid air campaign would attack political and infrastructure targets within Iraq while at the same time smashing Iraqi Army formations in and around Kuwait. In ground-air cooperation, this campaign diverged from AirLand Battle by largely disposing of BAI and establishing tight restrictions on the employment of both army and air force assets.[72] A thirty-seven-day air campaign against targets in Iraq and Kuwait began on January 16, 1991, and continued through a ground invasion that began on February 23. The air campaign did not convince Saddam Hussein to retreat from Kuwait or induce the collapse of his regime, but it did seriously degrade Iraqi military capabilities, contributing to a ground campaign that won an easy and decisive victory.[73] In an echo of the Strategic Bombing Survey, the USAF sponsored the *Gulf War Air Power Survey,* a five-volume work detailing air operations and examining their effectiveness.[74] Running to nearly 4,000 pages, the survey represented an exhaustive effort to determine the utility of particular kinds of airpower.[75]

The Gulf War saw the first employment of the joint force air component commander (JFACC), an air force officer tasked with organizing and executing the air component of the war. The JFACC fulfilled the air force's long-standing desire for centralized control of airpower, as the JFACC had authority over the entirety of coalition airpower, including navy and Marine Corps assets. While the other services had some complaints about JFACC priorities (in the case of the Gulf War, Lieutenant General Charles Horner fulfilled this role), the overwhelming superiority of American airpower assets made for relatively few difficult trade-offs.[76]

Evaluations of airpower effectiveness in the Gulf War revolve around the relative contribution of ground and air assets at driving Iraqi forces from Kuwait, and airpower triumphalism initially carried the day.[77] Colin Gray, for example, argues, "It is beyond argument that the heaviest lifting for the overall strategic effect was done by airpower. Even had Saddam's army sought to conduct a war of maneuver, it would have been unable to do so. . . . John Boyd was at least partially correct."[78]

Although airpower did not directly force Saddam from Kuwait, advocates claimed that air strikes broke the back of his army, cut Kuwait off from Iraq, and allowed coalition ground forces to easily defeat the rump Iraqi Army with very low casualties. These advocates concentrated on the morale effects of bombing on Iraqi frontline troops (who often surrendered en masse at the appearance of coalition ground forces), the effects of attacks on Iraqi command and control networks, the impact of interdiction of Iraqi logistics, and finally on the attrition of Iraqi fielded forces. Although most of these effects have traditionally fallen into tactical and operational conceptions of airpower, advocates argued that the USAF in the Gulf War had decisive effect at the strategic level.[79]

However, some critics later attacked this consensus. Daryl Press argued that the emerging narrative on the war overemphasized the impact of airpower. Specifically, Press argued that airpower failed to destroy deployed Iraqi forces, failed to prevent them from maneuvering, and failed to break their morale. According to Press, the more capable Iraqi formations retained much of their combat power and maneuvered in response to the U.S. ground offensive. Effects on morale were limited to poorly trained conscripts.[80] Stephen Biddle followed this analysis up by arguing that the coalition prevailed because the capabilities of its ground forces vastly exceeded those of the Iraqis in both technology and training, not because of the decisive effect of airpower.[81] Like Press, he suggested that the air campaign damaged Iraqi forces in the Kuwait theater of operations without destroying them. Biddle concluded that U.S. and British ground forces, employing much more sophisticated weapons and more advanced doctrine, could have destroyed the Iraqi army in the absence of a prolonged air campaign.[82]

As for the strategic campaign against Iraq, the air strikes against Iraqi infrastructure and political targets failed to drive Saddam Hussein from power or to reduce his control over the regime in any appreciable manner. In the face of attacks on its communications network, the Iraqi leadership resorted to older methods of sending messages, such as motorcycle messengers.[83] The war helped spur revolts in Kurdistan and in the Shiite south, but both of these failed to overthrow the regime. Western airpower did manage to reduce the ability of the Iraqi Army to restore order in Kurdistan, notably by limiting its ability to operate aircraft in the area. However, this required a long-term campaign of denial and did not affect the legitimacy of the Ba'athist regime. Indeed, the strongest claims that airpower advocates can make about the 1991 Gulf War involve the strategic impact of tactical airpower: the idea that air attacks so devastated the Iraqi military that it could not resist coalition attack.

Nevertheless, Operation Desert Storm represented one of the most successful collaborations of the air-ground team since the founding of the air force. Friction between the army and the air force existed, but not to the extent that it significantly hampered operations. The air force devoted resources to strategic as well as tactical and operational goals, but the central strategic effect of airpower came in the destruction of fielded Iraqi forces and in the preparation for the decisive advance of the U.S. Army and its allies. Extant intelligence limited air force effectiveness, but the concentration on the Iraqi Army (rather than on specific logistical or communications nodes) meant that the enemy still felt the full impact of American airpower.

However, the peace could not hold. Unsurprisingly, the army and the air force adopted the most favorable possible interpretations of their contributions to victory. The looming danger of post–Cold War austerity inclined both the army and the air force to emphasize their individual service contributions instead of the successful elements of their collaboration. The army focused on the continued mobility of Iraqi forces as well as the number of Iraqi vehicles destroyed during the ground offensive.[84] The air force, on the other hand, adopted a new vision of strategic warfare.

The seeds of the air force's narrative of victory had been sown in the 1980s, when USAF lieutenant colonel John Warden helped drive a rethinking of strategic airpower.[85] Warden argued that the enemy state represents an organic system and that by targeting the critical linkages of that system (key infrastructure, important decision makers, communications networks), airpower could shut down an entire state along with its military organizations. Warden borrowed Carl von Clausewitz's "center of gravity" concept and combined it with an understanding of the state as composed of five concentric "rings." The innermost ring included the enemy command structure, the next ring key production capabilities, the third ring transport and logistical capability, the fourth ring the population and its food sources, and the fifth ring the fielded forces of the enemy. Encapsulating much of the logic of strategic airpower, Warden contended that attacks on the outermost ring were the least efficient ways to win a war, with attacks on inner rings yielding progressively better results.[86] Warden was optimistic that intelligence and economic analysis would yield sufficiently good targeting data to allow an air campaign to attack decisive points in the innermost rings.

After 1991, these operational concepts found their way into the strategic realm. Instead of coordinating attacks during an offensive against an enemy military organization, the EBO concept may bring down the entire command structure of an enemy state. The use of PGMs against Saddam Hussein's regime in Iraq in 1991 would provide a case study for this idea.[87]

Warden helped develop the 1991 air campaign against Saddam Hussein, and he drove the reinterpretation of strategic airpower that followed the campaign. Warden argued that the large ground forces deployed in Operation Desert Shield and eventually for Operation Desert Storm were unnecessary to defeat Iraq. Indeed, Warden suggested that the destruction of the fielded forces of the Iraqi Army would prove counterproductive. A strategic campaign focused on attacking the sinews of the Hussein regime would leave Iraqi Army forces intact, and indeed enable them to seize power from the Ba'ath Party.[88] This argument took the classic strategic bombing approach to enemy military forces a step further. The destruction of enemy ground forces was not simply expensive and unnecessary—it was actively detrimental to the war effort.

Warden's new vision of strategic airpower helped reinvigorate the idea that airpower could have independent decisive impact. While strategic bombing of World War II concentrated on enemy civilian morale and industrial capacity, and the strategic bombing of the Cold War targeted infrastructure, modern EBO-style airpower seeks to cut the sinews that tie the state together.[89] Leaders who cannot communicate with their military subordinates cannot effectively lead. Air attacks can disrupt key government services and functions without laying waste to entire cities.[90] In the wake of a successful air campaign, invading armies might find enemy military organizations prostrate, paralyzed, and incapable of resistance. Warden played a role in the U.S. military's adoption of RMA concepts during the 1980s with his book *The Air Campaign: Planning for Combat*.[91] Warden harshly criticized the current U.S. Army doctrine, AirLand Battle, for placing airpower at the mercy of ground commanders involved in ground operations. Instead, Warden argued that attacks on the enemy leadership could lead to decisive outcomes.[92]

Warden helped restore a conventional strategic conception to the USAF and reaffirmed the idea that independent airpower could win decisive military and political victories. This amounted to a reformulation of classical airpower theory, based on the idea of leveraging intelligence and precision for strategic effect. Warden had, in effect, laid the foundation for neoclassical airpower theory. The influence of Warden's ideas was felt through the publication of his book and also through a series of campaign histories of the Gulf War. Major General Perry Smith called *The Air Campaign* "the most important book on air power written in the last decade." The implications of Warden's argument were made clear in *Global Reach—Global Power,* a white paper by three of Warden's associates arguing that the USAF could provide the uniquely capable vehicle for the projection of American power around the world.[93] Faster and more flexible than its army and navy counterparts, the air force could threaten enemies and potential enemies with destruction in short order and without the need for costly buildups or long-term occupations. Airpower thus represented a way of projecting U.S. power in an economical fashion.

Warden's vision of global U.S. dominance through airpower was compatible with an emerging consensus among civilian policymakers in Washington about the role that the United States could play in the international system.[94] Without the Soviet Union to worry about, the United States could think seriously about restructuring the international system according to its preferences. For some, including "neoconservatives" and "liberal hawks," this involved using force to support democratization and curtail authoritarianism as well as to maintain the liberal international economic order. The Iraq War and the NATO intervention in Kosovo seemed to support the idea that airpower could enable the United States to play this leadership role at a reasonable cost.

At the doctrinal level, the experience of the Gulf War led to the abandonment of many precepts of the AirLand Battle concept, including battlefield air interdiction. The ability of airpower to win war independently naturally meant that attention devoted to collaboration with other services was a waste of time. Indeed, in keeping with the logic that tactical airpower could now have independent strategic effect, the air force eliminated the old Tactical Air Command and Strategic Air Command organizational structures. Terrance McCaffrey argues that "service self-interest claims the lion's share of the accountability for BAI's disappearance. The USAF wanted to win a future air war alone. The only way to do that was to own the entire battlefield."[95] This interpretation suggests that the period of peace and cooperation between Vietnam and the Gulf War was the exception rather than the rule in relations between the U.S. Army and the U.S. Air Force.[96]

Airco DH-4 bombers were a mainstay of the early Army Air Service. (U.S. Air Force photo, courtesy of the National Museum of the United States Air Force.)

The Caproni Ca. 36 was one of the earliest strategic bombers. This aircraft is on display at the National Museum of the United States Air Force. (U.S. Air Force photo, courtesy of the National Museum of the United States Air Force.)

General William Lendrum "Billy" Mitchell, one of the founding fathers of the U.S. Air Force, commanded American air units in France in World War I. He was eventually court-martialed for insubordination relating to his views on airpower and an independent air force. (Courtesy of the National Museum of the United States Air Force.)

Early years of the Army Air Corps: Brigadier General Benjamin D. Foulois, Major General James. E. Fechet, and Brigadier General H. C. Pratt. (U.S. Air Force photo, courtesy of the National Museum of the United States Air Force.)

General Henry H. Arnold, commanding general of the U.S. Army Air Forces in World War II. (U.S. Air Force photo, courtesy of the National Museum of the United States Air Force.)

General Curtis E. LeMay. LeMay commanded the U.S. strategic bombing campaign against Japan and later led the Strategic Air Command. (U.S. Air Force photo, courtesy of the National Museum of the United States Air Force.)

Captain Claire Chennault (center) and the rest of an army flight demonstration team. Sergeant William C. McDonald (left), Sergeant John H. Williamson (right), and Captain Chennault would later participate in the training of Nationalist China's air force before World War II. (U.S. Air Force photo, courtesy of the National Museum of the United States Air Force.)

From left, an F-22 Raptor, an F-86 Sabre (bottom), a P-51 Mustang (top), and an F-4 Phantom participate in the Air Combat Command Heritage Flight during the 2010 Aviation Nation open house at Nellis Air Force Base. (U.S. Air Force photo by Airman First Class Daniel Hughes, courtesy of DefenseImagery.mil.)

Boeing B-29 flying near Mt. Fuji during World War II. (U.S. Air Force photo, courtesy of the National Museum of the United States Air Force.)

Convair B-36B, the first postwar strategic bomber and one of the largest combat aircraft ever built. (U.S. Air Force photo, courtesy of the National Museum of the United States Air Force.)

Boeing B-47B rocket-assisted takeoff on April 15, 1954. (U.S. Air Force photo, courtesy of the National Museum of the United States Air Force.)

(*Above*) Four U.S. Navy F-4U Corsair fighters, returning from a combat mission over Korea, fly above and to the starboard side of the carrier USS *Boxer* (CV-21). (Courtesy of DefenseImagery.mil.) (*Below*) Front view of a Convair B-58A Hustler. Soviet surface-to-air missile technology rendered the B-58 obsolete shortly after its introduction. (U.S. Air Force photo, courtesy of the National Museum of the United States Air Force.)

(*Above*) North American XB-70A Valkyrie in flight. Intended to replace the B-52, the B-70 was made obsolete by the development of surface-to-air missiles and intercontinental ballistic missiles. (U.S. Air Force photo, courtesy of the National Museum of the United States Air Force.) (*Below*) A C-7 Caribou transport aircraft used for airlifting supplies to short-runway forward outposts in Vietnam. The Caribou and most other fixed-wing aircraft were transferred from the U.S. Army to the air force on January 1, 1967, in accordance with the Johnson-McConnell agreement. (Courtesy of DefenseImagery.mil.)

Colonel John Robert Boyd, known as "40-second Boyd" because of his extraordinary proficiency as a fighter pilot. Boyd coined the term "OODA Loop" (Observe-Orient-Decide-Act) and helped set the terms for the design of a new generation of U.S. fighter and attack aircraft. (U.S. Air Force photo, courtesy of the National Museum of the United States Air Force.)

A Rockwell International B-1B is refueled by a McDonnell Douglas KC-10 Extender. Air refueling capability is central to the U.S. Air Force's "Global Reach, Global Power" concept. (U.S. Air Force photo, courtesy of the National Museum of the United States Air Force.)

Two U.S. Air Force A-10 Thunderbolt II aircraft fly in formation near a KC-10 Extender aircraft over Afghanistan in support of Operation Enduring Freedom, November 25, 2010. The A-10 has been at the center of several disputes between the air force and the army over close air support. (U.S. Air Force photo by Staff Sergeant Eric Harris, courtesy of DefenseImagery.mil.)

Colonel John Warden, airpower theorist and commandant of the Air Command and Staff College. (U.S. Air Force photo.)

(*Above*) The Military Sealift Command fleet replenishment oiler USNS *Laramie* (T-AO 203) and the amphibious assault ship USS *Kearsarge* (LHD 3) conduct a replenishment on the Red Sea, May 22, 2013. *Kearsarge* and other amphibious assault ships serve as platforms for the core of U.S. Marine Corps aviation. (U.S. Navy photo by Mass Communication Specialist Third Class Sabrina Fine.) (*Below*) F-35 test pilots Marine Corps major C. R. Clift and navy lieutenant commander Michael Burks fly a BF-2 and a BF-4 during a formation-flying-qualities test, August 22, 2012. The F-35B is capable of short takeoffs and vertical landings, enabling airpower projection from amphibious assault ships, ski-jump aircraft carriers, and expeditionary airfields. (U.S. Navy photo, courtesy of Lockheed Martin.)

(Above) An F-35 Lightning II maneuvers during its first flight over Eglin Air Force Base, Florida, April 23, 2009. The F-35 is expected to provide the core of the U.S. Air Force, U.S. Navy, and U.S. Marine Corps fighter fleets. (U.S. Air Force photo by Senior Airman Julianne Showalter, courtesy of DefenseImagery.mil.) *(Below)* A U.S. Air Force F-22A Raptor stealth fighter refuels from a KC-135 Stratotanker during an exercise over North Carolina, May 3, 2011. (Department of Defense photo by Senior Airman Gino Reyes, U.S. Air Force, courtesy of DefenseImagery.mil.)

RQ-4 Global Hawk drones perform high-altitude surveillance missions for the U.S. Air Force and the U.S. Navy as well as scientific missions for NASA. (U.S. Air Force photo by Bobbi Zapka, courtesy of the National Museum of the United States Air Force.)

A U.S. Marine Corps AV-8B Harrier aircraft waits as an MQ-1 Predator unmanned aerial vehicle passes by at Creech Air Force Base, Nevada, November 4, 2008. Both the Harrier and the Predator represent nontraditional airpower platforms. (U.S. Air Force photo by Senior Airman Larry E. Reid Jr., courtesy of DefenseImagery.mil.)

Major General
Charles Dunlap,
contemporary
airpower theorist
often credited with
coining the term
"lawfare." (U.S. Air
Force photo.)

The history of U.S. naval aviation is on display as an F6F Hellcat (top) flies alongside an
F/A-18C Hornet (bottom) during a battle of Midway commemoration ceremony aboard
the USS *Midway* (CV 41) Museum in San Diego, June 5, 2010. (U.S. Navy photo by Mass
Communication Specialist Second Class John Philip Wagner Jr.)

The Royal Navy aircraft carrier HMS *Illustrious* (R 06) and the U.S. Navy aircraft carriers USS *Harry S. Truman* (CVN 75) and USS *Dwight D. Eisenhower* (CVN 69) transition formation during a multiship maneuvering exercise in the Atlantic Ocean, July 29, 2007. (U.S. Navy photo by Mass Communication Specialist Second Class Jay C. Pugh.)

An F/A-18 Hornet embarked aboard the aircraft carrier USS *Nimitz* (CVN 68) intercepts and escorts a Russian Tu-95 Bear long-range bomber aircraft on February 9, 2008, south of Japan. Russian heavy bombers have shadowed U.S. carrier groups since the Soviet period. (U.S. Navy photo.)

An AV-8B Harrier from Marine Attack Squadron (VMA) 214 takes off vertically from the amphibious assault ship USS *Boxer* (LHD 4) in the Pacific Ocean, March 28, 2013. (U.S. Navy photo by Mass Communication Specialist Second Class Jason T. Poplin.)

7

Global Reach, Global Power in the Post–Cold War Era

Since 1947, the U.S. Air Force has been a part of the American military establishment, heavily involved in war fighting, procurement, and the development of strategy and doctrine. Today, the USAF has an important seat at the table for all decisions regarding the use of force and commands a sizable portion of the overall defense budget. The USAF continues to control the bulk of U.S. nuclear assets and flies combat missions daily in Afghanistan. The USAF remains an integral cog in the U.S. defense complex.

However, the demands on military forces have changed in ways that threaten to undermine the position of the USAF. The collapse of the Soviet Union robbed the USAF of its peer competitor force. Nuclear weapons became less relevant to U.S. security, making air force control of those assets a less important bureaucratic bargaining chip. Some aircraft, including bombers designed to penetrate Soviet air defenses, lost their missions. Bureaucratically, this forced the USAF to rethink its missions and repurpose its fleet. At the same time, the Soviet collapse eliminated many political obstacles to the use of airpower by making it easier for the United States to employ force against rogue states. As the last chapter detailed, Colonel John Warden supplied the strategic and operational logic of the new air force, built around highly effective fighter-bombers, stealth aircraft, precision-guided munitions, and information dominance.

Initially, the Kosovo War and the conflicts that made up the War on Terror seemed to support the air force's vision of power. However, two related developments in the conduct of war since 9/11 have cast doubt on the USAF's ability to adapt and endure. The first of these changes involved the development of a new model of ground-air cooperation that put a strong emphasis on joint effort, and the second was the rise to prominence of unmanned aerial vehicles, which threaten the air force's sense of identity. Together, these developments challenge not only the air force's anti-Clausewitzian tradition but also the wisdom of the bureaucratic boundaries that have divided the U.S. military establishment since 1947. This chapter concentrates on the former, the next chapter on the latter.

Kosovo

The 1999 Kosovo War represents a critical case in any evaluation of the effectiveness of airpower. At first glance, airpower worked; the Serbian army retreated from Kosovo after a three-month bombing campaign involving roughly 1,000 NATO aircraft. On closer inspection, the case for the effectiveness of airpower appears weaker, though hardly nonexistent.[1] The Kosovo War involved an almost profound imbalance of power between combatants, with a collection of the world's largest, wealthiest, and most powerful nations fighting against a small, isolated, and relatively poor Balkan state. If airpower could ever have an independent decisive effect it would have been in the Kosovo War.

The breakup of Yugoslavia produced several wars in the 1990s, the last of which involved the wayward Serbian province of Kosovo. Kosovo was crucial to Serbian national identity but populated mostly by ethnic Albanians, and their desires for regional autonomy were met with harsh Serbian violence. The North Atlantic Treaty Organization intervened in a growing conflict between Serbian armed forces and the Kosovo Liberation Army (KLA) in March 1999 after several years of failed diplomacy. The NATO air campaign, supported by KLA guerrilla attacks inside the province, forced Serbia to capitulate and withdraw in June, after eighty days of bombing.

The debate over the effectiveness of airpower in Kosovo revolves around three questions. First, did the Serbian government believe in the possibility of a NATO ground invasion of Kosovo and withdraw in order to prevent the destruction of its army? Second, what effect did the Kosovo Liberation Army attacks have on Serbia's ability to maintain control of the wayward province? Finally, what impact did political isolation have on Serbian decision making, especially after it became clear that Russia would not intervene on Serbia's behalf?

The threat of a NATO land invasion loomed over the Serbian decision to hold on to Kosovo.[2] Although Serbia could perhaps hold out against an extended air campaign, it could not hope to resist a direct invasion. However, key NATO members refused to commit to the threat of a land invasion. President Bill Clinton, working with a hostile Congress, resisted any public commitment to such an invasion.[3] As the air campaign dragged on, the ability of NATO to invade from bases in Greece, Albania, and Macedonia came into question. Throughout the war, disputes over targeting bedeviled NATO planners, as decisions required the consent of political actors within the coalition. These disputes detracted from the coherence of the campaign and reduced the effectiveness of the strategic effort. Planners selected targets in virtually ad hoc fashion based on the preferences and capabilities of different coalition players.[4] Lack of full commitment from Washington also hampered target selection, although this problem is endemic to air campaigns.[5]

The Kosovo Liberation Army had operated against Serbian forces in Kosovo since before the war. The KLA was a guerrilla-style organization composed of ethnic Albanians dedicated to Kosovar independence. Serbian reprisals against the KLA helped generate the NATO case for war, as the Serbian counterattacks targeted civilians. When the war began, the KLA began to step up its activities, in part because of the Serbian expulsion of a large portion of Kosovo's population. The ranks of the KLA swelled, and it carried out more aggressive attacks. Serbian forces had hunkered down in response to NATO air attacks and could not carry out antiguerrilla operations as freely as they had prior to the war. Eventually, the United States lent direct intelligence and training support to the KLA in the hopes of either forcing Serbian forces out of hiding or ejecting them from Kosovo altogether.[6] The activities of the KLA certainly limited the ability of the Serbians to control Kosovo, although they may not have been sufficient to force the Serbs out, even with NATO air support. But perhaps more important, the KLA offensive exposed the Serbian Army to direct air attack from NATO forces.[7] This substantially increased the amount of punishment NATO could apply to Serbian fielded forces.

For most of the war, Russia provided qualified diplomatic support to Serbia. Russia prevented the passage of a United Nations resolution endorsing the war, forcing the United States and its partners to use NATO as a legal and diplomatic venue.[8] As the war dragged on, however, Russian negotiators began to exert pressure on the Serbian government to bring the war to a close. In particular, the removal of pro-Serb Russian prime minister Yevgeny Primakov suggested hard limits on the Russian commitment to Serbia.[9] In April, Special Envoy Victor Chernomyrdin, seeking to bring the war to a close, began to engage in shuttle diplomacy between Serbia, Finland, and the United States. These efforts may have possibly undercut Serbian confidence in Russian support. Eventually, the Serbs agreed to Russian-Finnish mediation, acceding to most NATO demands.

Just as with the Operation Desert Storm, the army and the air force developed alternative narratives of the victory. The army pointed to the threat that a potential ground invasion posed to Serbian control of Kosovo, while the air force emphasized the strategic impact of the air campaign.[10] The air force appears to have the better case. While the Serbs may have believed the threat of a ground invasion, and their isolation from Russia might have had a major impact on their decision making, both concerns developed in the context of the air offensive. Without the air offensive, it is highly unlikely that the Milošević government would have taken seriously any threat of direct ground action to seize Kosovo.[11] Moreover, without the NATO commitment demonstrated by the air offensive, Russia may not have deserted its ally.[12] Finally, Serbian Army forces had managed to soundly defeat the Kosovo Liberation Army on several occasions prior to the initiation of the air campaign. Simply put, without the air campaign, Serbia probably would not have left Kosovo.

However, this admission creates almost as many questions as it resolves. If a concerted air campaign by NATO required almost three months to drive Serb forces from a single province, what independent utility does airpower have in more difficult cases? While the regime of Slobodan Milošević eventually fell, Serbian claims to Kosovo did not end. Moreover, some blame Milošević's fall on his failure to continue the war rather than on the air campaign itself. The Kosovo War also highlighted two broader connected problems associated with air campaigns. The first involved commitment to the cause: none of the NATO states seemed eager to make a sufficient effort to force Serbia from Kosovo on its own. The air campaign was a second-best option, allowing NATO to use force against Serbia without bringing European or American ground units into play, which could have created significant domestic political problems for many of the leaders. The coalition effort produced results largely because of its coalition nature, as it sent a costly signal to Moscow and Belgrade that the West was nearly united in its opposition to Serbian control over Kosovo. However, the political wrangling within the coalition over the operational and tactical details of the campaign detracted from its strategic coherence and effectiveness. Political tolerances varied across NATO states, making the development of a coherent effort to match strategic ends with strategic means difficult. Thus, the coalition was simultaneously necessary for success and self-undermining. Fortunately for NATO, the effort was enough for victory.

Post–Cold War Procurement

A Cold War understanding of airpower has continued to guide much procurement in the post–Cold War era, in large part because of the expansion of the procurement cycle. Projects with roots in the Cold War, such as the F-22 Raptor, remained major procurement priorities into the 2000s and 2010s because the cycle of development and production lasted decades. Other projects (such as the F-35 Joint Strike Fighter) began development after the end of the Cold War but nevertheless proceeded in a Cold War frame, with the expectation of combat against high-technology peer-competitor forces. Finally, virtually all of the major procurement projects in the post–Cold War era have experienced substantial cost overruns, whether due to overall program cuts or to problems with technology.[13]

The major fighter acquisition programs of the post–Cold War period have been the F-22 Raptor and the F-35 Lightning II Joint Strike Fighter. The F-22 is a high-performance "fifth-generation" fighter aircraft intended for air superiority missions against a capable, advanced opponent. Conceptualized as an answer to Soviet air superiority aircraft of the 1980s, the Lockheed Martin F-22 won a competition against the Northrup F-23. The air force initially intended to acquire 750 F-22s, but this number quickly began to drop as the reality of post–Cold War austerity set in. The USAF aggressively defended the program, retiring older aircraft and pushing studies (under assumptions that other government agencies found questionable) demonstrating the effectiveness of the Raptor over older aircraft.[14]

Critics argue that focusing on the F-22 has crippled the ability of the air force to maintain acceptable frontline strength. The ability of the F-22 to contribute to the modern ground-air team is limited, as it is optimized for air superiority missions. Given the demonstrated dominance of the F-15 in air superiority combat, the need for a new air superiority aircraft remains unclear.[15] The F-22 made a vanishingly small contribution to the wars in Iraq and Afghanistan, and did not appear in the Libyan Civil War. Secretary of Defense Robert Gates capped acquisition of the F-22 at 187 aircraft, in part because of plans to acquire over 1,000 F-35 Joint Strike Fighters.[16]

The F-35 Joint Strike Fighter was intended to complement the F-22's air superiority mission with a strike portfolio. The F-35 project aspired to supply the main tactical fighter-bomber for the USAF, USN, USMC, and several foreign air forces.[17] Each service would receive a variant tailored to its needs, based on the same airframe. For the air force this meant a conventional takeoff-landing fighter, for the navy a carrier-capable aircraft, and for the Marine Corps a VSTOL (vertical–short takeoff landing) jet.[18] Expected to be procured in far greater numbers than the F-22, the F-35 would take advantage of stealth characteristics and highly advanced electronics to defeat enemy antiaccess systems (including aircraft and air defenses).[19] The air force expected the F-22 to handle high-end air superiority missions, with the F-35 acting as the primary tactical bomber.

Despite high hopes, the F-35 program has suffered tremendous setbacks.[20] Lockheed Martin and the air force expected that advanced computer design systems would allow the F-35 to bypass many of the teething problems associated with the design process. Unfortunately, these hopes have not been realized, and the F-35 program has undergone repeated delays and cost overruns.[21] Testing has revealed technical problems with all three variants.[22] Reports have emerged that several countries originally expected to purchase the F-35 may back out, and even that the U.S. Navy may be getting cold feet.[23] A reduction in the overall F-35 buy runs the risk of creating a "death spiral" in which cost per unit metastasizes.[24] The problems associated with the F-35 cannot be laid solely at the feet of the air force; they are largely due to a selection process that emphasized commonality at the expense of mission effectiveness.

The latest major acquisition project (apart from a replacement for the KC-135 tanker fleet) involves a new strategic bomber. The air force seeks to augment and replace the current fleet of B-52s, B-1s, and B-2s with a long-range, subsonic, optionally manned stealth bomber.[25] This bomber, which would keep costs low by using proven legacy technologies, would be tasked with defeating advanced antiaccess capabilities. Projected totals remain in flux, but estimates suggest up to 100 aircraft.[26] Notably, while the new bomber project would retain the capacity for delivering nuclear weapons, conventional attack would play a larger role in frame and force development. This suggests, in contrast to the F-22, a distinctly post–Cold War appreciation of procurement needs. Replacing the current bomber force is surely a reasonable goal, although the ability of the USAF to keep costs down remains in serious question.[27]

OPERATION IRAQI FREEDOM

Operation Iraqi Freedom opened on March 20, 2003, as a U.S.-led coalition invaded Iraq from the south, overrunning and defeating conventional Iraqi forces over the course of four weeks. Major fighting ended on April 15, 2003, with the fall of Tikrit, although President George W. Bush did not declare the end of major combat operations until May 1, 2003.[28] An insurgency developed in the summer of 2003 that has lasted, with varying degrees of intensity, until the present day.

The U.S. Air Force undertook a variety of missions during the initial invasion of Iraq, ranging from close air support to interdiction to strategic attacks against Iraqi leadership targets. Unlike Operation Desert Storm, the air and ground offensives proceeded simultaneously. By most accounts the air-ground team performed very well, shattering organized Iraqi units and destroying the Iraqi government in a short time and with relatively low casualties. Iraqi forces, despite their experience with U.S. airpower in 1991, were not well prepared for the attack.[29]

Both the army and the air force performed effectively in Operation

Iraqi Freedom. Still, differences of opinion about the relative effectiveness of ground and air power fell along service lines. The army welcomed what it viewed as extremely effective interdiction and close air support, allowing it to advance and destroy Iraqi formations. Friction remained; even advanced intelligence assets sometimes misidentified Iraqi targets, and both services failed to fully appreciate the activities of light "Fedayeen" units. The most notable failure of American airpower came on March 23, when thirty Army Apache helicopters attempted to assault the Iraqi Medina division. The Iraqis drove the helicopters off before they could do significant damage. For its part, the air force concentrated on the effectiveness of attacks against the Iraqi communications and control networks. Finally, the army and air force continued to have problems delegating responsibility between artillery, army aviation, and air force assets.[30]

Despite the effectiveness of the air-ground team in the opening stages of Operation Iraqi Freedom, the support of large conventional formations in open battle against similar formations would become the aberration rather than the rule. In Iraq, Afghanistan, and eventually Libya, modern American airpower would operate on behalf of small U.S. and allied formations, themselves fighting against relatively small (and often irregular) enemy formations.

THE AFGHAN MODEL AND THE NEW AIR-GROUND TEAM

Hints of the ability of modern airpower to collaborate effectively with small-scale "proxy" ground forces emerged during the Kosovo War, when Kosovo Liberation Army attacks helped improve the effectiveness of NATO air operations against the Serbian Army.[31] This template of warfare came to maturity as the "Afghan model," a form of ground-air cooperation developed in the early stages of Operation Enduring Freedom and also executed during the 2011 Libyan Civil War.[32] The Afghan model involves the combination of special forces, allied proxy fighting forces, and heavy precision airpower to defeat the fielded forces of a target state.[33] Proxies screen the special operators from attack, fix enemy positions, and exploit tactical victories by seizing ground. Special forces operators identify targets and coordinate proxy ground assaults with precision strikes. Precision attacks from offshore aircraft and naval vessels either destroy enemy targets or sufficiently suppress them to allow proxy forces to overrun their positions.[34] Modern communications and reconnaissance technology, supported by space-based assets, make tight collaboration possible. If it works, the model can topple a government with minimal commitment of heavy allied ground forces.

The Afghan model differs in significant ways from older conceptions of the use of strategic airpower to topple governments. Whereas John Warden's vision of strategic airpower involved inducing a regime to concede or collapse by attacking "strategic" targets such as communication nodes, command complexes, and leadership concentrations, the Afghan model focuses on the destruction and disruption of enemy forces in the field.[35] While both the Afghan and Libyan campaigns involved attacks on the command and communications networks of the target, the primitive nature of these networks prevented these attacks from having decisive effect. Rather, the campaigns were won as proxy ground forces, supported by heavy precision air strikes, destroyed the ability of enemy ground forces to operate and resist.[36]

The campaigns over Libya and Afghanistan were not identical. Compared to the war in Afghanistan, the pace of the rebel advance in Libya was glacial. In Afghanistan, the Taliban stronghold of Kandahar fell on December 9, 2001, just two months and two days after the beginning of U.S. air strikes, while in Libya the loyalist stronghold Sirte did not fall for over seven months. The pace of air strikes over Afghanistan was more intense than those over Libya—by roughly a factor of three—and the strikes themselves were heavier.[37] While we may never know the precise composition of special forces in either the Afghan or the Libyan campaigns, the contingents were likely larger and more active in the former conflict. The organized military forces on both sides in the Afghanistan War were more experienced than their counterparts in Libya, a fact that may have made it easier to undertake the offensive that eventually seized Kandahar, as offensive infantry tactics generally take longer to master than defensive tactics. The geography of Libya, which forced most military operations into a relatively narrow corridor along the coast, also favored the use of airpower.[38]

The extent of cooperation between Libyan ground forces and NATO air forces was looser than in Afghanistan, as the legal justification for the intervention lay in protecting civilians, not overthrowing the Libyan state. This meant that NATO flew fewer close air support missions and more interdiction, as attacks on the movement and logistics of government forces could be framed as civilian protection. The length of the war also allowed Libyan government forces to adapt to the realities of NATO airpower, taking advantage of NATO rules of engagement to conduct operations that the Taliban could not. Nevertheless, the (relatively late) arrival of British special forces allowed closer coordination between NATO air assets and antigovernment Libyan forces, providing the foundation for defeating the loyalists.[39]

The distinction between the Afghan model and the more traditional understanding of decisive strategic airpower is subtle but important. As conceived by the airpower enthusiasts of the interwar period, or by the thinkers behind *Global Reach—Global Power,* airpower has decisive strategic effect because of its ability to defeat an enemy political actor without the need to defeat fielded enemy forces. In other words, the enemy can be defeated without being disarmed. The Afghan model rejects this, instead accepting the need for disarming the enemy (although this may not always mean the complete destruction of fielded forces). This more closely resembles the vision of air-ground cooperation put forward in David E. Johnson's *Learning Large Lessons: The Evolving Roles of Ground Power and Air Power,* which concentrates on the synergistic application of ground and air forces rather than on the decisiveness of either.[40] This puts the Afghan model back onto firmly Clausewitzian ground but drags it out of the vision of decisive airpower espoused by airpower advocates for nearly a hundred years.

However, the Afghan model is as much a political as a military concept. Ideally, the model minimizes domestic opposition in the intervening country, nationalist reactions in the target country, and international upheaval.[41] The focus on military rather than civilian infrastructure targets reduces both domestic and international opprobrium and presumably leaves the target country in better shape for reconstruction. The relatively small number of friendly troops, combined with the high standard of training for those troops, limits the prospect of casualties in the intervening country and antioccupation sentiment in the target.

The other political aspect of the Afghan model involves postconflict stability. Because that model eschews use of large-scale ground forces, it assigns de facto responsibility for postconflict management to the proxy/rebel forces. This has the upside of being cheaper for the intervening power and ideally avoids the nationalist backlash typically associated with a large-scale occupation.[42] However, it also puts tremendous stress on the proxy coalition. The rebels, who may not have previously worked extensively with each other for any purpose other than winning the war, suddenly need to assemble a working government coalition. The rebels also have to decide what to do with the surviving elements of the defeated government. All of these obstacles represent potentially disastrous pitfalls inherent to the Afghan model. As the United States and its allies learned in Afghanistan and Iraq, the overthrow of even unpopular leaders and political movements can leave the nucleus of a national insurgency. At the time of this writing, the war in Afghanistan continues, with U.S. and NATO troop deployments far larger than those envisioned in early 2002.

Airpower and Post-Stability Operations

The failure of the United States to establish stability in Iraq and Afghanistan reinvigorated an elderly debate about the role of airpower in COIN (counterinsurgency). The shift of the U.S. Army toward COIN and away from conventional warfare helped create conflict about both the proper employment of air assets and the proper prioritization of procurement. The debate over airpower in COIN involves two questions. First, do air strikes help or hurt a counterinsurgency effort when civilians' lives are at risk? Second, should defense planners prioritize technologically advanced aerial platforms geared toward high-intensity warfare or less expensive aircraft and capabilities that work well in COIN campaigns?

Ordnance delivered by aircraft can have a remarkably destructive impact on an insurgency. With good intelligence, aircraft can destroy targets in areas where ground assets are unavailable. However, without good intelligence, even precision-guided munitions cannot discriminate between friend and enemy. Bombs designed to kill a single sniper can destroy entire buildings, with consequent civilian toll.

Field Manual 3-24, known as the counterinsurgency manual, includes an appendix on the effectiveness of airpower in COIN situations. According to the FM 3-24: "Airpower provides considerable asymmetric advantages to counterinsurgents. If insurgents assemble a conventional force, air assets can respond quickly with precision fires. In a sudden crisis, air mobility can immediately move land forces where they are needed. In numerous COIN operations, airpower has demonstrated a vital supporting role. . . . Airpower enables counterinsurgents to operate in rough and remote terrain, areas that insurgents traditionally have used as safe havens."[43]

This reinforces the importance of close air support and air mobility to COIN operations. *FM 3-24* also emphasizes the importance of airpower to reconnaissance and intelligence collection, missions that the manual places at the forefront of any COIN effort. However, *FM 3-24* also sounds the alarm on the dangers of airpower: "Precision air attacks can be of enormous value in COIN operations; however, commanders exercise exceptional care when using airpower in the strike role. Bombing, even with the most precise weapons, can cause unintended civilian casualties. Effective leaders weigh the benefits of every air strike against its risks. An air strike can cause collateral damage that turns people against the host-nation (HN) government and provides insurgents with a major propaganda victory."[44] During his tenure as International Security Assistance Force commander in Afghanistan, General Stanley McChrystal issued strong restrictions on the use of airpower after several high-profile incidents in which civilians were killed.[45]

However, USAF officers, including, most notably, Major General Charles Dunlap (retired), have also argued that the focus on COIN runs the risk of reducing U.S. military effectiveness in more conventional operations.[46] Dunlap has further posited that the negative effects of airpower on counterinsurgency are overblown. *FM 3-24,* he argues, represents a bureaucratic effort on the part of the army and Marine Corps to marginalize the USAF. While the media devote considerable attention to the damage caused by air strikes, ground forces also commit atrocities: "Specifically, has collateral damage from airstrikes caused more enemy 'propaganda victories' than have, for example, the results of land force actions at such places as Abu Ghraib, Haditha, Hammadyia, and Mahmudiyah? Is there a difference between the impact of *unintended* civilian causalities from airstrikes and *intended* injury to civilians by rogue military members on the ground?"[47]

Indeed, Dunlap argues that *FM 3-24* fundamentally undervalues airpower and ignores the contributions that airpower has made to the conflicts in Iraq and Afghanistan. For example, at the height of the "surge," the 2007 deployment of five additional brigades to Iraq, air strikes increased by a factor of five.[48] This reflected an increase in the pace of U.S. operations but also suggested that "civilian-friendly" counterinsurgency campaigns nevertheless required the extensive use of airpower. Others have laid similar charges regarding General David Petraeus's tenure as commander of U.S. operations in Afghanistan.[49] However, while air strikes increased during the Iraqi surge, total munitions used during those air strikes remained flat, indicating a more complex picture than Dunlap paints.[50] Dunlap further argued that technological enhancements had increased the ability of aircraft to carry out precision strikes and to collect intelligence about enemy formations.[51] In a particularly caustic article in *Armed Forces Journal*, Dunlap denounced army COIN advocates as "boots on the grounds zealots," or "BOTGZ (pronounced bow-togs)" for short. Dunlap suggested that the COIN obsession with ground forces was mired in a romanticism reminiscent of the days of heavy cavalry formations. Instead, airpower would dominate future wars waged by Western powers such as Israel, the United Kingdom, and the United States. In long-term campaigns, ground forces would simply prove too expensive in blood and treasure to maintain abroad for long periods.[52]

The USAF pushback against the army and Marine Corps included the issuance of its own manual for governing the use of airpower in COIN as well as lauding the value of airpower in counterterrorist and counterinsurgent operations. *Air Force Doctrine Document 2-3* places counterterrorism and counterinsurgency under the rubric "irregular warfare," defined as "a spectrum of warfare where the nature and characteristics are significantly different from traditional war. It includes, but is not limited to, activities such as insurgency, counterinsurgency."[53] The *Irregular Warfare* manual emphasizes the need for unity of effort across military organizations and civilian agencies. Nevertheless, the manual also argued that airpower could solve some problems that traditional ground forces could not: "A sizeable ground force engaged in protracted COIN operations can inflame the populace against the COIN forces and can wear down the political will of the U.S. government and the local populace.

Air Force capabilities bring many advantages, including an 'economy of force' that enables the United States to have a smaller ground force, which reduces the problems associated with a large 'footprint' on the ground."[54]

The manual detailed the ways in which ground strike, reconnaissance, and air mobility missions could enhance a counterinsurgency campaign. For counterterrorism, the manual focused on reconnaissance, intelligence gathering, and ground strikes as missions that airpower could perform uniquely well.[55]

However, few beyond Dunlap seem to believe that the air force can take the lead in counterinsurgency operations. Rather, the emphasis on joint activity with other branches represents a defensive posture and pushback against the idea that airpower is harmful or irrelevant. This includes focusing on missions that the air force has never preferred, such as close air support and air mobility. The idea that airpower can have independent decisive effect seems virtually absent from the counterinsurgency dialogue. This indicates concern among the senior air force leadership about the ability of the USAF to maintain its position in the U.S. defense establishment.

The requirements of COIN-specialized aircraft also run contrary to USAF preferences. The Embraer EMB 314 Super Tucano, a propeller-driven aircraft built by a Brazilian firm, has drawn interest in the United States as a cheap counterinsurgency aircraft.[56] The Colombian Air Force has already used the Super Tucano in COIN operations directed against the Marxist rebel group FARC.[57] The Super Tucano costs roughly $14 million, considerably less than the fighter-bombers that currently conduct close air support.[58] While the plane is currently used only by South American air forces, both the U.S. Navy and the U.S. Marine Corps have expressed some interest. CENTCOM chief General James Mattis (USMC) has tried to build support within the military for the purchase of the Super Tucano or a similar aircraft.[59] However, Air Force Chief of Staff General Norton Schwartz denied that the USAF needed either a small turboprop attack aircraft or a small cargo lifter, arguing that existing aircraft (including the F-15 and F-16) fulfill all close air support needs.[60] An author at the blog Defense Tech explains how a light COIN aircraft like the Super Tucano could have helped in an engagement in Kunar province, Afghanistan:

The COIN plane would have 5 hours of loiter, more than enough time to recce the area before the meeting with the elder that was the bait of the ambush. The crew could have alerted the advisors and their Afghan charge well before they entered the village of the ambush setup. Even had they missed the emplacements, the COIN plane could have provided graduated levels of precise CAS and could have worked as a FAC-A [forward air controller (airborne)] for artillery and mortar support. Helicopters are great for this, but they were too far away and have limited loiter time. A COIN plane can be based at FOBs [forward-operating bases] or even COPs [command observation posts] with only a few hundred meters of runway and a skeleton maintenance crew.[61]

While the 2010 *Quadrennial Defense Review Report* directed the USAF to develop the capability to train foreign air forces on the use of counterinsurgency aircraft, Schwartz made clear that USAF interest in such aircraft was limited to this assistance mission.[62] As Greg Grant of Defense Tech writes, "Without Air Force buy-in, it's hard to see this effort goes anywhere. I'm not sure Mattis' [General James Mattis, USMC] powers of persuasion will have much impact on the Air Force's dominant constituency."[63]

Notably, the Afghanistan National Army Air Force operates only helicopters and light transport aircraft, a force structure designed for counterinsurgency. The Iraqi Air Force has also concentrated on helicopters, transport planes, and light attack aircraft, although the United States is scheduled to begin delivering F-16s to Iraq in 2014.[64] Both *FM 3-24* and the Air Force *Irregular Warfare* manual discuss developing partner air capacity as a key role of airpower in COIN. The extent to which an organization uninterested in COIN aircraft can train partners in COIN doctrine and tactics remains in question, however.

The Future of the Air-Ground Team

The success of the Afghan model in Libya and Afghanistan supplies only very tenuous and measured support for the idea that airpower has become decisive in modern warfare. The focus on tactical rather than strategic targets represents a profound retreat from the principles that guided the employment of airpower as recently as Operation Iraqi Freedom. Direct attacks on fielded enemy forces can hurt, but they also require great skill and lack the "multiplier effect" supposedly accrued by attacks against "strategic" targets such as communications networks and command nodes. Tactical campaigns also tie air assets to the whims of ground commanders, in this case a combination of special forces and proxy fighters. In the minds of many pilots, a tactical campaign turns an air force into an exceedingly expensive artillery branch.[65] While there is no doubt that such a campaign can have an effect, most advocates find it a waste of airpower's potential. The idea that airpower has decisive effect only in combination with ground forces seems commonsensical, but it challenges a century of airpower doctrine. Full realization of the cooperative demands of decisive war fighting could have wide-ranging consequences, including perhaps inducing Western militaries to reevaluate their military procurement policies and indicating to the targets of future Western interventions that if they're safe from ground attack, they can probably hold out against the bombs and missiles.[66] It should also be noted that the Afghan model has not to date been executed against a modern professional military organization. Given the difficulties that Libyan rebels had against ad hoc Loyalist forces in the Libyan Civil War, the ability of proxies to defeat a professional military, even with heavy air support, remains in serious question.

If Libya crumbles back into civil war in the wake of Gadhafi's fall, it will not reflect well on a strategic concept that promises large returns at minimal risk. On the other hand, if the experience of working together against Gadhafi's forces helped build relationships between the rebels that can serve as the foundation for a representative government, the slow course of the war in Libya may have had hidden benefits.[67]

The post–Cold War era provided ample opportunity for conflict and cooperation between ground and air forces. In all of these conflicts the U.S. joint air-ground team accomplished remarkable things, defeating opponents with few casualties while operating at great distance from the United States. The experience of the past ten years does not, however, offer much solace to those who hope that airpower can play a critical independent role in U.S. defense policy. Rather, air power complements and enables other forms of power, at sea and on land. In some cases the airpower can have truly dramatic effect, allowing the overturning of governments with minimal contribution of American soldiers. If extant trends in airpower technology and practice continue, we can expect that air, land, and sea assets will operate together in an ever-tighter embrace. In this context, maintaining the current bureaucratic barriers between services makes little sense.

In a very real sense airpower has "come of age": it has realized its genuine value as part of the air-ground team. However, acknowledging that airpower makes its greatest contribution as part of an air-ground team (regardless of how we allocate responsibility between components) undercuts the central arguments for air force independence; there is little more reason for an independent air force than an independent artillery service. Early airpower advocates understood this point, which is why they argued so bitterly for a strategic airpower rationale.

Finally, it bears brief note that the focus on the air-ground team that has developed over the past decade has arguably detracted from USAF concentration on other areas. In particular, several problems of nuclear management have developed in the past several years. In 2007, a B-52 took off from Minot Air Force Base in North Dakota improperly loaded with nuclear weapons, triggering a major investigation and the ousting of two senior leaders.[68] In another incident, nuclear parts were shipped to Taiwan in error.[69] Most recently, seventeen officers at a ballistic missile installation in North Dakota were disciplined for inadequate attention to duty. Jeffrey Lewis has argued that this lack of attention is symptomatic of a broader strategic and political retreat from the nuclear mission.[70] While the relevance of the nuclear mission to U.S. security is a matter for debate, the inability of the USAF to commit to its nuclear responsibilities is disquieting.

8

Drone Warfare

Over the past five years, the Predator drone has become the face of American airpower. Drones, operated by all of the services and by the CIA, have played a steadily larger role in American military aviation over the last decade. Best known for their use in the decapitation campaign against al-Qaeda in Pakistan, drones have quietly performed most of the missions normally associated with airpower during the War on Terror. Evolutionary in process and revolutionary in implication, the development of drone warfare threatens to upend the traditional categorization of airpower missions and potentially even the concept of military identity itself.

Air forces have employed drones since the Second World War, but with technological improvements their use expanded dramatically during the War on Terror. The attraction of drones has increased because they offer more for less: more information, more presence, and more coverage for lower cost. Drones also offer, for the moment, politically palatable options for the projection of power across national boundaries. The increasing use of drones by the United States has not gone unnoticed on the international stage, with global criticism of drone employment growing nearly as fast as global drone procurement.

This chapter examines the growth of American drone warfare from the Clausewitzian perspective developed in the introduction. How do drones contribute to the disarming of the enemy? Does drone warfare place technological novelty ahead of political applicability? Finally, how do drones change our approach to the fog of war? The answer in all three cases is that, while much remains to be learned, drone warfare suffers from many of the same problems associated with traditional airpower theory.

DEFINITION OF DRONES

The term *drone* generally applies to systems or vehicles that operate without human passenger-drivers. These vehicles either pilot themselves (through use of an internal computer) or are controlled by pilots in remote contact. While many different robotic systems (including ground and sea, and undersea vehicles) can fall under the term "drone," this chapter concentrates on unmanned aerial vehicles (UAVs). UAVs are what they sound like: aerial vehicles that do not carry pilots in the airframe. This definition includes a wide variety of different vehicles, from formerly manned vehicles (such as old fighter aircraft converted for use as targets) to craft nearly indistinguishable from toys to huge planes capable of remaining aloft for a day or more. The best-known drones include the RQ-11B Raven, a small reconnaissance craft that soldiers launch into the air by throwing, the RQ-1 Predator, a twenty-seven-foot, 1,200-pound UAV capable of reconnaissance and attack missions, and the RQ-4 Global Hawk, which can carry out intelligence collection missions for up to twenty-eight hours.[1]

Cruise missiles with internal or external navigation systems (such as the BGM-109 Tomahawk) are suicidal drones in the same sense that kamikazes were suicidal manned aircraft. Indeed, cruise missiles have played (and continue to play) many of the roles currently associated with drones, including long-range strike into and through unfriendly airspace. However, the ability of UAVs to conduct surveillance (communicating information back to their operators), fly multiple missions, and unite strike and surveillance missions within a single airframe sets them apart in terms of utility.

ORGANIZATION OF AMERICAN DRONES

Armed and unarmed drones play a major role in the future of the air force's conception of the air-ground team. Unarmed reconnaissance drones identify targets and maintain observation of combat areas, while armed drones provide local close air support. With long loiter capacity, armed drones also undertake interdiction and strategic missions by observing and targeting enemy movement well away from points of contact.

Service control of the drones depends on a complex set of agreements dictating drone usage between the army and the air force, but in general USAF drones bear the brunt of attack duties.[2] As of mid-2012, the USAF operated roughly 270 large and medium-sized drones, including the MQ-1B Predator, the RQ-4 Global Hawk, and the MQ-9 Reaper.[3]

However, as with manned aircraft, the air force lacks a monopoly over drone aircraft. In 2001, the U.S. Army operated 54 drones, a number that grew to over 4,000 by 2010. Army drones focus mainly on reconnaissance and intelligence collection in support of fielded forces, although the army has also pursued some drone options for sustainment and close air support missions. Command of drones lies at the battalion, brigade, or division level depending on mission and capability, with longer-range, longer-endurance drones typically operated by higher-level commands.[4] This leaves local commanders in control of many assets but also violates the principle of centralized control.[5] Army drones operate under restrictions similar to those faced by the rest of army aviation, which prevents airspace confusion with the air force but often forces the army to rely on air force assets for close air support, interdiction, and other missions. Altogether, the army operates around 6,700 drones (as of mid-2012), with small RQ-11B Ravens constituting the vast majority of aircraft.[6] The navy operates a variety of drones, primarily for reconnaissance and communications purposes.[7] The RQ-21A Scan Eagle, a basic recon drone launched from any number of different warships, constitutes the overwhelming majority of navy drones. However, in the future many expect that UAVs will become an important part of the carrier air group. The Marine Corps also operates a small drone fleet (about 60 total) with RQ-7B Shadows making up the bulk of the force.[8] Marine Corps drones play similar roles to army drones.

Two other organizations have played a significant role in increasing the prominence of drones within the U.S. national security bureaucracy. The Central Intelligence Agency and the Joint Special Operations Command (JSOC) have spearheaded the use of drones to conduct strategic decapitation campaigns in Pakistan, Somalia, and Yemen.[9] The exact size of the CIA's drone force remains classified, but advocates argue that it has had a major strategic impact on the ability of al-Qaeda to function. JSOC (a subunit of Special Operations Command that manages and coordinates U.S. special operations forces operating in Afghanistan, Pakistan, and elsewhere) has access to a variety of Department of Defense drones (precise numbers are classified) that it uses for reconnaissance, intelligence gathering, and strike missions.[10] The relationship between the CIA, JSOC, and the Department of the Defense is complex and often conflictual, but the organizations have worked together to conduct the most controversial aspects of the "drone war."[11]

Reports indicate that despite operational CIA control over drones it uses to conduct this campaign, the air force continues to maintain the aircraft itself.[12] This opaque and apparently complex arrangement may soon end, with control of UAVs shifted back to the Department of Defense (and presumably to the air force).[13] Critics of drone policy have argued that this shift will reduce the opacity of the drone war, as the U.S. government will be compelled to fully acknowledge strikes conducted by the Department of Defense in a way that it cannot with CIA strikes. Moving control of drones out of the CIA would place authority back within the normal chain of military command, more clearly subject to congressional oversight.[14] It would also, presumably, move the CIA back more clearly in the direction of intelligence gathering rather than operational warfare. Defenders of the current arrangement, however, argue that moving control of drones away from the CIA would limit the effectiveness of drone warfare as a policy tool.[15]

Finally, employment of drones for security purposes has expanded beyond military organizations. Police departments, border enforcement organizations, humanitarian organizations, and environmental groups have all explored the utility of drones for research and reconnaissance.[16] Like military organizations, these groups seek the benefits of combining long loiter time with relatively low cost. Police departments in particular have begun to use drones in roles previously assigned to helicopters.[17]

HISTORY OF DRONES

The first extensive use of remote control UAVs came in World War II, by which time radio and computer technology had advanced sufficiently to allow either remote or internal guidance.[18] The German Fritz X radio-controlled bomb destroyed several Allied ships in the Mediterranean during the latter half of the war, most notably the Italian battleship *Roma*.[19] German V-1 "Buzz Bombs," using a primitive internal computer, struck Great Britain in large numbers in 1944 and 1945.[20] Allied efforts trailed German innovation, perhaps because the Allies' vast resource advantage made UAVs unnecessary. After the war, a variety of surplus aircraft were converted to radio-controlled drones for training and testing purposes.[21]

The development of purpose-built drones for reconnaissance and attack missions by the USAF began in the 1950s, as the organization considered the implications of unmanned ballistic missiles and cruise missiles. Both types of delivery system had the potential to replace the bomber as the primary means for delivering nuclear weapons to the Soviet Union. The first deployable drones emerged out of cooperation between the air force and the National Reconnaissance Office (NRO) in the early 1960s. The NRO provided the vehicle for collaboration between the USAF and the CIA, as the latter was interested in the intelligence-gathering capabilities of drones. Critically, the NRO provided what amounted to a "free" source of money for drone development, insulated from other demands on the time, resources, and attention of the air force. Drones faced competition from aircraft such as the U-2 and the SR-71 but eventually demonstrated sufficient independent capability to justify continued development. Early reconnaissance drones were used in conjunction with Chinese Nationalists to spy on the People's Republic of China (PRC). U-2 spy aircraft operating from Taiwan provided valuable intelligence on Chinese air defenses and the PRC's nuclear program but suffered a high attrition rate. Although the Chinese also shot down some drones, unmanned violations of PRC airspace lacked the political impact made by manned aircraft. The air force would later use similar drones to probe the North Vietnamese air defense network.[22]

The air force took over drone development from the NRO in 1974. This granted the USAF greater autonomy but cut off a "free" source of funding. By the late 1970s, developments in Soviet ballistic missile technology created a demand for reconnaissance assets with persistent loiter capability, which neither the SR-71 nor the satellites of the time could provide. Research into a drone that could fill this gap did not result in a useable vehicle, but it did keep money flowing into the program. However, by the 1980s the air force began losing interest in drones. Stealth aircraft, such as the F-117 and the B-2, could strike Soviet targets during a general war and did not suffer from data link vulnerability. This need for operators to stay in contact with drones made them unreliable in high-intensity warfare and other critical situations. Air force planners worried that the Soviets could exploit the UAV's need to for a sophisticated data link during critical strike missions. Cruise missiles, which did not rely on such a link, also appeared more attractive.[23] By the early 1990s, USAF research into UAVs had virtually ceased.

In 1993, the Defense Airborne Reconnaissance Office (DARO) took over control of UAV research and development. DARO's governance of drone issues would be short lived, but it helped shepherd the RQ-1 Predator drone into existence. Created to answer a need for long-term loiter reconnaissance during the Bosnia conflict, the Predator used civilian satellite for data uplink and took advantage of the Global Positioning System. The USAF took control of the Predator in 1996.[24] The Predator served over Bosnia, in the Kosovo War, and in Operation Southern Watch (surveillance over Iraq). The Predator would serve as a forerunner for such craft as the RQ-4 Global Hawk and the MQ-9 Reaper. In 2001, a program to equip RQ-1Predators with Hellfire missiles came to fruition, with armed variants adopting the MQ-1 designation.[25] The first drone strikes were launched in October 2001.[26]

The critical parts of this story involve the free money available from the NRO and the inadvertent (from the perspective of drone developers) emergence of a robust, reliable data system for linking drones and operators. The former meant that the air force could work on drones without giving up other opportunities: drones would not have to justify themselves against fighters, bombers, transport aircraft, and the like, and consequently would be insulated from conflict within the air force. The latter meant that unmanned aircraft could perform missions with similar degrees of reliability to manned aircraft. Indeed, the explosion in availability of bandwidth and data storage in the 1990s meant that drones could return to their operators more data than the planners of the 1950s and 1960s could have possibly imagined. These developments set the stage for the combined attack-surveillance UAVs of the War on Terror.

Drones in the War on Terror

While the United States and other countries had operated drones in previous conflicts (in the first Gulf War, a group of Iraqi soldiers famously attempted to surrender to an RQ-2 Pioneer drone launched from the battleship *Wisconsin*), drone warfare as a significant phenomenon came to the attention of the strategic community during the War on Terror.[27] In Iraq and Afghanistan, fleets of drones deployed alongside traditional manned aircraft helped keep the cost of traditional air operations manageable.[28] Drones proved particularly useful in a counterinsurgency context because they shared many design features with COIN-specialized aircraft including, most notably, the capability to loiter over battlefields and low-traffic areas for long periods. This meant drones could perform close air support and reconnaissance missions that severely taxed conventional manned aircraft.[29]

Local operators control most drones (especially smaller variants), but some are operated from remote bases in the United States. Communications technology makes it possible for pilots to fly drones at great distances, although the drones still require local bases for refueling, rearming, and general maintenance. In some cases, drones have pilots in the United States who carry out offensive missions, while pilots on site conduct landings and takeoffs.[30]

The earliest use of Predator drones in attack roles came soon after the 2001 U.S. invasion of Afghanistan.[31] Predators conducted both close air support and "targeted" attacks against particularly important Taliban and al-Qaeda figures. The limited availability of U.S. troops on the ground, the unreliability of Afghan militia allies, and the forbidding nature of the Afghan terrain put a premium on the aforementioned characteristics of loiter capabilities. Still, manned aircraft have carried out the vast majority of attack sorties in Afghanistan from the beginning of the war all the way up to 2012.[32] Drones played a smaller role in Iraq, perhaps because of the greater availability of manned aircraft in that conflict.[33]

On November 4, 2002, the National Security Agency traced a cell phone belonging to Abu Ali al-Harethi to a sports utility vehicle on an isolated road in Yemen. Al-Harethi was suspected of masterminding the 2000 attack on the destroyer USS *Cole*, but had managed to elude capture by hiding in Yemen. With permission from Yemen's government, a CIA-operated Predator drone fired a Hellfire missile that destroyed al-Harethi's truck, killing everyone inside. This, the first known use of an armed drone outside Afghanistan, portended the development of a widespread campaign of assassination against al-Qaeda.[34] The campaign would soon expand beyond al-Qaeda. On June 18, 2004, a Predator drone killed Nek Muhammed Wazir, a Pashtun commander who had been leading military resistance to the Pakistani Army. Over the previous three years Taliban and al-Qaeda leaders had learned that they could take advantage of relative sanctuary across the Pakistani border. U.S. efforts to press the Pakistani military into action against these militants bore some fruit, but only to limited effect. Eventually, Pakistan and the United States came to an accord that allowed the United States to carry out attacks against targets on Pakistani territory in exchange for attacks against opponents of the Pakistani government.[35]

This agreement would open the door to the most controversial aspect of drone usage in the War on Terror. From 2004 on, the United States has conducted strategic bombing campaigns in Pakistan, Yemen, and Somalia with, ironically, only the peripheral participation of the conventional air force. U.S. drones strike suspected militants in home bases, far from combat areas, based on intelligence collected from human, electronic, and aerial sources. The precise contours of the division of responsibility between JSOC and CIA remain murky, but drones now play a central role in the war that the United States is waging against the al-Qaeda terrorist network.[36] According to a December 2011 *Washington Post* article, U.S. agencies have carried out over 240 drone strikes during the War on Terror, killing more than 1,600 people.[37]

Like the early recon drones used over China, attack drones have certain political advantages over manned aircraft, most notably cover for host governments. Although the CIA's drone campaign is not popular with the Pakistani public, the drones are likely more acceptable than strikes launched from manned aircraft. Civilian casualties in both Pakistan and Afghanistan have created political problems for the United States, but both manned aircraft and drones suffer from this problem. Just as drones gave the USAF a less politically sensitive way of studying Chinese nuclear and air defense capabilities in the 1960s, they allow the

United States to kill suspected terrorists in Pakistan with a relatively low political "footprint." Similarly, UAVs represented a low-cost, low-profile means for the United States to engage in Libya, where they were present at all stages of the campaign, including its final moments when Moammar Gadhafi's convoy was identified, fixed, and attacked by ground and air assets.[38]

We do not yet have a good sense of the effectiveness of the drone campaigns in Pakistan, Somalia, and Yemen.[39] The U.S. government insists that al-Qaeda networks have suffered significant attrition, and that this has dramatically limited their ability to conduct attacks against the West.[40] However, because of the murky state of intelligence in the areas under attack, precise information regarding al-Qaeda capabilities remains limited. Moreover, given that many drone strikes have focused on enemies of the Yemeni and Pakistani governments, the extent to which effort matches results remains in significant question.[41] Finally, foes of the drone campaign have argued that the civilian casualties associated with the attacks as well as mounting global dissatisfaction with the idea that the United States is waging a war with "killer robots" will in the medium and long run radicalize more anti-American militants.[42] Indeed, one (still classified) study has suggested that drone attacks may put civilians at greater risk than manned airstrikes.[43]

LEGALITY AND MORALITY OF DRONES

Legality

For most legal purposes, drones resemble manned aircraft. Drone strikes must abide by the restrictions associated with discrimination, proportionality, and the doctrine of double effect. The use of drones in support of ground combat creates no special or particularly interesting legal issues. UAVs insulate pilots from retaliation, but in many cases enemy ground forces under air attack cannot effectively respond in any case; the ability of Taliban soldiers to shoot down USAF B-1B bombers is already nil.

The more complicated problems involve the legality of the UAV-oriented strategic bombing campaigns in countries where the United States does not engage in direct combat. Although U.S. intervention in Pakistan, Somalia, and Yemen does not use drones exclusively, UAVs have come to symbolize the war that the United States has conducted in these countries. The United States appears to have governmental permission to use drones in both Yemen and Somalia. Despite concerns over the legitimacy of these two governments, formal permission for use of drones differs in no meaningful way from permission to use special forces or manned aircraft.[44]

In Pakistan, the debate turns on the extent to which the Pakistani government has granted secret permission, tacit permission, or both. As noted earlier, the Pakistani government reached an accord with the United States in 2004 that allowed drone strikes on condition that some of those attacks would target Pakistani militants.[45] In 2012, the *Wall Street Journal* reported that the CIA contacts its Pakistani counterpart once a month to indicate the scope and geographic extent of planned U.S. drone operations in Pakistani airspace.[46] Although the Pakistani Air Force could easily engage and destroy U.S. drone aircraft, just as it engaged and destroyed Soviet aircraft during the Soviet-Afghan War, it has not yet done so. This absence of action, despite Pakistani protests, indicates that the Pakistani government approves of, or at least tolerates, U.S. behavior.

However, legal specialists dispute the legality of such secret or tacit permission. In a March 2013 statement, the UN Special Rapporteur for Human Rights argued that the lack of clear consent on the part of Pakistani authorities for U.S. drone strikes in Pakistani territory effectively rendered those strikes illegal under international law.[47] Legal scholar Eric Posner describes Pakistani agreement to the drone war as "coerced consent," which has dubious legitimacy under international law (although Posner is known to be a harsh critic of international law).[48] Benjamin Wittes of the Brookings Institution also acknowledges, "It's going to be hard over time to sustain U.S. action in Pakistan based on an implied consent theory in the face of explicit non-consent—however insincere."[49]

Use of drones in this manner has arguably increased the foreign policy power of the U.S. executive, but this is widely argued to be necessary by counterterrorism specialists (although not by many other civilian and military authorities).[50] The contrast offered by the special forces raid that killed Osama bin Laden is instructive. That raid incurred a substantial amount of risk, flying into the teeth of Pakistani air defenses without prior notification. Equipment malfunctions and the potential for strong resistance in the compound combined to increase the prospect of American casualties. Perhaps the most controversial aspect of the U.S. drone campaign was the decision to kill Anwar al-Awlaki, an American citizen operating with al-Qaeda in Yemen. The killing of Awlaki by drone strike created concerns that the executive branch could order the execution of an American citizen without trial or due process.

In response, Attorney General Eric Holder argued that the government's decision to kill Awlaki through an internal, nonjudicial procedure nevertheless met the requirements of "due process."[51] The executive branch, under authority provided by Congress through the Authorization for the Use of Military Force (AUMF), can identify members of organizations at war with the United States and target those individuals for attack without judicial recourse. The executive may launch attacks against such individuals if it has reasonable information that the individuals pose an "imminent threat of violent attack," regardless of their location or citizenship.[52] The definition of "imminent threat" remains troublingly ambiguous. However, the rejection of geographic boundaries for combat has some support in the legal literature; legal scholar Michael Lewis argues that the Law of Armed Conflict applies to attacks on al-Qaeda regardless of geographic constraint. This means that U.S. citizens associated with al-Qaeda could conceivably be attacked on U.S. soil.[53] Indeed, some (including former deputy assistant U.S. attorney John Yoo) have argued that the power to order drone strikes derives from the inherent authority of the presidency rather than from congressional statute.[54]

It is worth noting that while these disputes over executive power have emerged specifically in response to drone strikes, the same issues would arise with strikes from manned aircraft. Had a bomb dropped by an F-16 killed Awlaki, concerns over executive power would remain. In this sense, concern about drones amounts to a proxy for broader critiques of American foreign and military policy. However, the drone wars are relevant to this book to the extent that the availability of drones enables policymakers to engage in strategic bombing campaigns against shadowy organizations with minimal legal oversight. The specific qualities of drones, including loiter capability and low political profile, make them ideal for hunting individual targets. F-16s can kill, but they cannot remain on station for twenty-four hours, and they tend to annoy the leaders of foreign states. Consequently, drones may make war (and especially foreign interventionist war) more likely.[55]

President Barack Obama has argued that drones represent a critical tool in the war against terrorist networks, and that their use is both legal and moral. According to the president, drones are preferable to either the deployment of ground forces or the use of manned aircraft, especially in states that cannot effectively police their own countryside. At the same time, Obama has called for an expansion of congressional oversight over the drone campaigns and for a general reduction in the number of drone strikes as circumstances warrant.[56]

What about autonomous drones? As of yet, humans have remotely piloted the UAVs tasked with killing, whether on or away from the battlefield. However, technology for the automation of attack UAVs already exists.[57] Indeed, some missions in high-intensity combat situations may require autonomy. If the data link between a UAV equipped for air-to-air combat and its remote pilot fails, the UAV will quickly fall victim to manned aircraft.[58] Only a UAV capable of carrying out its mission with a high degree of independence can hope to survive in complex and threatening electronic environments.

However, the development of autonomous machines with the capacity to kill creates deep difficult questions about adherence to humanitarian law. Human Rights Watch (HRW) argues "that fully autonomous weapons would not only be unable to meet legal standards but would also undermine essential non-legal safeguards for civilians," and that "fully autonomous weapons should be banned." Specifically, fully autonomous systems cannot meet the standards of reasoning necessary to successfully discriminate targets according the rules of distinction, proportionality, and military necessity. Moreover, drones lacking any human connection to target populations could enhance the ability of tyrannical governments to suppress their populations. Finally, legal accountability for the unlawful actions of drones remains murky. HRW suggests that governments and activists should pursue a multilateral treaty against the development and production of autonomous systems.[59]

Critics of HRW's position suggest that preemptive efforts to ban autonomous weapons are, as a policy matter, likely to fail, and that such efforts will handicap the development of effective robotic means of discriminating between targets.[60] The first position argues that efforts to limit autonomous weapons should concentrate on the development of norms of drone usage in major states rather than on treaty law. Such norms could develop incrementally as drone capability increases.[61] The second position contrasts the potential humanitarian shortcomings of autonomous drones with the actual legal shortcomings of traditional ground and air warfare.[62] Future autonomous drones will likely have better sensors and greater capacity to discriminate than soldiers or manned aircraft.[63] These arguments, especially the latter, echo older debates about the humanitarian problems of airpower.

Morality

The moral case for drones rests on two propositions. First, drones represent the "least worst case" solution for the difficulties associated with the War on Terror. Enemy militants shift quickly across borders, operate in shadowy groups, and are difficult to apprehend; drones are a low-cost, high-intelligence way of debilitating such militant groups. Second, in many cases, drone attacks simply replace ordnance delivery by manned aircraft, artillery, cruise missile, or other sources. The distinction between destroying a target with a bomb from an F-16 and one from a drone appears, at first glance, quite thin. Moreover, the long loiter capabilities of drones mean that operators can collect intelligence on potential targets that allows for better discrimination between civilians and legitimate targets.[64] Drones often also carry smaller ordnance than manned aircraft, further limiting collateral damage. However, the relatively low cost of drones, combined with the immunity they tend to provide their pilots, could create greater political incentive for specific strikes and for military action more generally.

The best critiques of the drone war concentrate on three arguments. First, legal or not, the drone war has created a deeply problematic set of legal precedents that threaten to expand executive power over war making. Second, regardless of whether drones facilitate a more discriminate use of force than other forms of ordnance delivery, the relative ease of their use by political authorities tends to increase civilian casualty levels.[65] Relatedly, drones facilitate interventionist war by the United States and similar states.[66]

It bears mention that drones, especially autonomous drones, also summon some of our worst fears about the vulnerability of humanity to machine destruction. Just since the 1980s, science fiction epics such as the *Terminator* films, the *Matrix* films, and the *Battlestar Galactica* television series have depicted horrific wars between humankind and autonomous machines.[67] These works build on earlier tropes about the threat automation presents to human society. The appearance of remotely piloted killing machines in the War on Terror thus found fertile imaginative ground for human fear.

Further research may indicate that there really is a psychological difference between being bombed by manned aircraft and stalked by killer UAVs.[68] On the other hand, just as the psychological terror of bombing eventually fades among its targets, the distinction between manned and unmanned aircraft may eventually dissipate. Similarly, some argue that drone warfare produces a disconnect between operators and the execution of military force.[69] However, drone operators seem to suffer from post-traumatic stress disorder at a rate similar to pilots who participate directly in air-to-ground combat.[70]

The extensive use of drones has spurred concern that use of drones by the United States sets a precedent that other countries may follow.[71] While a drone "race" may have taken place even without the large-scale Predator and Reaper campaign in Pakistan, Yemen, and Somalia, the extent and character of the race now on display has been driven by U.S. behavior. Other states, observing the effectiveness—or at least the capabilities—of U.S. drones, will work to create their own counterparts with an enthusiasm that they would not have had in absence of the U.S. example.[72]

DRONES AND AIR FORCE CULTURE

Do drones represent a challenge to air force culture and identity? In one sense, the extension of the remote is part of a trend in the projection of military force that accelerated early in the twentieth century. Pilots in World War I and World War II could kill without ever seeing the enemy, as could artillery operators on the Western Front. World War II saw the first major naval battles that ended without the ships of opposing sides ever coming into contact with one another. Identifying a target in Pakistan from Nevada, then killing that target, simply represents an extension of this trend. In another sense, however, the phenomenon of remote drone piloting represents a major discontinuity in the history of killing.[73] At least notionally, an F-16 pilot experiences a variety of hardships and dangers while doing his or her job. The enemy may shoot the aircraft down, or it may suffer a mechanical failure and crash. A drone pilot can drive to work in the morning, kill several targets, then drive home in the evening suffering no more direct physical threat than anyone else using American roadways. That said, drone pilots do exercise many of the same skills of targeting and discrimination expected of pilots operating manned craft.[74]

Drones also threaten to break the monopoly of air force officers on aerial combat. In all services other than the air force, both officers and enlisted personnel fight. Indeed, in the army enlisted personnel bear the overwhelming brunt of conflict. In the air force, however, officers piloting combat aircraft do almost all of the fighting. The expansion of drone warfare brings this practice into question. John Taplett has argued that the air force could save considerable amounts of money by assigning drone flight duties to enlisted personnel, with little loss of combat effectiveness.[75] Questions have also developed as to how promotion boards will evaluate the service and drone pilots, with some very early evidence indicating that drone operators suffer discrimination compared to traditional pilots.[76]

The decision in February 2013 to create a "drone medal" brought many of these issues to a head.[77] The medal recognized the contributions of drone operators and of troops assigned to cyber-warfare. The creation of this medal spurred controversy both within the military and with antiwar civilians. In the wake of this backlash, Secretary of Defense Chuck Hagel decided to cancel the medal in April, replacing it with an alternative device for recognizing "drone warriors."[78] This decision seems to have resolved the immediate controversy, but the place of drone operators within the U.S. Air Force (and the military more generally) remains in serious question. The civilian element of the backlash also raises questions about public perceptions of the air force.

Future development in drone technology may completely sever the connection between human pilot and airpower projection. Visual technology cannot yet compete with the ability of a human pilot to observe, identify, and engage targets. However, the need to service a human body also places hard limits on the speed and maneuverability of fighter aircraft. Remotely piloted drones face fewer such limitations. Drones have already been used in exceptional circumstances to conduct air superiority missions. While enforcing the "No Fly" zone over Iraq, a drone was once equipped with an air-to-air missile in order to counter an Iraqi effort to shoot down drones with conventional aircraft.[79] Several months before the South Ossetia War, a Russian fighter aircraft shot down a Georgian drone. The latter captured the attack on video, highlighting the vulnerability of drones to attack by conventional aircraft.[80] Nevertheless, within the foreseeable future drones will acquire the capability to defend themselves from manned aircraft.

Drone development has not ceased, although some have argued that the air force is shortchanging drone development in preference for manned aircraft.[81] Miniaturization continues to reduce the minimum size of effective drones, potentially creating a future in which armies and air forces deploy swarms of autonomous "killer drones" to accomplish basic missions such as reconnaissance and close air support.[82] The relevance of the traditional air force to such a project is unclear, given that the operators of such swarms would qualify as "pilots" only under the most expansive definitions. The United States and Israel are known to be exploring such technology; other countries may follow suit.[83]

DRONES AND AIRPOWER THEORY

The novelty of UAVs can obscure how well they fit within traditional airpower theory. Drones' capacity for combining persistent surveillance with precision-guided munitions makes them useful for air campaigns designed to detach the sinews of enemy military and governmental institutions. Indeed, if neoclassical airpower theory is about leveraging intelligence and surveillance to achieve political and strategic effect, drones are ideal platforms. Drones' vulnerability to surface and air attack (at least by sophisticated opponents) is ameliorated by their lower material and human costs.[84] While certain very sophisticated opponents could potentially prevent drones from functioning within part of the battle space (either by making it inhospitable for slow, defenseless aircraft or severing the data link that drones depend on), forcing an enemy to pay the costs of defeating drones is probably, on balance, worth it to many attackers. In any case, an opponent sophisticated enough to defeat drones can also probably inflict unacceptably high losses on manned aircraft.

This book has concentrated on the friction between airpower theory and a Clausewitzian approach to war. How do the drone campaigns of the War on Terror, and the emerging norms and practices of drone warfare, fit into the Clausewitzian framework?

How Do Drones Contribute to the Disarming of the Enemy?

Drone attacks against al-Qaeda undoubtedly contribute to the degradation of the organization's capabilities. The assassination of key members of the organization deprives it of human capital, and steps taken to avoid drones (such as limiting communications and limiting gatherings of individuals) inhibit its ability to act.[85] However, it is unclear how these assassinations fall into a broader strategic framework for victory. Drone strikes have made the United States exceedingly unpopular in Pakistan and in other parts of the world. This unpopularity has consequently made it much more difficult for the United States to work with partners in the War on Terror, whether in Pakistan, Yemen, or Afghanistan. The overall strategic impact of the drone campaign is, therefore, difficult to assess.[86] Nevertheless, in the terminology described by this book, the drone war appears to have Clausewitzian characteristics in that it represents an effort to win by destroying the military capability of the enemy organization.

Does Drone Warfare Place Technological Novelty Ahead of Political Applicability?

There is good reason to believe that the novelty of drones, a mostly new kind of warfare, is sufficiently impressive to civilians that they overstate the degree to which the method meets strategic needs. Drones give governments a simple military solution to complex political and military problems. In the case of the War on Terror in particular, they allow the U.S. government to forego the difficulties associated with either capturing and prosecuting members of al-Qaeda or physically occupying the space in which al-Qaeda operates. Like many airpower campaigns, the drone war has arguably escaped the bounds its initiators imagined, but while mission creep is common to air campaigns, it is not solely a feature of airpower.

Indeed, the air force as an institution does not appear to bear any guilt in this situation. The USAF's standoffish relationship with drones—not particularly hostile, nor altogether friendly—does not resemble its older relationship with the manned bomber, for example.[87] Indeed, in the War on Terror the drone-led strategic bombing campaign against al-Qaeda has largely been executed by entities other than the air force, with only marginal air force participation. And so while the drone war surely involves some degree of technological fetishism, the problem cannot, in this case, be laid at the feet of the USAF.

Do Drones Change Our Approach to the Fog of War?

One of the key attractions of drones is their ability to clear away some of the fog of war. The loiter capability allows drones to study targets for a longer period, leaving analysts with more information for drawing conclusions about the position of a target within the enemy organizational framework. Indeed, the assassination of al-Harethi is a textbook example of how intelligence can be used to identify and destroy key network members.[88] The overwhelming majority of drones perform specifically this duty, whether at tactical, operational, or strategic levels. Consequently, drones represent an attempt to lift the fog of war off of both the battlefield and the social milieu that armed forces are intended to protect.

However, implementation indicates that imperfections remain. Estimates of the death toll of drone attacks in Pakistan vary dramatically, including differences on the legal status of targets and civilians.[89] Indeed, "signature strikes" are defined by imperfect intelligence; targets are identified by their suspicious patterns of behavior rather than by intelligence indicating specific culpability in terrorist or militant activity.[90]

More important, evaluation of the impact of drone warfare on the militant networks that it targets is inherently difficult. While U.S. intelligence agencies have some tools for evaluating the strength of militant networks, these metrics remain hazy and difficult to test. Moreover, it may be beyond the capacity of the state to evaluate whether members of the Chechen diaspora are more likely to launch attacks against the United States because of their concern about Pakistani villagers living under the threat of drone strikes.[91]

Debate over drone warfare remains fraught with misperception and misunderstanding. The emerging opposition to the use of drones by the United States is unfocused, with many arguments blurring the lines between the technology itself and broader critiques of American foreign and military policy. The difference between killing someone with a drone and killing the same person with an F-16 surely means little to the person killed. However, critics are correct to identify troubling trends in drone usage. If drones allow policymakers to believe that wars (or even antiterrorist campaigns) can be won cheaply and easily, they may lead to more such conflicts. Perhaps more worrisome, the trend toward automation in military drone technology is fraught with deeply troubling questions about human control of machines and the responsibility of individuals for crimes against humanity.

The future of drone warfare depends, to some extent, on decisions made within the air force and in the U.S. Department of Defense more broadly. However, the genie has undoubtedly left the bottle. Many countries have undertaken the development of advanced drones, similar to the ones employed by the United States. While no other nation has embarked on a drone campaign similar to that of the United States, we can guess that drones will eventually prove as useful to foreign leaders as they have to the U.S. government. Thus, while the answer to the question that animates this book (how shall we structure America's airpower?) affects the future of drone technology, it will not determine that future.

Indeed, perhaps the most fascinating part of the story of the Rise of the Drone (so to speak) is how little the story depends on the U.S. Air Force. The USAF fostered early drones because it had free money with which to do so, but it never saw drones as central to its future. The bulk of American drones operate outside of air force control. Most surprising, the United States is conducting a strategic bombing campaign that involves the air force only at the margin. While (in the view of this book) these developments exclude the air force from a great deal of the blame associated with the drone wars, they also suggest that the USAF is no more than a minor player in what is thus far the most important question of twenty-first-century airpower theory.

The practice of drone employment is compatible with the body of twentieth-century airpower theory. But drones undoubtedly lack the romanticism associated with manned flight, and there is no question that this romanticism still cuts to the heart of air force identity. Obviously, given its commitment to the F-35 and to the Long Range Strike Bomber (LRS), the air force remains interested in manned aviation (although the LRS may have unmanned capabilities). Discussions of organizational culture and bureaucratic position tend to render debates over the future of the air force dull and dry, but we cannot forget that one of the great appeals of airpower remains the sheer joy of flight. As drones, abetted by bureaucracy and economics, slowly take missions away from manned aircraft, this romanticism may fade, and much airpower advocacy may fade with it.

9

The Way Forward

This book has made the case that organizational dynamics have repeatedly caused friction between the U.S. Air Force and its sibling services, and that this pattern will likely continue for as long as the air force retains its independence. Consequently, the book argues for folding the air force back into its constituent services. However, abolishing the air force is not the only alternative for reforming the U.S. armed forces. This chapter briefly examines the institutional arrangement of airpower in two other countries, presents some alternative policy options, sets forth a plan for abolishing the air force, and studies the process of institutional reform in Canada.

FOREIGN ALTERNATIVES

This section briefly examines alternative systems of institutional airpower. These systems represent other configurations of airpower and have different implications for the relationship between ground, sea, and air military forces. Each case study includes a brief description of the institutional arrangements and an evaluation of the consequences of that arrangement. These arrangements do not represent "optimal" ways of managing; indeed, there is no optimal way of organizing military institutions. Different states face different environments and have different strategic cultures. Different organizations have different internal cultures. What might have worked for the Soviet Union in 1950 would not necessarily have worked for Israel in 1970 or for the United States today. Rather, the purpose is to provide a sketch of how alternative institutional arrangements function so as to better evaluate how similar arrangements might work in the U.S. context. On many metrics, U.S. airpower clearly outperforms the services described here. In other ways, these foreign services give good account of themselves.

Soviet Union

Institutional Structure   Although the USSR toyed with the idea of strategic bombing in the 1920s and 1930s, the tactical concepts concentrating on support of Red Army ground forces came to dominate Soviet procurement and doctrine before and during World War II.[1] Like the United States, the Soviet Union divided airpower responsibilities across several organizations. During the post–Cold War period, the Strategic Rocket Forces, the Soviet Army, the Military Air Force (with Long-Range Aviation, Frontal Aviation, and Transport Aviation branches), the Soviet Navy, and the Air Defense Force each controlled some aviation assets.

The Soviet Navy operated a broad array of aircraft, including a maritime version of the primary Soviet strategic bomber, the Tu-95 (naval designation Tu-142), and frontline Soviet medium bombers, such as the Tu-16 and the Tu-22M.[2] This stands in stark contrast to U.S. practice, in which the use of strategic bombers for tactical maritime purposes was rarely considered. Moreover, when strategic bombers were equipped for naval warfare (B-52Gs armed with Harpoon antiship missiles, for example), the bombers themselves remained under control of the USAF. The Soviet Navy also operated sea-based helicopters and fixed-wing carrier aviation.[3]

In the 1930s the Soviets created the Air Defense Forces (PVO), which operated interceptor aircraft, radar, and air defense artillery.[4] The PVO became an autonomous separate service in 1954, as Soviet concern over U.S. strategic bombers grew.[5] The PVO retained its independence until 1998, when it was folded into the Russian Air Forces.

The division of responsibility in the Military Air Force resembled the USAF in some ways, although Long-Range Aviation did not dominate in the same sense as Strategic Air Command.[6] Rather, the Military Air Force pursued minimum deterrence capability with a portion of its strategic bombers, assigning the rest (and the bulk of medium bombers) to tactical tasks (including the delivery of tactical nuclear weapons). Frontal aviation remained under control of ground commanders and concentrated on short-range fighter and attack aircraft designed to operate in support of the advancing Soviet Army.[7] The Soviet Army itself was the primary operator of attack and transport helicopters.

Consequences   The overall impact of Soviet military institutions on aviation is difficult to assess. The Soviet Union did suffer from some interservice conflict during the Cold War. As memory of World War II waned, the Soviet Navy, the PVO, and the Strategic Rocket Forces all asserted their relevance (and in some cases primacy). In the late 1970s, Marshal Nikolai Ogarkov embarked on a campaign to enforce what would now be known as "jointness." In particular, the Air Defense Force received severe criticism in the latter part of the Cold War for developing doctrine that stood apart from the rest of Soviet war-fighting capacity.[8] This was not surprising, given that the Air Defense Force had been allocated a "strategic" mission (national defense against nuclear attack) that in many cases did not involve close cooperation with the other Soviet services.

The establishment of a separate missile force and the focus on ground warfare left the Soviet air forces with a strategic strike capability that was, by U.S. standards, limited. However, Soviet military thinking was carefully attuned to the potential for revolutionary technological advances and followed the development of military aviation closely. The Soviet Army became comfortable with the concept of modern mechanized warfare by the end of the 1920s, understanding that aviation would inevitably play a role in this kind of combat. While the Soviets sometimes lacked the technological and industrial prowess to pursue airpower capabilities to their fullest extent, the overall Soviet force posture represented a sensible reaction to strategic and tactical realities.

The relative quality of Soviet military equipment remains an important point of debate. First, Soviet equipment proved competitive with Western equipment for much of the Cold War, and many argue that when properly handled Soviet aircraft performed as well as their American counterparts. Evidence for this proposition is less than 100 percent clear, however. Accepting *arguendo* that the Soviet military aviation complex produced inferior equipment, part of the responsibility would lie with the less advanced nature of Soviet industry.[9] However, the idea that an institutional framework that favored visionary development of airpower might have produced better equipment cannot be ruled out.

From an American point of view, the Soviet Union consistently lacked an appreciation of strategic airpower and consequently the tools with which to carry out a strategic campaign.[10] The Soviet Union remained substantially behind the United States in such technologies as in-flight refueling. Without a strategic mission for short-range aircraft to undertake, the Soviets never perceived much need for refueling capability. From a different perspective, however, the bureaucratic arrangement of the Soviet strategic arm limited many of the more outlandish aspects of strategic airpower culture. Without air force independence or the legacy of a World War II strategic bombing campaign, the Soviets built far fewer bombers than the United States, focusing production on the Tu-95 Bear, an aircraft with capabilities very roughly in between the B-36 and the B-52. About 500 Tu-95s were built by the Soviet Union, as compared to a total of 1,244 B-36s, B-52s, and B-58s.[11] Focusing on ICBMs instead of bombers, the Soviets' only other major strategic bomber project was the Tu-160 Blackjack, built in the 1980s with a full production run of 35 aircraft. The Soviets also built a total of about 2,400 medium bombers, including the Tu-16 Badger, the Tu-22 Blinder, and the Tu-22M Backfire, all of which were capable of nuclear and conventional missions.[12] Indeed, the Soviet Air Forces directed most of their efforts toward national air defense and victory in conventional war.[13] Soviet ICBMs belonged to the Strategic Rocket Forces, an organization separate from the Long-Range Aviation (heavy bomber) division of the Soviet Air Forces.[14]

The Soviet aviation system produced some innovative aircraft and gave Soviet ground forces confidence that they would receive air support over the battlefield. The Soviet willingness to flexibly deploy strategic aircraft in tactical roles prefigured U.S. willingness to do the same. Moreover, the Soviet aviation system helped avoid wasteful spending on dinosaurs such as the B-36, the B-58, and the B-70. The Soviet experience demonstrates that a solid institutional structure cannot overcome basic societal and economic disadvantages.

Israel

Institutional Structure   The Israeli Air Force (IAF) constitutes one arm of the Israeli Defense Force (IDF), sharing the designation with the ground arm and the sea arm. Historically, the IAF has had better representation in elite military and political circles than the Sea Arm but has remained subordinate to the Ground Arm. Two of the twenty IDF chiefs of staff have come from the air force, with only one (Lieutenant General Dan Halutz) enjoying the bulk of his career with the air force.[15] An attempt to win full independence for the IAF failed in the early 1950s.[16]

The IAF controls virtually all of the air assets of the Israeli Defense Force, including helicopters, transport aircraft, and maritime aircraft. Largely because of the institutional closeness between the Ground Arm and the air force, an independent helicopter force attached to the Ground Arm has never appeared necessary. The IAF also operates Israel's ballistic missile forces, and since 1970 the vast bulk of the IDF's air defense network. The IAF has no internal divisions specific to strategic versus tactical aviation, although helicopters, fixed wing, and air defense have their own "groups."

Consequences   The organizational unity of the Israeli Defense Force helped produce close collaboration between air and ground forces. Indeed, Israeli doctrine required tight cooperation between air units tasked with close support and advancing ground forces. However, over time the need for large-scale armored maneuver from the Israeli Defense Force has declined, with major regional antagonists either coming to an accommodation with Israel (Egypt), or accepting that the balance of power does not favor a conventional war (Syria). While the IAF continued to play an important tactical role in conflicts such as the 1982 Lebanon War, policymakers increasingly tasked it with strategic missions detached from direct support of ground troops.[17]

Dima Adamsky has traced the path of the Revolution in Military Affairs concept through the IDF, suggesting that during the 1990s and 2000s the IDF increasingly adopted the attitude that effects-based operations could be decisive in war. These beliefs stood in tension with the traditional combined arms focus of the IDF, creating some intraorganizational conflict. Adamsky argued that the IDF effectively carried out an EBO-oriented campaign against Syria during the Lebanon War, even if it did not adopt EBO terminology.[18]

The 2006 war against Hezbollah represented a shift in the Israeli reliance on airpower. In this campaign, the Israeli Air Force conducted a wide-ranging campaign against political and infrastructure targets throughout Lebanon as well as direct attacks in service of an IDF ground advance (this campaign was discussed in greater detail in chapter 3). However, Hezbollah capably resisted Israeli efforts, declaring victory once the IDF withdrew.[19] Some commentators disagree with the notion that the course of the war resulted from a significant doctrinal shift in the IDF.[20] After the war, a commission investigating the conduct of the conflict concluded that a disjuncture between means and ends, and especially between the needs of an air campaign and the needs of a ground campaign, had severely reduced IDF effectiveness. Israeli political and military leaders expected that the air campaign would suffice and did not sufficiently prepare for the ground campaign that became necessary.[21]

The IAF lacks the long history of institutional hostility with its ground counterpart, and indeed relations between the arms appear to remain strong. The shift to a more strategic approach has resulted from a broader shift in Israel's international situation. As Israel no longer depends for survival on its ability to defeat Egyptian and Syrian armored formations, the IAF has had the opportunity to develop a new vision of its contribution to warfare. However, the 2006 war provoked grave questions about the effectiveness of this vision.

LESSONS

Institutional structure is not destiny. Rather, institutions set the stage on which bureaucratic conflict and institutional culture interact. Particular constellations of culture and bureaucracy may serve the interests of a nation at a given time but not under alternative conditions. Moreover, culture itself can be a moving target. Nevertheless, institutions surely do interact with strategic and organizational culture to push military capability in certain directions. Moreover, states use a vast number of different institutional structures to arrange their airpower assets. Lessons from this brief investigation include:

- There is no single configuration of military power that will serve all nations at all times.

- Institutional culture changes. Sometimes bureaucratic arrangements that worked with one set of organizational cultures lose their relevance or become inadequate over time. Conversely, sometimes institutional cultures "grow into" their bureaucratic spaces.

- A good institutional configuration does not remedy all national security problems. The Soviet Union collapsed despite its sensible division of military authority.

- Nations should be as flexible as possible with regard to institutional arrangements. Constraints include the political process, the need to formulate serious doctrinal and procurement strategies, and the need to develop healthy organizational morale.

Change in institutional structure does not necessarily imply that the previous structure has failed. Rather, it can simply indicate recognition that the environment has changed sufficiently to make previous arrangements obsolete or inadequate. It is crucial, however, that nations recognize when technological and political conditions have changed, and act to prepare their security bureaucracies accordingly.

ALTERNATIVES

This book is not the first effort to identify problems with the air force and propose solutions. In 1994 Carl Builder called upon the air force to redefine and reconceptualize its organizational mission as follows: "The mission of the Air Force is the military control and exploitation of the aerospace continuum in support of the national interests."[22] Builder argued that such a redefinition would change air force culture sufficiently to modify both the fixation with technology (the airplane in particular) and the fixation with the strategic mission (victory in war without disarming the enemy). In other words, Builder proposed a cultural fix for the structural problem of the air force's relations with other services. Builder would rely on the redefinition of mission to eliminate some of the long-standing cultural tensions between the air force and its sibling services as well as to remedy the problem of the "quick, cheap, decisive war" that continues to problematize civil-military relations.

RAND analyst David Johnson argues that ground and air power have become tightly intertwined, and that in recent wars interservice conflict between the air force and the army has had destructive effects. Johnson acknowledges that precision-guided munitions and information supremacy have granted an extraordinary leap in the effectiveness of airpower against conventional military formations and even against irregular combatants. Johnson suggests, however, that future military operations will involve the conjunction of ground and air elements, and that despite the focus on "jointness" in U.S. military doctrine, interservice competition continues to introduce an unacceptable level of friction. Johnson argues that the problems of friction could be ameliorated by a series of reforms that make clear the air force's responsibility for "deep operations" and that give joint commanders the confidence to override service preferences while planning for war fighting.[23] Effectively, this would privilege the air force at the expense of the army, solving the problem of interservice conflict by making the USAF the dominant partner in the army–air force relationship.

In *Airpower for Strategic Effect,* Colin Gray argues that interservice conflict and certain organizational pathologies amount to the cost of doing business. Gray accepts that airpower advocates have vastly overstated the impact of airpower but argues that context matters: the airpower we enjoy today would not have come about without a great deal of exaggeration.[24] Doing nothing is always an option; the United States will enjoy dominance at almost every level of escalation into the medium-term future, possibly making reform a less than pressing priority. Given the existence of a cottage industry for national security reform of various sorts, an argument that we can get by with the institutions we have is refreshing.

THE NEW LOOK

While all of these proposals represent serious efforts to remedy significant problems with U.S. military institutions, none grapples with the core problem. The United States needs airpower, but bureaucratic infighting and historical tensions limit its effectiveness. These problems will grow as the air force takes over the space and cyber realms. The 1947 reorganization transformed the landscape of American military power, and eliminating air force independence would have a similar effect. The most immediate question involves the reallocation of USAF assets, including aircraft, weapons, personnel, bases, and missions, to the surviving services.

To reiterate the four principles set forth in the introduction:

- Principle of organic mission: Each service should, insofar as possible, organically include the assets necessary to undertake its most likely missions. No reorganization can completely eliminate the need for jointness, but the best structures minimize the need for crossing service boundaries in the normal course of events.

- Principle of redundancy: When possible, the potential for redundant capabilities between army and navy air assets should be retained. For critical missions, each service should have the capability to cover the shortfalls of the other.

- Principle of efficiency: As much as possible, reorganization should favor a more efficient distribution of assets and responsibilities, resulting in the elimination of unnecessary maintenance, administration, and other costs.

- Principle of organizational culture: Divisions of responsibility should take into account the necessity for each service to establish and maintain a healthy organizational culture, built around a coherent vision.

Under this proposed reorganization, the navy would become (in very broad terms) the "stage-setting" service, focusing primarily on the defense and maintenance of the liberal international order (insofar as such order serves the national interests of the United States), while the army would become the "war-fighting" service, focusing on the destruction of fielded enemy forces and their supporting infrastructure. The reorganization would divide the missions and assets of the USAF along the following lines.

Cyber

Responsibility for cyber-warfare and defense should pass to the navy. As discussed earlier, the navy has a robust, long-standing concept of the commons that supports a positive vision of cyberspace and cyber-security. This concept makes national cyber-defense more comfortably at home in the navy than in the army, although the army would obviously retain responsibility for defense of its own networks. We can expect that the navy will focus on defense, resilience, and the maintenance of network security rather than on offense and deterrent capability.[25] Moreover, we can expect that the navy will take seriously the idea that defense of the commons is a global responsibility, and that it will work to achieve cooperative outcomes with foreign cyber-defense organizations.[26]

Global Strike Command

The USAF currently manages the bulk of the U.S. nuclear deterrent. The USAF's writ includes both ICBMs and strategic bombers capable of carrying nuclear weapons. Many of these assets are located at bases deep within the United States. Nevertheless, because the USN currently manages a substantial number of nuclear weapons on its nuclear ballistic missile submarines and other platforms, allocating USAF nuclear assets to the USN makes the most sense. As an alternative the United States could create a new service dedicated specifically to ballistic missiles as nuclear delivery systems. Missile defense might also fit in this service's writ. However, it is unlikely that the benefits of such reorganization would outweigh the bureaucratic problems and administrative costs. Consequently, the personnel, bases, and infrastructure associated with the management of the bomber and ICBM elements of the nuclear triad should shift to navy control. To cut costs and because of the general obsolescence of the concept, the bomber element of the triad should stand down, with existing bombers converted to conventional missions.

Air Combat Command

In accordance with a broad division of responsibility between "stage-setting" and "war-winning" capabilities, and with the distribution of nuclear weapons toward the navy, the USN would take control of the bulk of the "strategic" assets of the USAF. However, the principles of redundancy and of organic mission sets suggest that the army should claim control of some of the strategic bomber force. Strategic bombers often play tactical roles, utilizing long ranges and heavy payloads to good local effect. Army-operated strategic bombers can also carry out some strike and interdiction missions more efficiently in context of a general army air campaign than in a joint army-navy campaign. Consequently, the strategic bomber force of the U.S. Air Force (B-1Bs, B-52Hs, and B-2s) should be divided between the army and the navy, with some of the navy assets repurposed for maritime patrol and strike roles. Each service would also operate a sufficient number of reconnaissance and long-range strike drones. Finally, the services would share the extant tanker fleet, which serves both strategic and tactical purposes.

Assets associated with the tactical support of fielded U.S. forces will shift to the army. This includes close air support aircraft such as the A-10 but also air superiority and multirole aircraft such as the F-15, F-16, F-22, and F-35. While these aircraft can carry out strategic strike and interdiction missions, they can also perform tactical roles. Moreover, the inclusion of air superiority allows the army to set the terms on which it will meet enemy forces. The shift of tactical assets to the army would allow a greater degree of mission coherence in many of the tasks now assigned to U.S. fighting forces in Afghanistan as well as in potential future conflicts. The army would also take control of the bulk of air force drones. As noted above, the army would also take control of some "strategic" air force assets, including a portion of the bomber fleet. The shift of these assets would require the army to take control of the bulk of the physical infrastructure of the air force, including bases and training facilities, as well as the bulk of air force personnel.

Space Command

Space assets play an enabling role for all modern military functions. U.S. military satellites carry out surveillance, monitor enemy communications, and provide the foundation for the communications system that undergirds modern military operations. Historically, the air force has acted as the primary "space" service, responsible for procurement, defense, and maintenance of most space systems.[27] In the modern combatant command structure, space operations have come under the aegis of

U.S. Strategic Command.[28] Both the navy and the army will require space assets to continue operation. While some duplication may be possible and even beneficial from a redundancy point of view, the services will have to share other assets. The navy and the army will divide the personnel currently associated with space responsibilities and will undertake to maintain the training and competence of new personnel assigned to this command. This arrangement could lead to either free riding or bureaucratic imperialism, but there is little other choice for the maintenance of crucial military space infrastructure.

Air Mobility Command

Transport assets will receive greater attention under the new look. First and foremost, plans to retire the C-27J would be cancelled, with surviving units transferred back from the reserves to active service.[29] Assets, including the OV-22 fleet, will primarily shift to the army, with some allowance for the needs of the Marine Corps. This element of the reorganization links control of the asset with need for and use of the asset, and prioritizes a capability long neglected under the current bureaucratic structure. An arrangement that puts control of both rotary and fixed-wing transport assets under the same command also eliminates wasteful redundancies, allowing the most efficient platforms and technologies to thrive.

Procurement

The reorganization would force a hard look at many procurement priorities. The Pentagon would have to look very carefully at the new bomber project, evaluating its capabilities against existing platforms and against the promise of Prompt Global Strike, the multiplatform effort to ensure capability to deliver munitions to any target in the world within one hour.[30] Conceivably, the new bomber could deploy with both the navy and the army, fulfilling different roles with each. However, careful analysis (shorn of parochial air force service interest) may reveal that the bomber unnecessarily duplicates other capabilities.

While the F-35 Joint Strike Fighter continues to produce headaches for all associated with it, in the near term there appears little good option but to continue to pursue procurement of the F-35A. However, the army should procure new versions of "legacy" aircraft such as the F-15 to fulfill missions not requiring the most advanced stealth technology. Also, the army should take an extremely critical look at any plans for the development of a follow-up "sixth-generation" fighter aircraft.[31] The future of strike and air superiority may well lie with drone technology, and the army is well positioned to take an unbiased look at the need for maintaining manned air superiority capability.

The U.S. Army should undertake active efforts to procure so-called COIN aircraft, fixed-wing, propeller-driven planes with significant armament and long loiter time.[32] While the process of reorganization may outlast the war in Afghanistan, procurement of COIN aircraft would serve both to make the United States a better partner for states with internal security problems and to preserve a capability for unforeseen future conflicts.

Jointness

The reorganization would hardly eliminate the need for a continued emphasis on jointness, although the nature of that emphasis would shift. The removal of the air force from tactical, operational, and strategic decision making would improve performance by streamlining the process and by orienting planning around mission-based, rather than service-based, metrics and criteria. Many aspects of jointness would continue, such as career incentives for officers to develop expertise in interservice collaboration.

Institutional Flexibility

Some strict bureaucratic rules are necessary. While it makes some sense for the navy to possess an "army" focused around amphibious operations, it makes less sense for the army to operate nuclear submarines or air defense cruisers. Similarly, the possession of strategic nuclear weapons by several different organizations both creates waste and enhances the danger of nuclear accidents.[33] However, the experience of the U.S. military in the wake of the 1947 separation of the USAF and of the Key West agreement demonstrates the folly of hard-and-fast rules of service responsibility. Such rules, although revised many times, helped slow or restrict technological and doctrinal innovation in several different areas. The rules also created tension between organizations competing for missions and for procurement dollars.[34] Strict rules based on technological or doctrinal differentiation (rotary versus fixed wing, tactical versus strategic) invariably fail to take into account important changes in technology and in the relevance of particular doctrines. Accordingly, rules for sharing responsibility for the management of assets like Air Force Space Command, on which both the navy and army depend for communications and information technology, must be sufficiently flexible to allow innovation, yet not so flexible as to allow one service or the other to shirk. That such capabilities are absolutely critical to the functioning of the modern U.S. military should incline both services to take their maintenance seriously.

THE PROCESS OF AMALGAMATION

While many air forces have won their independence, very few have lost it. Massive state bureaucracies learn how to defend themselves, both publicly and inside the corridors of government. The most notable case for an air force losing its independence is close at hand: the Royal Canadian Air Force was folded into a unified Canadian military structure in 1967. Service unification accomplished some, but not all, of the goals envisioned by its advocates in the 1960s. The process of unification also uncovered some unexpected problems.

In September 1918, the Canadian government created the Canadian Air Force and Royal Canadian Naval Service from existing squadrons of Canadian fliers in Europe.[35] The institution went through several reorganizations in the ensuing years, resulting by 1924 in the Royal Canadian Air Force (RCAF).[36] The World War II RCAF, flying British and American aircraft, peaked at over 200,000 personal before declining to 12,000 after the end of the war.[37] The postwar division of responsibilities between the RCAF, the Canadian Army, and the Royal Canadian Navy (RCN) mirrored that of the British defense establishment, with the RCAF having primary responsibility both for rotary aircraft and for maritime patrol missions.[38] However, the RCN developed its own air arm, operating three aircraft carriers plus some antisubmarine aircraft.[39]

Serious study of unifying the Canadian Army, Royal Canadian Air Force, and Royal Canadian Navy began in the 1950s.[40] Financial concerns drove interest in amalgamation, although frustration with redundancy and military bureaucracy also played a role. Minister of National Defence Paul Hellyer spearheaded the legislative project of melding the three services into one organization. Hellyer believed that eliminating redundancy could achieve considerable savings.[41] Hellyer also found the lack of responsiveness from the Canadian military during the Cuban missile crisis disturbing. Rather than consult the Canadian government, the three services followed the standard operating procedures set forth by the requirements of their partners in the NATO alliance. This raised serious civil-military relations questions, not to mention the specter of inadvertent Canadian participation in a general war.[42]

The project of amalgamation began with the Liberal Party's White Paper on Defence and continued with the December 1966 Canadian Force Reorganization Act. Justification for unifying the Canadian Forces was primarily but not solely financial.[43] The Canadian government believed that the military system as it existed had created a bevy of organizational and civil-military problems. The policy transition began in 1964 with the Act to Amend the National Defence Act. The individual service chiefs were replaced by a collective chief, and several other positions were eliminated. Reorganization into new integrated functional commands (Maritime, Mobile, Air Defence, Air Transport, Material, and Training) began in 1965. In April 1967, the Canadian Force Reorganization Act officially eliminated the three separate services and reconfigured them into a single force.[44]

Hellyer pursued unification in a quick, almost haphazard fashion; many officers did not believe that full unification would arrive until the 1970s.[45] The lack of veto points in the Canadian system and the speed of the process may also have made it more difficult to drum up public and bureaucratic opposition to unification. Nevertheless, unification incurred serious resistance in the services. Several high-ranking senior officers retired during the process of unification, and Rear Admiral William Landymore, commander of Maritime Command, and six other admirals resigned their posts in protest of the unification decision.[46] Minister of Defence Hellyer's relations with the uniformed military were not good, even prior to the unification effort.[47] Hellyer moved to a different portfolio during the course of the transition, and then left government entirely. The government of Prime Minister Pierre Trudeau displayed little interest in military affairs, and Canadian public opinion did not treat military reunification as a salient issue.[48] Consequently, civilian follow-through of the process of unification was hardly ideal.

Evaluation and Comparison

Canadian service unification experienced some successes and some failures. The effort to break service culture failed almost entirely, as the individuals within the Air, Maritime, and Land Force commands remained loyal to their units and home services. In the 1980s, the practice of using the same uniforms was effectively ended, as the Canadian Forces were divided along "environmental" lines, with sea, land, and air representing the trades.[49] The amalgamation succeeded at eliminating some administrative redundancies, however. Some money was saved, although changing macroeconomic conditions (primarily 1970s inflation) make evaluating the full financial impact difficult.[50] In 1975, Air Defence Command and Air Transport Command became Air Command, which also had responsibility for tactical and maritime air. A 1979 government task force attempted to evaluate the costs and benefits of amalgamation. It identified some problems but was reluctant to render a verdict on whether unification had been a positive or negative undertaking. The Canadian government has displayed little interest in revisiting the question of unification, however, instead pushing a series of small tweaks and reforms to the existing military organization.[51]

The problem of morale received a great degree of attention from military critics of unification. Although quantitative evaluations of changes in morale over time are difficult to come by, most anecdotal accounts suggest that morale in the Canadian Forces dropped after unification. The losses of separate uniforms and of separate rank structure appear to have played some role in this drop. However, funding for the Canadian military also decreased substantially in the period after unification, for economic reasons mostly unrelated to the reorganization.[52] This decrease in funding undoubtedly contributed to a loss in morale, as did resistance within the navy. Of the former services, the navy may have reacted worst. Integration of the army and air force went relatively smoothly, but long-standing cultural differences with the navy were harder to bridge.[53] Also, naval personnel were not well represented at the highest levels of the Canadian command staff, perhaps because of the geographic concentration of maritime forces on the coasts.[54]

Other evaluations of unification suggest that while the process suffered from some problems, the decision essentially placed Canada on the right side of military history. Canadian service unification substantially accomplished many of the goals envisioned by the Goldwater-Nichols reforms twenty years before the latter became law in the United States.[55] Daniel Gosselin argues that Hellyer's unification may have been ahead of its time and that the Canadian Forces continue to move in a direction that emphasizes jointness and cooperation. Gosselin argues that unification is winning a "tug of war" against the "strong services" concept, largely because of the same developments in doctrine and technology that have driven the United States towards jointness.[56] Gosselin has also argued that the 2005 Canadian Forces Transformation, a modernization and reorganization effort spearheaded by General R. J. Hillier, moved the Canadian Forces further on the joint path.[57] K. W. Bailey, another Canadian Forces officer, largely agrees with the sentiment. Bailey argued that whatever the political problems of the process of unification, the Canadian Forces cannot hope to maintain credible combat capability without a greater emphasis on jointness.[58] Finally, a 1976 article by Lieutenant Colonel J. H. Pocklington argued that amalgamation had strong positive effects for officer professionalism.[59]

However, Canadian opinion on the wisdom and effectiveness of service unification varies considerably. Historian and defense analyst Geoffrey Shaw has a notably dim view of unification: "The kindest and most liberal summation one could give to the Hellyer reforms for unification and integration is that as a military/social experiment they were demonstrated to not work. In effect, none of the goals spelled out by Hellyer were attained in any meaningful sense. A blunter estimation, and in accordance with all the soldiers this writer has talked to, would have to state that the Hellyer plan was an unmitigated disaster for Canada's Armed Forces."[60]

Others have argued that the unification of the Canadian Forces had little other than cosmetic effect. For example, Douglas Bland contends that reform has not produced unity, nor has it allowed distinct service cultures to develop in a way that would maximize efficiency and effectiveness.[61] This perspective suggests that the 2005 Canadian Forces Transformation ought to be seen as the end point of the Canadian Forces' unification rather than a new round of reform.

Lessons of the Canadian Experience

This book does not propose unifying the three U.S. services. First, the army and the navy pursue sufficiently distinct objectives of war to justify separate organizations. While military forces on land and sea interact (and have always interacted), in most cases they do not play an organic role in each other's operations. Moreover, the development of separate services with unique traditions and cultures based around environmental distinctions is not inherently destructive. Indeed, such traditions and cultures play a necessary role in military life. They are only destructive when they have negative political effects or when they inhibit cooperation between services.

Nevertheless, the Canadian experience does hold lessons for the United States, or for any other country that wishes to restructure its military forces. The first and most important lesson is this: it is possible for a country to redesign its military forces in the face of changed circumstances. While the Canadian military is considerably smaller than its American counterpart, there is little good reason to believe that scale should prevent institutional reform. After all, the creation of the USAF in the first place required restructuring on a scale larger (in terms of personnel and aircraft) than the elimination of the USAF would require today. Similarly, the Goldwater-Nichols reforms brought significant institutional change to a military much larger than the one the United States possesses today. Indeed, if scale really matters, then U.S. military institutions are more ready for massive reform than at any time since World War II.

The second lesson is that airpower can persist in the absence of an organizationally independent air force. Airpower advocates worry that air assets will wither in the absence of a dedicated service with its own access to power and state coffers. This has not happened to Canadian airpower. While Canadian military aviation has lacked a truly strategic component since the 1950s, the key shift from strategic to tactical happened well prior to the amalgamation of forces. Canada continues to employ airpower, both in the service of hemispheric defense and in support of Canadian ground and naval operations around the world.

It is difficult to predict the fallout from the abolition of the U.S. Air Force with any certainty. In 1947, few foresaw major conflicts over ICBMs, helicopters, and supercarriers. The test for any institutional arrangement comes in its ability to successfully adapt to changing circumstances and to prepare the nation to fight whatever wars may come. The scenario set forth in this chapter is of necessity speculative. Military doctrine, military procurement, and war fighting are complicated endeavors, so complex that it is difficult to predict how a change as significant as eliminating the U.S. Air Force will affect outcomes. In general, however, U.S. defense policy appears less reckless, more capable, and less expensive without an independent air force than with one.

Conclusion

By its own admission, the U.S. Air Force is in crisis. Its ability to manage the nuclear weapons placed in its care remains in deep question.[1] Its two newest fighter aircraft, the F-22 and F-35, have wildly exceeded cost projections and have suffered technical problems that have resulted in several months of grounding.[2] Other procurement programs have also suffered setbacks. A next-generation bomber project may (literally) never get off the ground.[3] It is true that the USAF crisis is part of a general crisis for the U.S. military establishment, as two long-term irregular wars, a financial collapse, and technological change have served to shift the foundations that underpin U.S. military power. But the problems facing the air force go to the core of the USAF's identity and the justification of its purpose. This justification is no longer compelling—if it ever was. The United States needs airpower, but it does not need a separate military service dedicated to providing that airpower.

On July 4, 2010, Air Force Chief of Staff General Norton A. Schwartz detailed his vision of the future of the USAF in a speech titled "The Way Ahead." He outlined three challenges facing the air force as it approaches the future: restoring credibility to the nuclear enterprise, enhancing the USAF contribution to today's fight, and recapturing acquisition excellence. The first of these challenges referred to recent problems in USAF nuclear weapons handling and readiness, the second to the ongoing debate about how the air force could contribute to Afghanistan and Iraq, and the third to procurement debates swirling around the F-22, F-35, and USAF tanker program. In his introduction, General Schwartz summarized his belief about what the USAF could contribute:

> Let me be very clear: I see our Air Force rising, strong and capable—an Air Force delivering consistent, credible Global Vigi-

lance, Global Reach and Global Power for America—in what is likely to be a very challenging future.

The Airman's distinctive focus on air, space and cyber power, and the asymmetric advantage the Air Force provides, continues to be indispensable to this Nation. America relies on us to gain and maintain control of the air and space, and increasingly cyberspace, wherever and whenever needed. Beyond that, our ability to exploit that control remains a cornerstone of this Nation's ability to shape, deter and, if necessary, fight and win—anywhere our interests and those of our allies and partners are at stake.[4]

The mention of global reach and global power refers to John Warden's vision of decisive independent airpower, but the rest of the statement—and indeed, of the speech—suggests a far more humble vision of what the air force can provide. Key objectives include maintaining older USAF capabilities (such as nuclear readiness) and improving the contribution that the air force makes to the joint fight. The speech evokes no confidence in the idea that the air force can independently provide a decisive impact on world events. This represents an important downward revision in expectations for what independent airpower can achieve.

To be sure, technology has changed profoundly since World War II, and John Warden rejected the arguments of Douhet on terror bombing. Precision-guided munitions and advanced information technology might, in fact, provide the technological fix necessary to make strategic airpower truly decisive. However, Warden and similar theorists continue to dreadfully underestimate the *robustness* of political and bureaucratic organizations. Like the original strategic bombing theorists, Warden treats state and society as a delicate structure, in danger of collapsing if the right support beams are taken away. Just as Douhet and Harris believed that cities would collapse into anarchy in response to bombing, Warden believed that states and organizations could be induced to collapse if the right buttons were pushed. Instead, however, organizations such as the Iraqi Army and the Serbian state demonstrated a remarkable ability to keep operating, even as many of their crucial organs came under concerted attack.

Strategic bombing theory, as first described in military terms in the

Smuts Report, offered a way out of the horrors of the Western Front. If bombers could literally fly over the enemy army, attack enemy cities, and induce something along the lines of the Bolshevik Revolution in Russia, then the slaughter would be unnecessary. Building huge armies and grinding them to dust on foreign soil appeals to very few civilian leaders or military commanders. At the best of times, such an effort requires tremendous blood and treasure, and in a democracy it represents a very serious national commitment. Strategic bombing offers the prospect of victory without the investment or the mess. Consequently, countries infatuated with strategic bombing have consistently used it to try to avoid committing ground forces in a decisive manner.

But such hopes have consistently foundered on the robustness of states, societies, and organizations. Rather than collapse, social organizations have defended themselves and adapted to new circumstances. States and military organizations learn to communicate in new (and sometimes very old) ways. Industrial systems manage to work around "bottlenecks" created by the destruction of "critical" factories and industrial sectors. Strategic bombing has proven adept at destroying physical infrastructure but not at destroying the networks of human relationships that knit social institutions together. A police officer without a police station is still a police officer if the neighborhood *treats* him or her as a police officer. Moreover, as an empirical matter, the death and destruction caused by strategic bombing seem to actually increase the strength and vitality of these networks of human relationships.

The belated realization of the limits of airpower is a welcome development. However, if the air force cannot provide independent decisive effect, and instead exists only to support the other services in their aims, then it becomes harder to justify the organization's independent existence. As explained in earlier chapters, airpower advocates insisted that the air force needed independence because the requirements of the other services would hamstring airpower's ability to deliver decisive effect. The nature of this decisive effect has changed over time, but the logic remains the same: airpower must be free to be itself. To rhetorically construct the contributions of airpower in terms of support for the other services undermines the very foundation of air force independence. The independent air force has created a vast number of doctrinal, procurement, and bureaucratic problems; if it exists only to support the other services, then why bother keeping it around? The air force wants to emphasize its contribution to the current fight but paints itself into a corner by doing so.

The USAF's current force structure represents a similar corner. The air force has repurposed Cold War weapons for low-intensity counterinsurgency conflicts. The B-1B Lancer, for example, was designed to penetrate Soviet airspace at low altitude and deliver nuclear weapons. For a time during the command of General Stanley McChrystal, it loitered over Afghanistan, taking pictures instead of dropping bombs because of COIN-oriented strike restrictions.[5] Indeed, even conventional war planning has become ever more "joint." AirSea Battle, the operational doctrine designed to provide guidance during a U.S. war with China, concentrates directly on bridging the gap between the navy and the air force and eliminating interservice friction.[6] The boundaries between services, at least as far as airpower is concerned, have become more impediment than defense.

THE PROCESS OF REFORM

At first glance, prospects for folding the U.S. Air Force back into the older two services appear bleak. However, the first and most important step for any kind of major institutional revision is to start talking about why and how it should be undertaken. This book should be understood as part of the opening gambit for a restructuring of U.S. military institutions.

The USAF does not lack for friends. The Air Force Association (AFA) is a powerful lobbying group that brings together veterans, families, and others with an interest in supporting the U.S. Air Force.[7] The AFA commonly argues for increased attention to USAF priorities and lobbies Congress for additional personnel and procurement funding. The AFA also undertakes campaigns to move public opinion in directions that benefit the air force. More important, however, the USAF has substantial and long-standing ties with numerous industry groups that maintain and hope for major procurement contracts. These industry groups in turn have contacts in Congress that they have painstakingly developed over the past fifty years. The defense industry wins friends in Congress by apportioning factories and other facilities as widely as possible over a swath of states and congressional districts. As procurement reform is a major benefit of abolishing the USAF, many elements of Congress and industry would no doubt resist major change. Finally, public opinion will likely be wary about any project to reform U.S. airpower, as the air force has long enjoyed a positive image in American society.[8]

Unlike in the United Kingdom, the uniformed military services have shown reluctance to engage in fratricidal conflict, at least since the 1950s. In part, this results from Secretary of Defense Robert McNamara's efforts in the early 1960s to encourage competition between the services for procurement funding. McNamara's effort failed disastrously and led to a closing of the ranks such that the services and their lobbyists essentially remained mute about the shortcomings of their siblings.[9] While underlying tensions persist, the other services cannot be relied upon to advocate the abolition of the USAF.

Nevertheless, several concurrent crises have helped to bring the utility of the air force into public question. The (possibly temporary) victory of COIN advocates within the U.S. Army and the growth of drone use created tension for the USAF. The first challenges the importance of the air force in the two wars in which the United States finds itself entangled. The second challenges some of the foundational notions of military professionalism. These crises may help provide an intellectual foundation for rethinking the independent existence of the USAF.

U.S. involvement in Afghanistan and Iraq, together with the global financial collapse, precipitated a third crisis: the United States cannot long afford its military institutions without making significant changes. Professional analysts, both civilian and military, are warning of the possibility of substantial cuts in U.S. military spending. Recent political conflict over the "debt ceiling" in the United States has put the question of defense cuts front and center. This political and fiscal environment has two major implications for this argument. First, policymakers will look for ways to cut administrative cost without undercutting military capability. The "Canadian option," undertaken specifically in order to cut administrative costs, may become more attractive. Second, the prospect of severe cuts in procurement funding may help break the wall that the army, air force, and navy have erected between themselves and civilian procurement officials. As the cash flow tightens, the services and their lobbying arms may feel less reticent about criticizing each other's procurement priorities. The financial crisis may thus provide a material foundation for reconsidering the need for an organizationally independent air force.

Consequently, while the prospects for major reform may appear bleak, there are financial and theoretical reasons for reconsidering the USAF. Under the right conditions, the existence of these conditions could help trigger a transformation in how the United States organizes its military forces. The end of U.S. involvement in Iraq and Afghanistan, whenever that end comes, may provide a contingent moment in which a rethinking of the institutional structure of the U.S. military can take place.

The Legislative Context

The U.S. Constitution allows Congress to "raise and support" armies and to "provide and maintain" a navy but has little to say on the specifics of the organization of the armed forces. Consequently, the existence of the U.S. Air Force is not a constitutional issue. Rather, the USAF is a legislative and administrative reality brought into existence by the National Security Act of 1947. Similar legislation could eliminate the air force and return its constituent parts to the older military organizations.

The 1986 Goldwater-Nichols Department of Defense Reorganization Act was the last piece of legislation to have a major impact on the organizational structure of the U.S. military establishment. Goldwater-Nichols accomplished several major goals, including making "jointness" a priority and reorganizing the chain of command such that the chairman of the Joint Chiefs of Staff and the combatant commanders take precedence over the service chiefs.[10] If the 1947 act prepared the United States to face the postwar world, the Goldwater-Nichols Act set the terms for U.S. military engagement with the post–Cold War international system. In particular, Goldwater-Nichols helped make the combatant commanders the "rock stars" of America's world-girdling military establishment. For example, CENTCOM, the regional combatant command that covers the Middle East, has been led by H. Norman Schwarzkopf, Anthony Zinni, Tommy Franks, William "Fox" Fallon, and of course David Petraeus. As Dana Priest detailed in The Mission, these regional combatant commanders have enormous latitude over diplomatic and military activity within their areas, acting in some sense as "Imperial Proconsuls."[11]

Of course, neither the 1947 act nor the Goldwater-Nichols Act was intended for the world we live in today. The collapse of the Soviet Union and the development of the "rogue" state (a term troubled in both conception and deployment) have fundamentally changed the national security environment the United States currently faces. These environmental changes, however, did not bring about a significant transformation of the U.S. defense establishment. The intelligence community experienced the largest reforms, although even in that case the shift is small in magnitude compared to that enacted in 1947.

A new National Security Act, driven by concerns about the fiscal unsustainability of the U.S. defense posture as well as the belief that the current U.S. national security apparatus does not well serve the future grand strategic interests of the United States, could fundamentally redefine the American military bureaucracy. The abolition of the air force would require a legislative effort of this magnitude. Given the veto-laden nature of the American political system, the prospect of such an act can appear distant. However, the combination of fiscal concerns and the continuing shift to a post–Cold War, post–War on Terror strategic environment makes the possibility of significant reform greater now than it has been in the past.

FINAL CONCLUSIONS

While much of this book has focused on how the modern security context exposes the deficiencies of the U.S. Air Force, my argument is not that COIN, drones, or the collapse of the Soviet Union has rendered the air force obsolete. Rather, I argue that creating the USAF in 1947 was a mistake, just as creating the RAF in 1918 was a mistake. Enthusiastic aviators, working with civilian leaders who wanted to make war cheap, deceived themselves into thinking that airpower could solve all military problems. The delusion of airpower has helped make conflict more likely, interservice rivalry more destructive, and wars more devastating. Thus, that the air force cannot deal productively with the situation in Afghanistan does not justify its elimination—sixty years of failure justify its elimination. However, profound changes in the security environment have, in the past, led to major legislative action that restructured the U.S. defense establishment. The magnitude of the shift from Cold War to post–Cold War is as great as the changed environment of 1947. Moreover, the War on Terror exposes some of the most glaring shortcomings of the theory of independent decisive airpower. If the simultaneous crises of fiscal collapse and foreign war put the United States in the mood for a major restructuring of the national security bureaucracy, then elimination of the air force should be one of the items up for consideration. The national security bureaucracy of the United States does not turn on a dime, meaning that we need to take full advantage of every opportunity for reform.

This book has argued strongly against the bureaucratic institutionalization of airpower. However, no part of the case made in these pages should be understood as an attack on the courage or importance of military aviators. Since the beginning of manned flight, pilots have suffered from some of the most dreadful loss rates of any military profession. During periods of World War I, pilots new to the front could measure their expected life span in days. Aircraft, then and now, are temperamental, difficult machines not particularly well suited to taking fire. Moreover, whatever the large-scale impact of the strategic bombing campaigns of World War II, Vietnam, and later, the pilots and crews who flew the missions believed, almost to an individual, that they were risking their lives to end the war more quickly. During the darkest days of World War II, these aviators represented one of the few ways in which Britain and the United States could resist Nazi Germany. Similarly, aviators who trained to fly missions deep into the Soviet Union did so in the belief that the safety of their country demanded such preparation. The same can be said of Soviet pilots preparing to fly into the teeth of U.S. air defenses or Israeli pilots bombing Hezbollah targets. The problems of air forces have nothing to do with the virtue or courage of individual aviators.

Likewise, it bears repetition that this book should not be interpreted as dismissive of military aviation. Modern military operations require well-built, well-maintained aircraft designed to fulfill their missions and flown by competent, well-trained military professionals. No professional force in the world can operate without sufficient air support. Armies and navies require reconnaissance aircraft, fighters, bombers, attack planes, helicopters, light and heavy transports, and drones in order to perform the tasks assigned to them. This book simply argues that the best organizational venue for such aircraft is within armies and navies rather than within independent air forces.

Folding the air force into the army and the navy will allow for a return to a genuinely Clausewitzian understanding of the relationship between politics, war, and victory. We must not imagine that wars can be won through disregarding complexity and eschewing the need to disarm the enemy; the combination of assets on land and at sea will allow for operational, strategic, and industrial planning that carefully links military and political goals. Disarmed enemies cannot resist, and it makes far more sense to concentrate our military planning around this fact rather than engage in quasi-magical speculation about the ability of airpower to disrupt complex organizations and societies.

Finally, even when military professionals doubt the effectiveness of airpower in certain situations, the siren song of airpower continues to appeal to civilians committed to doing *something*.[12] However, reintegrating the air force into the navy and the army will hopefully help change civilian mind-sets on the utility of military power. Military interventions are expensive, destructive, and ought not to be pursued on a lark. Strategic air campaigns *are* military interventions; they simply hope to achieve goals at minimal cost.[13] Civilians *ought* to think of military intervention as costly, deadly, and fraught with political difficulty. Removing the air force, which has an institutional predisposition to portraying war as cheap and easy, would hopefully go some distance toward changing how we have come to think about war.

Acknowledgments

I would like to thank Matthew Yglesias for persuading me, way back in 2007, to write the initial "Abolish the Air Force" article for the *American Prospect*. I'd also like to thank Harold Meyerson of the *American Prospect* for giving the idea a platform, and Noah Shachtman, Michael Goldfarb, John Noonan, Jason Sigger, and Sharon Weinberger for participating in a roundtable on the initial article. Iain Ballantyne of *Warships: International Fleet Review* also supplied critical early support for the project. A grant from the National Security Network made possible research in the United Kingdom.

Thanks are due my dissertation committee, composed of Jonathan Mercer, Elizabeth Kier, David Bachman, and Mary Callahan. Beth Kier in particular helped develop my interest in the politics of the national security bureaucracy. I would also like to thank Stephen Biddle, Stephen Peter Rosen, and Richard Betts for developing and hosting the Summer Workshop on the Analysis of Military Operations and Strategy, where I developed an understanding of military operations and made a number of enduring friends.

For substantive advice along the way, I would like to thank Adam Elkus, Yoav Gortzak, Will Ruger, Sean Kay, and Nick Sarantakes, all of whom offered productive criticism and suggestions about content and strategy.

I'd like to thank my research assistants Erin Petrey, Mary Ryan Hawkins Conrad, Tyler Scott, Will Marshall, and Patrick Smith for helping with editing, citation, idea formation, and general sanity maintenance during the process of writing and researching.

Thanks also to the war game team at the Patterson School: Captain Andrew Betson, Nick Paden, Patrick Davey, Trevor Sutherland, and Katie Putz. This team was enormously helpful in terms of structuring and thinking through the implications of folding the air force into the other services. Particular thanks go out to Captain Betson, who regularly added helpful comments and identified useful sources for the manuscript.

For advice on publishing, disseminating, and in general coming up with a plausible idea, I'd like to thank David Axe, Dan Nexon, Dan Drezner, Stephanie Carvin, and Charli Carpenter. Thanks are also due to my colleagues at the Patterson School of Diplomacy and International Commerce, Carey Cavanaugh, Karen Mingst, John Stempel, Evan Hillebrand, Stacy Closson, and George Herring.

None of this would have been possible without the blogging platforms of Lawyers, Guns and Money and Information Dissemination. Scott Lemieux, David Watkins, and Raymond Pritchett deserve the heartiest of thanks for helping to build those blogs.

Most of all, I would like to thank my wife, Davida Isaacs, for research, editing, argumentation, and general all-around wonderfulness.

Notes

Introduction

1. David Axe, "Buyer's Remorse: How Much Has the F-22 Really Cost?" *Wired: Danger Room,* December 14, 2011, http://www.wired.com/dangerroom/2011/12/f-22-real-cost/.

2. Philip Ewing, "The Air Force's Record-Breaking B-1 Deployment," *DoD Buzz,* August 2, 2012, http://www.dodbuzz.com/2012/08/02/the-air-forces-record-breaking-b-1-deployment/.

3. This memorable phrase came from an extremely critical anonymous review of an early version of this book. The phrase is so apt I felt I had to include it in the final product.

4. Philip Meilinger, "Giulio Douhet and the Origins of Airpower Theory," in *The Paths of Heaven: The Evolution of Airpower Theory,* ed. Philip Meilinger (Maxwell AFB, AL: Air University Press, 1997), 1.

5. Carl H. Builder, *The Icarus Syndrome: The Role of Air Power Theory in the Evolution and Fate of the U.S. Air Force* (New Brunswick, NJ: Transaction, 1994).

6. Carl von Clausewitz, Michael Howard, Peter Paret, and Bernard Brodie, *On War* (Princeton, NJ: Princeton University Press, 1984), 81, 77, 85.

7. Tami Davis Biddle, *Rhetoric and Reality in Air Warfare: The Evolution of British and American Ideas about Strategic Bombing, 1914–1945* (Princeton, NJ: Princeton University Press, 2002), 104–5, 12–13.

8. David MacIsaac, "Voices from the Central Blue: The Air Power Theorists," in *Makers of Modern Strategy: From Machiavelli to the Nuclear Age,* ed. Peter Paret (Princeton, NJ: Princeton University Press, 1986), 628.

9. See, for example, John Warden III, "Strategy and Airpower," *Air and Space Power Journal,* Spring 2011, 65; Grant Hammond, *The Mind of War: John Boyd and American Security* [Kindle edition] (Washington, DC: Smithsonian Institution, 2001), 2971; Christopher Bassford, *Clausewitz in English: The Reception of Clausewitz in Britain and America, 1815–1945* (New York: Oxford University Press, 1994); Phillip S. Meilinger, "Airpower and Collateral Damage: Theory, Practice, and Challenges," *Air Power Australia Essay on Military Ethics and Culture,* April 15, 2013, http://ww.ausairpower.net/APA-EMEAC-2013-02.html; Mark Clodfelter, *Beneficial Bombing: The Progressive Foundations of American Air Power, 1817–1945* (Lincoln: University of Nebraska Press, 2010), 41, 58.

10. John A. Warden III, "Employing Air Power in the Twenty-first Century," in *The Future of Air Power in the Aftermath of the Gulf War*, ed. Richard H. Shultz Jr. and Robert L. Pfaltzgraff Jr. (Maxwell AFB, AL: Air University Press, 1992), 62.

11. Barry D. Watts, *The Foundations of U.S. Air Doctrine: The Problem of Friction in War* (Maxwell AFB, AL: Air University Press, 1984), 2.

12. Biddle, *Rhetoric and Reality in Air Warfare*, 12–13.

13. Ibid.; see also Warden, "Strategy and Airpower."

14. James Q. Wilson, *Bureaucracy* (New York: Basic Books, 1989), 181.

15. Biddle, *Rhetoric and Reality in Air Warfare*, 81.

16. Charles J. Gross, *American Military Aviation: The Indispensable Arm* (College Station: Texas A&M University Press, 2002), 7.

17. See Conrad Crane, *American Airpower Strategy in Korea, 1950–1953* (Lawrence: University of Kansas Press, 2000); Mark Clodfelter, *The Limits of Air Power: The American Bombing of North Vietnam* (New York: Free Press, 1989).

18. On the origins of this term, see Rene F. Romero, *The Origin of Centralized Control and Decentralized Execution* (Fort Leavenworth, KS: U.S. Army Command and General Staff College, 2003).

1. American Airpower and the Military Services

1. Graham T. Allison, "Conceptual Models and the Cuban Missile Crisis," *American Political Science Review* 63, no. 3 (1969): 689–718.

2. Elizabeth Kier, *Imagining War: French and British Military Doctrine between the Wars* (Princeton, NJ: Princeton University Press, 1997), 5.

3. Clausewitz et al., *On War*, 119.

4. Gross, *American Military Aviation*, 144–45.

5. Joint Staff, *Close Air Support: Joint Publication 3-09.3* (Washington, DC: Department of Defense, July 8, 2009), ix.

6. John A. Warden III, *The Air Campaign: Planning for Combat* (Washington, DC: National Defense University Press, 1988), http://www.au.af.mil/au/awc/awcgate/warden/wrdchp07.htm.

7. Gross, *American Military Aviation*, 7.

8. Diana Wueger, "Leave the A-10, Take the Cannoli," *Gunpowder and Lead*, February 10, 2012, http://gunpowderandlead.org/2012/02/leave-the-a-10-take-the-cannoli/.

9. Clifford R. Krieger, "Air Interdiction," *Airpower Journal* (Spring 1989), http://www.airpower.au.af.mil/airchronicles/apj/apj89/spr89/krieger.html.

10. Warden, *The Air Campaign*, http://www.au.af.mil/au/awc/awcgate/warden/wrdchp06.htm.

11. Terrance J. McCaffrey III, *What Happened to Battlefield Air Interdiction: Army and Air Force Battlefield Doctrine Development from Pre–Desert Storm to 2001* (Maxwell AFB, AL: Air University Press, 2004), 1–2.

12. Gross, *American Military Aviation*, 6.

13. Ibid., 7.

14. Secretary of the Air Force, *Countersea Operations Air Force Doctrine Document 2-1.4* (Washington, DC: Air Force Doctrine Center, September 15, 2005), vii.

15. Gross, *American Military Aviation*, 118.

16. Ibid., 7.

17. Biddle, *Rhetoric and Reality in Air Warfare*, 161.

18. Colin S. Gray, *Airpower for Strategic Effect* (Maxwell AFB, AL: Air University Press, 2012), 213.

19. CBS Evening News, "At Saddam's Bombed Palace: New Details about the First Strike on Saddam," May 28, 2003, http://www.cbsnews.com/stories/2003/05/28/eveningnews/main555948.shtml.

20. BBC News, "Dual Attack Killed President," April 21, 1999, http://news.bbc.co.uk/2/hi/europe/325347.stm.

21. Warden, *The Air Campaign*, http://www.au.af.mil/au/awc/awcgate/warden/wrdchp01.htm

22. Joint Staff, *Countering Air and Missile Threats: Joint Publication 3-01* (Washington, DC: Department of Defense 2012), I-4.

23. "Air Ministry Memorandum," June 1921, AIR 5/166, National Archives, Kew, Richmond, UK.

24. Martin Van Crevald, *Age of Airpower* [Kindle edition] (New York: Public Affairs, 2011), 896–916.

25. Builder, *The Icarus Syndrome*, 182.

26. Suzanne C. Nielsen and Don M. Snider, introduction to *American Civil-Military Relations: The Soldier and the State in a New Era*, ed. Suzanne C. Nielsen and Don M. Snider (Baltimore: Johns Hopkins University Press, 2009), 6.

27. "Goldwater-Nichols Department of Defense Reorganization Act of 1986: Public Law 99-433," 99th Cong. (October 1, 1986), https://acquisition.navy.mil/rda/media/files/policy_memos/goldwater_nichols_department_of_defense_reorganization_act_of_1986.

28. Builder, *The Icarus Syndrome*, 198–99.

29. Clodfelter, *Beneficial Bombing*, 8, 36.

30. Van Crevald, *Age of Airpower*, 896–916.

31. "Notes for Questions for Lord Cavan, 8-6-1923," June 8, 1923, AIR 9/5, National Archives, Kew, Richmond, UK.

32. Builder, *The Icarus Syndrome*, 165.

33. Clark A. Murdock et al., *Beyond Goldwater Nichols: Defense Reform for a New Strategic Era, Phase 1 Report* (Washington, DC: Center for Strategic and International Studies, 2004), 16.

34. "Goldwater-Nichols Department of Defense Reorganization Act of 1986."

35. Leo J. Blanken and Jason J. Lepore, "Redundancy in Military Force Structure Planning" (unpublished paper, July 17, 2008).

36. See, for example, Eliot A. Cohen and John Gooch, *Military Misfortunes: The Anatomy of Failure in War* (New York: Vintage Books, 1991).

37. Steven Metz, "Strategic Horizons: Does America Need Two Armies?" *World Politics Review*, January 9, 2013, https://www.worldpoliticsreview.com/articles/12612/strategic-horizons-does-america-need-two-armies.

38. Daniel W. Drezner, "When Is It a Good Thing to Have Multiple Bureaucracies Tackling the Same Problem?" *Foreign Policy Magazine Blog: Daniel W. Drezner Global Politics, Economics, & Pop Culture*, July 19, 2010, http://drezner.foreignpolicy.com/posts/2010/07/19/two_cheers_for_bureaucratic_redundancy.

39. Marshall L. Michel III, *Clashes: Air Combat over North Vietnam, 1965–1972* (Annapolis, MD: Naval Institute Press, 1997), 232–33.

40. Crane, *American Airpower Strategy in Korea*, 29–30.

41. See, for example, Allan R. Millett, "Why the Army and the Marine Corps Should Be Friends," *Parameters* 24 (Winter 1994–1995): 30–40.

42. Andrew F. Krepinevich, *The Army and Vietnam* (Baltimore: Johns Hopkins University Press, 1986), 175.

43. See, for example, Joao Resende-Santos, *Neorealism, States, and the Modern Mass Army* (New York: Cambridge University Press, 2007).

44. John W. Meyer, John Boli, George M. Thomas, and Francisco O. Ramirez, "World Society and the Nation State," *American Journal of Sociology* 103, no. 1 (1997): 144–81.

45. See, for example, Kimberly Zisk Marten, *Engaging the Enemy: Organization Theory and Soviet Military Innovation, 1955–1991* (Princeton, NJ: Princeton University Press, 1993).

46. Jasjit Singh, "Indian Air Power," in *Global Air Power* [Kindle edition], ed. John Andreas Olsen (Washington, DC: Potomac, 2011), 4670–86.

47. Ibid.

48. James M. Hasik, "Mimetic and Normative Isomorphism in the Establishment and Maintenance of Independent Air Forces" (unpublished paper, September 24, 2013), 6.

49. *Full Metal Jacket*, directed by Stanley Kubrick (Warner Bros. Pictures, 1987).

50. Colin Gray, "Understanding Airpower: Bonfire of the Fallacies," *Strategic Studies Quarterly* 1, no. 2, (2008): 67.

51. Bob Seals, "In Defense of the Horse: Major General John K. Herr, Chief of Cavalry," *The Long Riders Guild Academic Foundation*, May 7, 2009, http://www.lrgaf.org/military/john-herr.htm.

52. Robert H. Larson, *The British Army and the Theory of Armored Warfare, 1918–1940* (Newark: University of Delaware Press, 1984), 16.

53. Wilson, *Bureaucracy*, 181.

54. Kier, *Imagining War*, 19–20.

55. U.S. Air Force, *Command and Control: Air Force Doctrine Document 2-8* (Washington, DC: U.S. Air Force, 2007), ii.

56. Romero, *Origin of Centralized Control and Decentralized Execution*, 2–3.

57. Wilson, *Bureaucracy*, 192.

58. Gray, *Airpower for Strategic Effect*, 77.

59. Ibid., 78.

60. Sharon K. Weiner, "The Politics of Resource Allocation in the Post–Cold War Pentagon," *Security Studies* 5, no. 4 (1996): 128.

61. Robert Farley, "A User's Guide to Interservice Conflict," *World Politics Review*, December 8, 2010, http://www.worldpoliticsreview.com/articles/7254/ over-the-horizon-a-users-guide-to-inter-service-conflict.

62. Steven L. Rearden, *History of the Office of the Secretary of Defense: The Formative Years, 1947–1950* (Washington, DC: Office of the Secretary of Defense, 1984), 410.

63. Ibid., 386.

64. Gray, *Airpower for Strategic Effect*, 77.

65. Tacit knowledge "is the component of knowledge that is normally not reportable since it is deeply rooted in action and involvement in a specific context. It thus reflects the active participation of the knower in the situation at hand. It has two parts: the technical form that applies to specific settings and the cognitive form, constituting mental models which help people perceive and define their world." Joseph A. Raelin, "A Model of Work-Based Learning," *Organization Science* 8, no. 6 (1997): 564.

66. Andrew Boyle, *Trenchard* (London: Collins, 1962), 397.

67. Rearden, *History of the Office of the Secretary of Defense*, 386.

68. Ibid., 387.

69. Meilinger, "Giulio Douhet and the Origins of Airpower Theory," 32.

70. Murdock et al. *Beyond Goldwater Nichols*, 5.

2. Air Force Independence and Air Force Culture

1. Kier, *Imagining War*, 27–28.

2. Ibid.

3. Alastair Iain Johnston, "Thinking about Strategic Culture," *International Security* 19, no. 4 (1995): 34.

4. Kenneth M. Pollack, *Arabs at War: Military Effectiveness, 1948–1991* (Lincoln: University of Nebraska Press, 2002), 76–77.

5. Gray, *Airpower for Strategic Effect*, 62.

6. Robert M. Farley, "Transnational Determinants of Military Doctrine" (PhD diss., University of Washington, 2004), 7.

7. Lynn Eden, *Whole World on Fire: Organizations, Knowledge, and Nuclear Weapons Devastation* (Ithaca, NY: Cornell University Press, 2004), 50.

8. David E. Johnson, *Learning Large Lessons: The Evolving Roles of Ground Power and Air Power in the Post–Cold War Era* (Santa Monica, CA: RAND, 2007), 150.

9. Giulio Douhet, *The Command of the Air* (Washington, DC: Air Force History and Museums Program, 1998), 367–68.

10. Perry McCoy Smith, *The Air Force Plans for Peace, 1943–1945* (Baltimore: Johns Hopkins University Press, 1970), 15.

11. Carl Builder, *The Masks of War: American Military Styles in Strategy and Analysis* (Baltimore: Johns Hopkins University Press, 1989), 67, 71.

12. Ibid., 30.

13. Ibid., 69–73.

14. Gian Gentile, *How Effective Is Strategic Bombing? Lessons Learned from World War II and Kosovo* [Kindle edition] (New York: NYU Press, 2001), 186.

15. Builder, *The Icarus Syndrome,* 30; Clodfelter, *Beneficial Bombing,* 65.

16. Clint Stockings and Clifton Fernandes, "Airpower and the Myth of Strategic Bombing as Strategy," *ISAA Review* 5, no. 2 (2006): 6.

17. Johnson, *Learning Large Lessons,* 182.

18. Phillip S. Meilinger, "Ten Propositions regarding Airpower," *Air and Space Power Journal* (Spring 1996), http://www.airpower.au.af.mil/airchronicles/cc/meil.html.

19. Rearden, *History of the Office of the Secretary of Defense,* 386.

20. Builder, *Masks of War,* 73; D. M. Drew, *Basic Aerospace Doctrine of the United States Air Force* (Washington, DC: Department of the Air Force, 1992), 8, 18.

21. Johnson, *Learning Large Lessons,* xvi.

22. James M. Ford, *Air Force Culture and Conventional Strategic Airpower* (Maxwell AFB, AL: Air University Press, 1992), ix.

23. Warden, "Employing Air Power in the Twenty-first Century," 62.

24. Hammond, *The Mind of War,* 2975.

25. Johnson, *Learning Large Lessons,* 184.

26. Meilinger, "Ten Propositions regarding Airpower."

27. James P. Tate, *The Army and Its Air Corps: Army Policy toward Aviation, 1919–1941* (Maxwell AFB, AL: Air University Press, 1998), 5. See also Maurer Maurer, *Aviation in the U.S. Army, 1919–1939* (Washington, DC: Officer of Air Force History, 1987).

28. Maurer, *Aviation in the U.S. Army,* 13.

29. Ibid., 16.

30. Robert L. O'Connel, *Sacred Vessels: The Cult of the Battleship and the Rise of the US Navy* (New York: Oxford University Press, 1991), 2.

31. Ibid.

32. Builder, *The Masks of War,* 23.

33. Builder, *The Icarus Syndrome,* 166.

34. Ibid., 151.

35. Smith, *The Air Force Plans for Peace,* 18.

36. Builder, *The Masks of War,* 104–5.

37. Michael J. Eula, "Guilio Douhet and Strategic Air Force Operations: A Study in the Limitations of Theoretical Warfare," *Air University Review,* September–October 1986, http://www.airpower.maxwell.af.mil/airchronicles/aureview/1986/sep-oct/eula.html.

38. Eden, *Whole World on Fire,* 74–75.

39. Watts, *The Foundations of U.S. Air Doctrine,* 106–7, 110.

40. Meilinger, "Ten Propositions regarding Airpower."

41. Biddle, *Rhetoric and Reality in Air Warfare,* 224.

42. Clodfelter, *Beneficial Bombing,* 103–6, 129.

43. John Andreas Olsen, *John Warden and the Renaissance of American Air Power* (Kindle edition) (Washington, DC: Potomac, 2007), 1288.

44. Clodfelter, *Beneficial Bombing,* 57; Gentile, *How Effective Is Strategic Bombing?* 341.

45. Clodfelter, *Beneficial Bombing,* 141; Robert Jervis, "Rational Deterrence: Theory and Evidence," *World Politics* 41, no. 2 (1989): 202.

46. Warden, "Strategy and Airpower," 68.

47. Clodfelter, *Beneficial Bombing,* 37–38.

48. James Scott, *Seeing Like a State: How Certain Schemes to Improve the Human Condition Have Failed* (New Haven, CT: Yale University Press, 1998), 4–7.

49. Ibid., 309–10.

50. Abraham M. Denmark and Dr. James Mulvenon, eds., *Contested Commons: The Future of American Power in a Multipolar World* (Washington, DC: Center for New American Security, January 2010), 5.

51. Ibid.

52. Barry Posen, "Command of the Commons: The Military Foundation of U.S. Hegemony," *International Security* 28, no. 1 (2003): 5.

53. Alex Vacca, "Military Culture and Cyber Security," *Survival: Global Politics and Strategy* 53, no. 6 (2011–2012): 159–60.

54. Kelly Martin and Oliver Fritz, "Sustaining the Air Commons," in Denmark and Mulvenon, *Contested Commons,* 79.

55. Vacca, "Military Culture and Cyber Security," 165–66.

56. Ibid., 162.

57. Frank Hoffman, "The Maritime Commons in the Neo-Mahanian Era," in Denmark and Mulvenon, *Contested Commons,* 79.

58. "A Cooperative Strategy for 21st Century Seapower" (Washington, DC: U.S. Navy, Marine Corps, and Coast Guard, October 2007).

59. Andrea Shala-Esa, "Six U.S. Air Force Cyber Tools Designated as 'Weapons,'" *NBC News,* April 9, 2013, http://www.nbcnews.com/technology/six-u-s-air-force-cyber-tools-designated-weapons-1C9277187; Vacca, "Military Culture and Cyber Security," 167.

60. Vacca, "Military Culture and Cyber Security," 171.

61. Chris C. Demchak, *Wars of Disruption and Resilience: Cybered Con-

flict, Power, and National Security (Athens: University of Georgia Press, 2011), 12–13.

62. Max Lord, "Starfleet or Aerospace Force: Structural and Doctrinal Aspects of Service Domination in Space Operations" (working paper, University of Kentucky, April 28, 2013), 1–2.

63. Robert S. Dudney, "Five Roads to Space Dominance," *Air Force Magazine*, July 2011, http://www.airforcemag.com/MagazineArchive/Pages/2011/July%20 2011/0711space.aspx.

64. Ibid.

65. Lord, "Starfleet or Aerospace Force," 4.

66. Eric Sterner, "Beyond the Stalemate in the Space Commons," in Denmark and Mulvenon, *Contested Commons*, 108; John E. Hyten, "A Sea of Peace or a Theater of War? Dealing with the Inevitable Conflict in Space," *Air and Space Power Journal* 16, no. 3 (2002): 81.

67. Builder, *The Icarus Syndrome*, 151.

68. White House, "National Security Council," January 25, 2012, http://www .whitehouse.gov/administration/eop/nsc.

69. Alexander L. George, "The Case for Multiple Advocacy in Making Foreign Policy," *American Political Science Review* 66, no. 3 (1972): 751.

70. Morton H. Halperin, "The Decision to Deploy the ABM: Bureaucratic and Domestic Politics in the Johnson Administration," *World Politics* 25, no. 1 (1972): 65–66.

71. George, "The Case for Multiple Advocacy in Making Foreign Policy," 751.

72. Ibid., 752.

73. A. C. Grayling, *Among the Dead Cities: The History and Moral Legacy of the WWII Bombing of Civilians in Germany and Japan* (New York: Walker, 2006), 46–47.

74. Allison, "Conceptual Models and the Cuban Missile Crisis," 706.

75. Clodfelter, *Limits of Air Power*, 52.

76. Andrew L. Stigler, "A Clear Victory for Air Power: NATO's Empty Threat to Invade Kosovo," *International Security* 27, no. 3 (2002–2003): 125.

77. David Halberstam, *War in a Time of Peace: Bush, Clinton, and the Generals* (New York: Touchstone, 2002), 471.

3. Airpower, Morality, and Lawfare

1. Meilinger, "Airpower and Collateral Damage."

2. Grayling, *Among the Dead Cities*, 184.

3. Kristen M. Thomasen, "Air Power, Coercion, and Dual-Use Infrastructure: A Legal and Ethical Analysis," *International Affairs Review* 17, no. 2 (2008), http://www.iar-gwu.org/node/40; Clodfelter, *Beneficial Bombing*, 42.

4. Thomasen, "Air Power, Coercion, and Dual-Use Infrastructure."

5. Ibid.

6. Meilinger, "Airpower and Collateral Damage."

7. Grayling, *Among the Dead Cities,* 184.

8. Clodfelter, *Beneficial Bombing,* 132.

9. BBC, "Casualties in the Two World Wars from Combatant Nations," August 4, 2004, http://www.bbc.co.uk/dna/h2g2/A2854730.

10. Meilinger, "Airpower and Collateral Damage."

11. Michael Walzer, *Just and Unjust Wars* (New York: Perseus Books Group, 2006), 129, 144–45.

12. Ibid., 153–54.

13. Peter R. Faber, "The Ethical-Legal Dimensions of Strategic Bombing during WWII: An Admonition to Current Ethicists" (paper presented at Joint Services Conference on Professional Ethics XVII, January 25–26, 1996), http://web .duke.edu/jscope/papfab.htm.

14. Meilinger, "Giulio Douhet and the Origins of Airpower Theory," 12.

15. Gene Dannen, "Draft Rules of Aerial Warfare, The Hague, February 1923," *International Law on the Bombing of Civilians,* 1999, http://www.dannen .com/decision/int-law.html#C.

16. Phillip Meilinger, "Trenchard, Slessor, and Royal Air Force Doctrine before World War II," in Meilinger, *Paths of Heaven,* 56.

17. Peter Gray, *The Leadership, Direction and Legitimacy of the RAF Bomber Offensive from Inception to 1945,* Birmingham War Studies (London: Continuum, 2012), 66, 120.

18. Meilinger, "Trenchard, Slessor, and Royal Air Force Doctrine," 56.

19. Thomasen, "Air Power, Coercion, and Dual-Use Infrastructure."

20. Jonathan F. Keiler, "The End of Proportionality," *Parameters* 39 (Spring 2009): 53.

21. Biddle, *Rhetoric and Reality in Air Warfare,* 80–81.

22. Ibid., 202, 229–30, 246, 199–202.

23. Gray, *Leadership, Direction, and Legitimacy,* 167.

24. Gentile, *How Effective Is Strategic Bombing?* 264–308.

25. Biddle, *Rhetoric and Reality in Air Warfare,* 227–28.

26. Steven Brakman, Harry Garretsen, and Marc Schramm, "The Strategic Bombing of German Cities during World War II and Its Impact on City Growth," *Journal of Economic Geography* 4, no. 2 (2004): 205.

27. Grayling, *Among the Dead Cities,* 104.

28. Williamson Murray and Allan R. Millet, *A War to Be Won: Fighting the Second World War* (Cambridge, MA: Belknap Press of Harvard University Press, 2000), 190.

29. John S. Craig, *Peculiar Liaisons: In War, Espionage, and Terrorism in the Twentieth Century* (New York: Algora, 2004), 162.

30. Van Crevald, *Age of Airpower,* 2674.

31. Ibid.

32. Bret Fisk, "The Tokyo Air Raids in the Words of Those Who Survived," *Asia-Pacific Journal,* January 17, 2011, http://japanfocus.org/-Bret-Fisk/3471.

33. Van Crevald, *Age of Airpower,* 2674, 2700.

34. Grayling, *Among the Dead Cities,* 233.

35. Ibid., 242.

36. Walzer, *Just and Unjust Wars,* 258–62.

37. Ibid., 251–55.

38. Grayling, *Among the Dead Cities,* 277.

39. Ibid., 184–85, 188, 202–3.

40. Itai Brun, "The Second Lebanon War, 2006," in *A History of Air Warfare* [Kindle edition], ed. John Andreas Olsen (Washington, DC: Potomac, 2010), 308, 304.

41. Ibid., 307.

42. Robert A. Pape, *Bombing to Win: Air Power and Coercion in War* (Ithaca, NY: Cornell University Press, 1996), 236.

43. Brun, "The Second Lebanon War," 302.

44. Ibid., 306.

45. Lazar Berman, "Beyond the Basics: Looking beyond the Conventional Wisdom Surrounding the IDF Campaigns against Hizbullah and Hamas," *Small Wars Journal,* April 28, 2011, http://smallwarsjournal.com/jrnl/art/beyond-the-basics.

46. Brun, "The Second Lebanon War," 308.

47. Yaakov Katz, "High-Ranking Officer: Halutz Ordered Retaliation Policy," *Jerusalem Post,* July 24, 2006, http://fr.jpost.com/servlet/Satellite?cid=1153291987290&pagename=JPost/JPArticle/ShowFull.

48. Amos Harel and Eli Ashkenazi, "IAF Strikes Religious Building in Southern Lebanon: 4 Wounded," Haaretz.com, July 21, 2006, http://www.haaretz.com/news/iaf-strikes-religious-building-in-southern-lebanon-4-wounded-1.193505.

49. Shimon Golding, "New Yorkers Rally for Israel," *Jewish Press,* July 19, 2006, http://www.jewishpress.com/pageroute.do/18897/.

50. Nimrod Raphaeli, "Hizbullah-Israel War: Economic Consequences for Lebanon," *Memri Economic Blog,* July 22, 2008, http://memrieconomicblog.org/bin/content.cgi?article=227.

51. Amnesty International, "Israel/Lebanon—Deliberate Destruction or Collateral Damage? Israeli Attacks on Civilian Infrastructure," August 23, 2006, http://reliefweb.int/sites/reliefweb.int/files/resources/2F9C6C700F570D8FC12571D300486106-amnesty-lbn-23aug.pdf , 4.

52. "War Criminals at Harvard," *Harvardcriminals.blogspot.com,* May 2007, http://harvardwarcriminals.blogspot.com/2007/05/dan-halutz.html

53. Amnesty International, "Israel/Lebanon," 3.

54. Donald Macintyre and Eric Silver, "Israel Widens Bombing Campaign as Lebanese Militia Groups Retaliate," *Independent,* July 14 2006, http://www.independent.co.uk/news/world/middle-east/israel-widens-bombing-campaign-as-lebanese-militia-groups-retaliate-407859.html.

55. Amnesty International, "Israel/Lebanon," 2.

56. Caroline B. Glick, "The Path to the Next Lebanon War," *Jerusalem Post,* July 11, 2011, http://www.jpost.com/Opinion/Columnists/Article.aspx?id=228892.

57. David Gardner, "Israel's Perceived Lawlessness Hurts Its Cause," *Financial Times,* February 25, 2010, http://www.ft.com/intl/cms/s/0/43c961e4-224a-11df-9a72-00144feab49a.html#axzz1WANFcCt2.

58. Michael Walzer, "Responsibility and Proportionality in State and Nonstate Wars," *Parameters* 39 (Spring 2009): 44–49.

59. Amnesty International, "Israel/Lebanon," 3.

60. "Odin's Eye," *Warship: International Fleet Review* (October 2006): 8.

61. Jeffrey Gingras and Tomislav Ruby, "Morality in Modern Aerial Warfare" (Air Command and Staff College Research Report, April 2000), 26; Clodfelter, *Beneficial Bombing,* 151.

62. Charles J. Dunlap Jr., "Law and Military Interventions: Preserving Humanitarian Values in 21st Century Conflicts" (paper presented at Humanitarian Challenges in Military Intervention Conference, Carr Center for Human Rights Policy, November 29, 2001), 2.

63. Charles J. Dunlap Jr., "Lawfare: A Decisive Element of 21st Century Conflicts," *Joint Force Quarterly* 54, no. 3 (2009): 36.

64. Dunlap, "Law and Military Interventions," 5.

65. Wikileaks, *Collateral Murder,* http://collateralmurder.com/.

66. Dunlap, "Law and Military Interventions," 4–5.

67. Noah Shachtman, "Does Petraeus Mean a Return of Afghanistan Air War?" *Danger Room,* June 23, 2010, http://www.wired.com/dangerroom/2010/06/does-petraeus-mean-a-return-to- all-out-war/. Also see "Noah Shachtman, "How the Afghanistan War Got Stuck in the Sky," *Danger Room,* December 8, 2009, http://www.wired.com/magazine/2009/12/ff_end_air_war/all/1.

68. Charles J. Dunlap Jr., *Shortchanging the Joint Fight? An Airman's Assessment of FM 3-24 and the Case for Developing Truly Joint COIN Doctrine* (Maxwell AFB, AL: Air University Press, 2008), 24.

69. Charles J. Dunlap Jr., "America's Asymmetric Advantage," *Armed Forces Journal,* September 2006, http://www.armedforcesjournal.com/2006/09/2009013.

70. Drunkenpredator, "Orwells and Oppenheimers: Drone Opponents' Marriage of Convenience," *Gunpowder and Lead,* May 3, 2012, http://gunpowderandlead.org/2012/05/orwells-and-oppenheimers-drone-opponents-marriage-of-convenience/.

71. Jeffrey Gingras and Tomislav Ruby, "Morality and Modern Air War," *Joint Force Quarterly,* Summer 2000, 107.

72. Gingras and Ruby, "Morality in Modern Aerial Warfare," 2.

73. Ibid., 13.

74. Ibid., 22, 27.

75. Meilinger, "Airpower and Collateral Damage."

76. Charles A. Blanchard, "About," *Air Force General Counsel Blog,* November 8, 2012, http://afgeneralcounsel.dodlive.mil/sample-page/.

77. Crane, *American Airpower Strategy in Korea,* 123.

78. Charles J. Dunlap Jr., "Collateral Damage and Counterinsurgency Doctrine," *Small Wars Journal,* February 5, 2008, http://smallwarsjournal.com/jrnl/art/collateral-damage-and-counterinsurgency-doctrine.

4. The Struggle for the RAF and the Roots of American Airpower

1. Liam Fox, *Chief of Air Staff's Air Power Conference,* July 14, 2011, http://www.rusi.org/events/past/ref:E4D6635E4D5ADE/info:public/infoID:E4E1F18A71C987/.

2. Tony Mason, "British Air Power," in Olsen, *Global Air Power,* 449.

3. Christopher J. Luck, *The Smuts Report: Interpreting and Misinterpreting the Promise of Airpower* (Maxwell AFB, AL: Air University Press, 2007), https://www.afresearch.org/skins/rims/q_mod_be0e99f3-fc56–4ccb-8dfe-670c0822a153/q_act_downloadpaper/q_obj_8a72589a-4dd7–4177–85ce-d0d176a9ee40/display.aspx?rs=publishedsearch, 21.

4. John H. Morrow, "The First World War, 1914–1919," in Olsen, *A History of Air Warfare,* 7, 9.

5. Mason, "British Air Power," 532.

6. Luck, *The Smuts Report,* 18–19, 25.

7. Biddle, *Rhetoric and Reality in Air Warfare,* 23.

8. Ibid., 30.

9. Ibid., 38–39.

10. "Note by the Air Staff on the Reasons for the Formation of the Royal Air Force," citing Curzon report of 1916, 4, AIR 9/5, Plans Archives, vol. 47, Separate Air Force Controversy, 1917–1936, National Archives, Kew, Richmond, UK.

11. See F. S. Crawford, *Jan Smuts: A Biography* (Garden City, NY: Doubleday, 1943).

12. Luck, *The Smuts Report,* 33.

13. Ibid., 36.

14. "Note by the Air Staff on the Reasons for the Formation of the Royal Air Force."

15. Ibid.

16. Ibid., 9.

17. Luck, *The Smuts Report,* 40.

18. "Future Development of the Air Services, No. 5," AIR 1/16/15/1/74: Air

Service: Future Developments of Memorandum, National Archives, Kew, Richmond, UK.

19. Boyle, *Trenchard,* 43, 198, 196.

20. Ibid., 204, 219, 222.

21. Ibid., 229, 230, 232.

22. Morrow, "The First World War," 22.

23. Luck, *The Smuts Report,* 49.

24. Boyle, *Trenchard,* 288.

25. Morrow, "The First World War," 23, 22.

26. Gray, *Leadership, Direction, and Legitimacy,* 58–59.

27. MacIsaac, "Voices from the Central Blue," 628–29.

28. Gray, *Leadership, Direction, and Legitimacy,* 59.

29. For the most widely accepted definition of the term, see Peter Haas, "Introduction: Epistemic Communities and International Policy Coordination," *International Organization* 46, no. 1 (1992): 1–35.

30. Biddle, *Rhetoric and Reality in Air Warfare,* 104–5, 201; Pape, *Bombing to Win,* 265.

31. Biddle, *Rhetoric and Reality in Air Warfare,* 56–59.

32. Richard Overy, *The Bombing War: Europe, 1939–1945* (London: Allen Lane, 2013), 15–16.

33. Gentile, *How Effective Is Strategic Bombing?* 214.

34. Douhet, *The Command of the Air.*

35. Stockings and Fernandes, "Airpower and the Myth of Strategic Bombing as Strategy," 8.

36. Gentile, *How Effective Is Strategic Bombing?* 214.

37. Meilinger, "Giulio Douhet and the Origins of Airpower Theory," 9.

38. Ibid., 14, 20, 18.

39. Basil Henry Liddell Hart, *The Decisive Wars of History* (London: Bell & Sons, 1929), 2–3.

40. Grayling, *Among the Dead Cities,* 132–33; Gray, *Leadership, Direction, and Legitimacy,* 97.

41. "Memorandum on Naming of RAF Ranks," August 4, 1919, AIR 1/9/15/1/28: Is the organization of the Air Force as an independent fight force justified? National Archives, Kew, Richmond, UK.

42. Meilinger, "Trenchard, Slessor, and Royal Air Force Doctrine," 42.

43. Vincent Orange, *Slessor: Bomber Champion* [Kindle edition] (London: Grub Street, 2006), 1515.

44. Mason, "British Air Power," 643.

45. Boyle, *Trenchard,* 268, 397, 472, 439.

46. Gray, *Leadership, Direction, and Legitimacy,* 85.

47. Mason, "British Air Power," 587, 643.

48. "Air Staff Memorandum on the Obligations of the Air Force," June 1921,

AIR 1/26/15/1/125: R.A.F. obligations in defense of the Empire—statement for the Imperial Defence Committee, National Archives, Kew, Richmond, UK.

49. Boyle, *Trenchard*, 450.

50. "The Role of the Air Force in Relation to the Army: Memorandum by the Secretary of State for War," May 26, 1921, AIR 9/5 Plans Archives, vol. 47, Separate Air Force Controversy, 1917–1936, National Archives, Kew, Richmond, UK.

51. Mason, "British Air Power," 892.

52. "Notes for Questions for Lord Cavan, 8-6-1923."

53. See also Johnson, *Learning Large Lessons*, 13, on the artillery/interdiction debate in the U.S. Army.

54. Kier, *Imagining War*, 105.

55. "Note by the Air Staff on the Reasons for the Formation of the Royal Air Force."

56. Gray, *Leadership, Direction, and Legitimacy*, 101; Grayling, *Among the Dead Cities*, 132–33.

57. Boyle, *Trenchard*, 470.

58. Meilinger, "Trenchard, Slessor, and Royal Air Force Doctrine," 50.

59. Ibid., 576; Gray, *Leadership, Direction, and Legitimacy*, 59.

60. Mason, "British Air Power," 732, 759; Gray, *Leadership, Direction, and Legitimacy*, 184.

61. Mason, "British Air Power," 764.

62. Ibid., 892; Orange, *Slessor*, 1426.

63. Kier, *Imagining War*, 91, 116.

64. Gray, *Leadership, Direction, and Legitimacy*, 175.

65. Orange, *Slessor*, 2234.

66. Stephen Peter Rosen, *Winning the Next War: Innovation and the Modern Military* (Ithaca, NY: Cornell University Press, 1991), 97–98.

67. Orange, *Slessor*, 1054.

68. James S. Corum, "Airpower Thought in Continental Europe between the Wars," in Meilinger, *The Paths of Heaven*, 152, 154–56, 161, 166–67, 172, 175. See also Overy, *The Bombing War*, 41–42.

5. From Army Air Service to Air Force

1. Gross, *American Military Aviation*, 16.

2. Richard P. Hallion, "U.S. Air Power," in Olsen, *Global Air Power*, 1612.

3. Jeffrey S. Underwood, "Presidential Statesmen and U.S. Airpower," in Robin Higham and Mark Parillo, eds., *The Influence of Airpower upon History: Statesmanship, Diplomacy, and Foreign Policy since 1916* (Lexington: University Press of Kentucky, 2013), 178.

4. Maurer, *Aviation in the U.S. Army*, xxi, xxii.

5. W. H. Sitz, *USMC: A History of U.S. Naval Aviation* (Washington, DC: United States Navy Department Bureau of Aeronautics, 1930), 5.

6. Maurer, *Aviation in the U.S. Army*, 113.

7. Gross, *American Military Aviation*, 54.

8. William J. Ott, "Maj. Gen. William 'Billy' Mitchell: A Pyrrhic Promotion," *Air and Space Power Journal*, December 1, 2006, 30.

9. Thomas Greer, *The Development of Doctrine in the Army Air Arm, 1917–1941* (Washington, DC: Office of Air Force History, 1985), 14.

10. Maurer, *Aviation in the U.S. Army*, 44.

11. James P. Tate, *The Army and Its Air Corps: Army Policy toward Aviation, 1919–1942* (Maxwell AFB, AL: Air University Press, 1998), 12, 13.

12. Maurer, *Aviation in the U.S. Army*, 44.

13. Ibid., 165.

14. Greer, *Development of Doctrine in the Army Air Arm*, 16.

15. Gross, *American Military Aviation*, 41–42.

16. Alfred F. Hurley, *Billy Mitchell: Crusader for Air Power* (Bloomington: Indiana University Press, 2006), 75; Biddle, *Rhetoric and Reality in Air Warfare*, 52; Clodfelter, *Beneficial Bombing*, 18.

17. Gentile, *How Effective Is Strategic Bombing?* 214.

18. Peter R. Faber, "Interwar US Army Aviation and the Air Corps Tactical School: Incubators of American Airpower," in Meilinger, *The Paths of Heaven*, 186.

19. Greer, *Development of Doctrine in the Army Air Arm*, 24.

20. Gross, *American Military Aviation*, 56.

21. Tate, *The Army and Its Air Corps*, 15–16.

22. Roger G. Miller, *Billy Mitchell: Stormy Petrel of the Air* (Washington, DC: Office of Air Force History, 2004), 33.

23. O'Connel, *Sacred Vessels*, 257.

24. Gross, *American Military Aviation*, 56.

25. Maurer, *Aviation in the U.S. Army*, 127–29.

26. Paul Bergman and Michael Asimow, *Reel Justice: The Courtroom Goes to the Movies* (Kansas City: Andres McMeel, 2006), 302.

27. Gross, *American Military Aviation*, 56–57.

28. Smith, *The Air Force Plans for Peace*, 33–34.

29. Phillip S. Meilinger, *Airpower: Theory and Practice* (Oxford: Frank & Cass, 2003), 87.

30. Spencer Tucker, *Who's Who in Twentieth Century Warfare* (New York: Taylor & Francis Library, 2005), 101.

31. Gross, *American Military Aviation*, 59.

32. Ibid., 67–69.

33. Maurer, *Aviation in the U.S. Army*, 284–85.

34. Miller, *Billy Mitchell*, 24.

35. Sitz, *USMC*, 34–35.

36. Maurer, *Aviation in the U.S. Army*, 283–84.

37. Gentile, *How Effective Is Strategic Bombing?* 270.

38. Smith, *The Air Force Plans for Peace*, 32, 34, 28.

39. Gentile, *How Effective Is Strategic Bombing?* 294, 318.

40. Gross, *American Military Aviation*, 78.

41. Maurer, *Aviation in the U.S. Army*, 446.

42. Overy, *The Bombing War*, 60.

43. Ibid., 64.

44. Ibid., 78, 83, 108, 614–15.

45. Albert L. Raithel Jr., "Patrol Aviation in the Atlantic in World War II," *Naval Aviation News*, November–December 1994, www.history.navy.mil/download/ww2-33.pdf, 31–35.

46. John Pomeroy Condon, *Corsairs and Flattops—Marine Carrier Air Warfare, 1944–45* (Annapolis, MD: Naval Institute Press, 1998), 87–88.

47. "The Air Forces," *Aerofiles*, January 21, 2012, http://aerofiles.com/airforces.html.

48. Murray and Millet, *A War to Be Won*, 311–13.

49. Clodfelter, *Beneficial Bombing*, 117–18.

50. Murray and Millet, *A War to Be Won*, 311–13.

51. Gross, *American Military Aviation*, 128.

52. Pape, *Bombing to Win*, 92.

53. Gerhard L. Weinberg, *A World at Arms: A Global History of World War II* (Cambridge: Cambridge University Press, 1994), 858.

54. Ibid.

55. Ibid., 869.

56. Clodfelter, *Beneficial Bombing*, 224.

57. Overy, *The Bombing War*, 613–17.

58. Murray and Millet, *A War to Be Won*, 334.

59. Grayling, *Among the Dead Cities*, 104.

60. John Fahey, "Britain, 1939–1945: The Economic Cost of Strategic Bombing" (PhD diss., University of Sydney, 2004), 3–5.

61. Richard Rhodes, *The Making of the Atomic Bomb* (New York: Simon & Schuster, 1986), 605.

62. Overy, *The Bombing War*, 627.

63. Gentile, *How Effective Is Strategic Bombing?* 474.

64. Ibid., 571.

65. Ibid., 968.

66. Ibid., 2149.

67. Tate, *The Army and Its Air Corps*, 183.

68. Smith, *The Air Force Plans for Peace*, 27.

69. Ibid., 60.

70. Dean Allard, "Interservice Differences in the United States, 1945–1950:

A Naval Perspective," *Airpower Journal,* Winter 1989, http://www.airpower.au.af
.mil/airchronicles/apj/apj89/win89/allard.html.

71. Ibid.

72. Ibid.

73. Ibid.

74. SecDef Histories, "James V. Forrestal," *Department of Defense,* August 25,
2011, http://www.defense.gov/specials/secdef_histories/bios/forrestal.htm.

75. Richard Irving Wolf, ed., *The United States Air Force: Basic Documents
on Roles and Missions* (Washington, DC: Office of Air Force History, 1987), 161.

76. L. Parker Temple III, *Shades of Gray: National Security and the Evolution
of Space Reconnaissance* (Reston, VA: American Institute of Aeronautics and As-
tronautics, 2005), 15, 16.

77. Allard, "Interservice Differences in the United States."

78. Ibid.

79. L. Douglas Keeney, *15 Minutes: General Curtis LeMay and the Countdown
to Nuclear Annihilation* (New York: St. Martin's, 2011), 221.

80. Robert Frank Futrell, *Ideas, Concepts, Doctrine: Basic Thinking in the
United States Air Force, 1907–1960* (Maxwell AFB, AL: Air University Press,
1989), 529–31.

81. Alex Abella, *Soldiers of Reason: The RAND Corporation and the Rise of the
American Empire* (Orlando: Harcourt, 2008), 14.

82. Ibid., 18.

83. Ibid., 44, 68.

84. Ibid., 139.

85. Rhodes, *The Making of the Atomic Bomb,* 605.

86. Keeney, *15 Minutes,* 45–46.

87. Ibid., 47.

6. American Airpower in the Era of Limited War

1. See, for example, Crane, *American Airpower Strategy in Korea.*

2. Pape, *Bombing to Win,* 160–63. For an important critique of Pape, see
Barry D. Watts, "Ignoring Reality: Problems of Theory and Evidence in Security
Studies," *Security Studies* 7, no. 2 (1997–1998): 115–71.

3. Crane, *American Airpower Strategy in Korea,* 87–88, 75, 83.

4. Ibid., 59, 33, 82–83, 84, 120.

5. Pape, *Bombing to Win,* 172–73.

6. Ibid., 240.

7. Gross, *American Military Aviation,* 175.

8. Dale Smith, "Speed Freak," *Air and Space,* January 2006, http://www
.airspacemag.com/history-of-flight/speed-freak.html.

9. Keeney, *15 Minutes,* 175.

10. Gross, *American Military Aviation*, 175, 178.

11. Keeney, *15 Minutes*, 221.

12. Smith, "Speed Freak."

13. Gross, *American Military Aviation*, 189.

14. Builder, *The Icarus Syndrome*, 151.

15. Ibid., 33.

16. Christopher Paine, "Pershing II: The Army's Strategic Weapon," *Bulletin of the Atomic Scientists* 36, no. 6 (1980): 25.

17. Keeney, *15 Minutes*, 241.

18. Wolf, *The United States Air Force*, 243–45.

19. Tom Cooper, "Algerian War, 1954–1962," *Western and North African Database*, November 12, 2003, http://www.acig.org/artman/publish/article_354.shtml.

20. Earl H. Tilford, *Crosswinds: The Air Force's Setup in Vietnam* (College Station: Texas A&M University Press, 1993), 183.

21. Kevin J. Dougherty, "The Evolution of Air Assault," *Joint Force Quarterly* 21 (Summer 1999): 54.

22. Ray L. Bowers, *Tactical Airlift: United States Air Force in Southeast Asia* (Washington, DC: Office of Air Force History, 1983), 673–74, 651–52.

23. Clodfelter, *Limits of Air Power*, 73.

24. Pape, *Bombing to Win*, 175.

25. Thomas C. Schelling, *Arms and Influence* (New Haven, CT: Yale University Press, 1966), 74–75.

26. Pape, *Bombing to Win*, 187; Clodfelter, *Limits of Airpower*, 84.

27. Clodfelter, *Limits of Airpower*, 52, 28, 53, 59.

28. Lien-Hang T. Nguyen, *Hanoi's War: An International History of the War for Peace in Vietnam* (Chapel Hill: University of North Carolina Press, 2012), 91.

29. Clodfelter, *Limits of Airpower*, 64–65, 73, 77, 130; Van Crevald, *Age of Airpower*, 6332.

30. Pape, *Bombing to Win*, 194.

31. Clodfelter, *Limits of Airpower*, 152, 167.

32. Van Crevald, *Age of Airpower*, 6446.

33. Nguyen, *Hanoi's War*, 330.

34. Clodfelter, *Limits of Airpower*, 200.

35. Ibid., 129, 164.

36. Jim Cunningham, "Rediscovering Air Superiority: Vietnam, the F-X, and the 'Fighter Mafia,'" *Air and Space Power Journal*, August 25, 2011, http://www.airpower.maxwell.af.mil/airchronicles/cc/jim.html.

37. C. R. Anderegg, *Sierra Hotel: Flying Air Force Fighters in the Decade after Vietnam* (Washington, DC: Air Force History and Museums Program, 2001), 4, 8.

38. Michel, *Clashes*, 181, 186.

39. Anderegg, *Sierra Hotel*, 33, 186.

40. Cunningham, "Rediscovering Air Superiority"; Anderegg, *Sierra Hotel*, 33.

41. Anderegg, *Sierra Hotel,* 14.

42. Ibid.; Olsen, *John Warden,* 1689.

43. Clodfelter, *Limits of Airpower,* 208.

44. Hammond, *The Mind of War,* 1628.

45. Gross, *American Military Aviation,* 225.

46. Hammond, *The Mind of War,* 1866.

47. Gross, *American Military Aviation,* 221, 233.

48. Richard D. Newton, "A Question of Doctrine?" *Airpower Journal,* Fall 1988,   http://www.airpower.au.af.mil/airchronicles/apj/apj88/fa188/newton.html.

49. Dougherty, "The Evolution of Air Assault," 54.

50. Douglas N. Campbell, *The Warthog and the Close Air Support Debate* (Annapolis, MD: Naval Institute Press, 2003), 65.

51. Ibid., 77–78, 1–3.

52. Arden B. Dahl, "The Warthog: The Best Deal the Air Force Never Wanted" (unpublished paper, National War College, 2003), http://www.dtic.mil/cgi-bin/GetTRDoc?AD=ADA442118, 1; Campbell, *Warthog,* 172–73.

53. Robert Coram, "The Hog That Saves the Grunts," *New York Times,* May 27, 2003.

54. Anderegg, *Sierra Hotel,* 120, 122, 126, 135.

55. Harold R. Winton, "Partnership and Tension: The Army and Air Force between Vietnam and Desert Shield," *Parameters,* Spring 1996, 100.

56. Ibid., 105; Cunningham, "Rediscovering Air Superiority."

57. Olsen, *John Warden,* 1655.

58. Cunningham, "Rediscovering Air Superiority."

59. Builder, *The Icarus Syndrome,* 141.

60. Dima Adamsky, *The Culture of Military Innovation* (Stanford, CA: Stanford University Press, 2010), 2–3.

61. Hammond, *The Mind of War,* 235, 2975.

62. Adamsky, *The Culture of Military Innovation,* 2–3.

63. Ibid.; Stockings and Fernandes, "Airpower and the Myth of Strategic Bombing as Strategy," 12–13.

64. Adamsky, *The Culture of Military Innovation,* 30.

65. Richard G. Davis, *The 31 Initiatives: A Study in Air Force–Army Cooperation* (Washington, DC: Office of Air Force History, 1987), 32.

66. Winton, "Partnership and Tension," 107, 108.

67. McCaffrey, *What Happened to Battlefield Air Interdiction,* 2.

68. Winton, "Partnership and Tension," 110; McCaffrey, *What Happened to Battlefield Air Interdiction,* 18.

69. See especially Grant Hammond, "Paths to Extinction: The US Air Force in 2025" (Air Force 2025 Research Paper, August 1996), 3.

70. McCaffrey, *What Happened to Battlefield Air Interdiction,* 27, 25, 28, 26.

71. Olsen, *John Warden,* 2379.

72. McCaffrey, *What Happened to Battlefield Air Interdiction,* 38.

73. Thomas A. Keaney and Eliot A. Cohen, *Gulf War Air Power Survey Summary Report* (Washington, DC: Department of the Air Force, 1993), 23–24.

74. See Keaney et al., *Gulf War Air Power Survey,* http://www.airforcehistory .hq.af.mil/Publications/Annotations/gwaps.htm.

75. Gentile, *How Effective Is Strategic Bombing?* 2993.

76. Johnson, *Learning Large Lessons,* 35, 36–37.

77. Edward Luttwak, "Airpower in US Military Strategy," in Shultz and Pfaltz-graff, *The Future of Air Power,* 20.

78. Gray, *Airpower for Strategic Effect,* 212.

79. Luttwak, "Airpower in US Military Strategy," 19, 30.

80. Daryl Press, "The Myth of Air Power in the Persian Gulf War and the Future of Warfare," *International Security* 26, no. 2 (2001): 7, 27, 36.

81. Stephen Biddle, "Victory Misunderstood: What the Gulf War Tells Us about the Future of Conflict," *International Security* 21, no. 2 (1996): 148.

82. Ibid., 139. For alternative interpretations and critics of Biddle, see Thomas G. Mahnken and Barry D. Watts, "What the Gulf War Can (and Cannot) Tell Us about the Future of Warfare," *International Security* 22, no. 2 (1997): 151–62; and Thomas A. Keaney, "The Linkage of Air and Ground Power in the Future of Conflict," *International Security* 22, no. 2 (1997): 147–50.

83. Pape, *Bombing to Win,* 230, 238–40.

84. Johnson, *Learning Large Lessons,* 47, 25.

85. Winton, "Partnership and Tension," 115.

86. Warden, "Employing Air Power in the Twenty-first Century," 64–66.

87. Ibid., 69.

88. Olsen, *John Warden,* 2393.

89. Stockings and Fernandes, "Airpower and the Myth of Strategic Bombing as Strategy," 12–13.

90. Pape, *Bombing to Win,* 322.

91. See Warden, *The Air Campaign.*

92. Olsen, *John Warden,* 1104.

93. Ibid., 1334, 2157.

94. Department of the Air Force, *The Air Force and U.S. National Security: Global Reach—Global Power* (Washington, DC: Air Force, June 1990), 1.

95. McCaffrey, *What Happened to Battlefield Air Interdiction,* 60, 59, 58, 69.

96. Winton, "Partnership and Tension," 116.

7. Global Reach, Global Power in the Post–Cold War Era

1. Ivo Daalder and Michael O'Hanlon, *Winning Ugly: NATO's War to Save Kosovo* (Washington, DC: Brookings Institution Press, 2000), 202.

2. Ibid., 203–4.

3. Stigler, "A Clear Victory for Air Power," 125.

4. Benjamin Lambeth, *NATO's Air War for Kosovo: A Strategic and Operational Assessment* [Kindle edition] (Santa Monica, CA: RAND, 2001), 2040, 4240.

5. Wesley Clark, *Waging Modern War* (New York: Public Affairs, 2001), 240.

6. Daalder and O'Hanlon, *Winning Ugly,* 135, 58–59, 150–51, 152.

7. Lambeth, *NATO's Air War for Kosovo,* 5093.

8. Stigler, "A Clear Victory for Air Power," 140.

9. "Frontline: War in Europe: A Kosovo Chronology," *PBS.ORG Frontline,* July 29, 2010, http://www.pbs.org/wgbh/pages/frontline/shows/kosovo/etc/cron.html.

10. Johnson, *Learning Large Lessons,* 82.

11. Daalder, and O'Hanlon, *Winning Ugly,* 204.

12. Lambeth, *NATO's Air War for Kosovo,* 2045. See also Karl Mueller, "Deus ex Machina? Coercive Air Power in Bosnia and Kosovo" (unpublished paper, School of Advanced Air Power Studies, Maxwell AFB, AL, November 7, 1999), 10.

13. David Axe, "Why Can't the Air Force Build an Affordable Plane?" *Atlantic,* March 26, 2012, http://www.theatlantic.com/national/archive/2012/03/why-cant-the-air-force-build-an-affordable-plane/254998/.

14. Christopher Niemi, "The F-22 Acquisition Program: Consequences for the US Air Force's Fighter Fleet," *Air and Space Power Journal,* November–December 2012, 56, 57, 59.

15. Ibid., 71.

16. Sharon Weinberger, "Gates: F-22 Has No Role in War on Terror," *Danger Room,* February 2, 2008, 40–41, http://www.wired.com/dangerroom/2008/02/gates/.

17. Adam Ciralski, "Will It Fly?" *Vanity Fair,* September 16, 2013, http://www.vanityfair.com/politics/2013/09/joint-strike-fighter-lockheed-martin; see also "F-35 Joint Strike Fighter (JSF) Lightning II," GlobalSecurity.org, September 3, 2012, http://www.globalsecurity.org/military/systems/aircraft/f-35.htm.

18. "F-35 Joint Strike Fighter (JSF) Lightning II."

19. Ibid.

20. Colin Clark, "Gates Fires JSF Program Manager," *DoD Buzz,* February 1, 2010, http://www.dodbuzz.com/2010/02/01/gates-fires-jsf-program-manager/.

21. Richard Whittle, "JSF's Build and Test Was 'Miscalculation,' Adm. Venlet Says; Production Must Slow," *AOL Defense,* December 1, 2011, http://defense.aol.com/2011/12/01/jsf-build-and-test-was-miscalculation-production-must-slow-v/; Government Accountability Office, *GAO-06-356: Joint Strike Fighter: DOD Plans to Enter Production before Testing Demonstrates Acceptable Performance* (Washington, DC: U.S. Government, March 2006), http://www.gao.gov/new.items/d06356.pdf.

22. Government Accountability Office, *GAO-06–356: Joint Strike Fighter.*

23. David Pugliese, "Experts: Canada's Potential F-35 Cut Would Hurt Mission," *Defense News,* December 15, 2012, http://www.defensenews.com/article/20121215/DEFREG02/312150002/Experts-Canada-8217-s-Potential-F-35-Cut-Would-Hurt-Mission; Chiaa Vasarri, "Italy to Cut F-35 Fighter Jet Orders as Part of Defense Revamp," *BloombergBusinessweek,* February 16, 2012, http://www.businessweek.com/news/2012–02–16/italy-to-cut-f-35-fighter-jet-orders-as-part-of-defense-revamp.html.

24. Stephen Trimble, "F-35 versus Spinney's 'Death Spiral,'" *Flight Global: The Dew Line,* January 14, 2010, http://www.flightglobal.com/blogs/the-dewline/2010/01/f-35-versus-spinneys-death-spi.html.

25. Colin Clark, "Gen. Welsh Dismisses Talk of Scrapping Air Force; Pledges to Protect KC-46, F-35A, Long Range Bomber," *Breaking Defense,* September 17, 2013, http://breakingdefense.com/2013/09/17/gen-welch-dismisses-talk-of-scrapping-air-force-pledges-to-protect-kc-46-f-35a-long-range-bomber/.

26. David Axe, "Why the U.S. Wants a New Bomber: Interview with David Deptula," *Diplomat,* May 6, 2012, http://thediplomat.com/2012/05/06/why-the-u-s-wants-a-new-bomber/?all=true.

27. Axe, "Why Can't the Air Force Build an Affordable Plane?"

28. Johnson, *Learning Large Lessons,* 107.

29. Ibid., 109.

30. Ibid., 113, 119, 125–26, 134.

31. Daalder and O'Hanlon, *Winning Ugly,* 150–51.

32. Robert Farley, "Over the Horizon: Libya and the Afghan Model," *World Politics Review,* March 23, 2011, http://www.worldpoliticsreview.com/articles/8277/over-the-horizon-libya-and-the-afghan-model.

33. Stephen Biddle, "Allies, Airpower, and Modern Warfare: The Afghan Model in Afghanistan and Iraq," *International Security* 30, no. 3 (2005–2006): 161–63.

34. Farley, "Over the Horizon: Libya and the Afghan Model."

35. Robert Farley, "Over the Horizon: In Libya, the Strategic Air Campaign That Wasn't," *World Politics Review,* May 18, 2011, http://www.worldpoliticsreview.com/articles/8890/over-the-horizon-in-libya-the-strategic-air-campaign-that-wasnt.

36. Christian F. Anrig, "Allied Air Power over Libya: A Preliminary Assessment," *Air and Space Power Journal* 25, no. 4 (2011): 101.

37. Ibid., 104.

38. Raymond Pritchett, "The Missing Capabilities from Sea," *Information Dissemination,* March 31, 2011, http://www.informationdissemination.net/2011/03/missing-capabilities-from-sea.html.

39. Frederic Wehrey, "The Hidden Story of Airpower in Libya (and What It Means for Syria," *Foreign Policy,* February 11, 2013, http://mideast.foreignpolicy.com/posts/2013/02/11/the_hidden_story_of_airpower_in_libya.

40. Johnson, *Learning Large Lessons*, 191.

41. Chris Rawley, "Libya Lessons: Supremacy of the SOF-Airpower Team . . . or, Why Do We Still Need a Huge Army," *Information Dissemination*, September 15, 2011, http://www.informationdissemination.net/2011/08/libya-lessons-supremacy-of-sof-airpower.html.

42. Dunlap, "America's Asymmetric Advantage."

43. Headquarters Department of the Army, *Field Manual 3-24, Counterinsurgency*, December 15, 2006, E-1, http://usacac.leavenworth.army.mil/CAC2/COIN/repository/FM_3-24.pdf.

44. Ibid., E-1–2.

45. Shachtman, "Does Petraeus Mean a Return of Afghanistan Air War?" Also see Shachtman, "How the Afghanistan War Got Stuck in the Sky."

46. Dunlap, *Shortchanging the Joint Fight?* 65–66.

47. Dunlap, "Collateral Damage and Counterinsurgency Doctrine."

48. Julian E. Barnes, "Battle Centers on Surge," *Wall Street Journal*, August 27, 2010, http://online.wsj.com/article/SB10001424052748704913704575453530793746968.html.

49. Noah Shachtman, "Petraeus Gone, Afghan Air War Plummets," *Danger Room*, November 8, 2011, http://feeds.wired.com/~r/WiredDangerRoom/~3/eNpb7xUwTUc/.

50. Nicholas Beaudrot, "I'm Tired of Waiting on a Plane That Don't Have Wings," *Attackerman.firedoglake.com*, December 2, 2009, http://attackerman.firedoglake.com/2009/12/02/im-tired-of-waiting-on-a-plane-that-dont-have-wings/.

51. Dunlap, "Collateral Damage and Counterinsurgency Doctrine."

52. Dunlap, "America's Asymmetric Advantage."

53. *Irregular Warfare: Air Force Doctrine Document 2-3* (Washington, DC: U.S. Air Force, 2007), viii.

54. Ibid., 20; see also Noah Shachtman, "Air Force Lashes Out at Grunts in New War Manual," *Danger Room*, August 13, 2007, http://www.wired.com/dangerroom/2007/08/air-force-capab/.

55. *Irregular Warfare*, 20, 25, 26.

56. "US Air Force Reconsiders the Spad," *Strategy World.com*, April 27, 2009, http://www.strategypage.com/htmw/htairfo/articles/20090427.aspx.

57. "Colombia Finalizes Deal for Super Tucano COIN Aircraft," *DefenseIndustryDaily.com*, December 12, 2005, http://www.defenseindustrydaily.com/colombia-finalizes-deal-for-super-tucano-coin-aircraft-01606/.

58. "Embraer EMB 314 Super Tucano," *AircraftCompare.com*, November 23, 2012, http://www.aircraftcompare.com/helicopter-airplane/Embraer-EMB-314-Super-Tucano/110.

59. Greg Grant, "Mattis Still Supports Light COIN Plan Air Force Wants Dead," *DefenseTech*, http://defensetech.org/2010/07/29/mattis-still-supports-light-coin-plane-air-force-wants-dead/.

60. Greg Grant, "Shwartz Shoots Down COIN Plane," *DoD Buzz*, May 6, 2010, http://www.dodbuzz.com/2010/05/06/schwartz-shoots-down-light-fighter/.

61. Christian Lowe, "Could the COIN Plan Have Saved Lives?" *Defensetech* .org. September 14, 2009, http://defensetech.org/2009/09/14/could-the-coin-plane-have-saved-lives/.

62. *Quadrennial Defense Review Report* (Washington, DC: Department of Defense, 2010), 29, 39.

63. Grant, "Mattis Still Supports Light COIN Plan Air Force Wants Dead."

64. Defense Industry Daily Staff, "The New Iraqi Air Force: F-16IQ Block 52 Fighters," *Defense Industry Daily*, September 16, 2013, http://www .defenseindustrydaily.com/iraq-seeks-f-16-fighters-05057/.

65. Robert Farley, "Over the Horizon: Drawing the Right Lessons on Airpower from Libya," *World Politics Review*, October 26, 2011, http://www .worldpoliticsreview.com/articles/10458/over-the-horizon-drawing-the-right-lessons-on-airpower-from-libya.

66. Farley, "Over the Horizon: In Libya, the Strategic Air Campaign That Wasn't."

67. Farley, "Over the Horizon: Libya and the Afghan Model Revisited." See also Joshua Hammer, "Vengeance in Libya," *New York Review of Books*, December 15, 2011, http://www.nybooks.com/articles/archives/2012/jan/12/vengeance-libya/?pagination=false.

68. Thom Shanker, "2 Leaders Ousted from Air Force in Atomic Errors," *New York Times*, June 6, 2008, http://www.nytimes.com/2008/06/06/washington/06military.html?hp&_r=0.

69. Josh White, "Nuclear Parts Sent to Taiwan in Error," *Washington Post*, March 26, 2008, http://articles.washingtonpost.com/2008-03-26/news/36791585_1_nuclear-warheads-nuclear-missile-nuclear-weapons.

70. Jeffrey Lewis, "Death Wears Bunny Slippers," *Foreign Policy*, May 16, 2013, http://www.foreignpolicy.com/articles/2013/05/16/death_wears_bunny_slippers_nuclear.

8. Drone Warfare

1. Peter Singer, *Wired for War: The Robotics Revolution and Conflict in the Twenty-first Century* [Kindle edition] (New York: Penguin, 2009), 611, 689.

2. *The U.S. Air Force Remotely Piloted Aircraft and Unmanned Aerial Vehicle Strategic Vision* (Washington, DC: Department of Defense, 2005), 5, 13–14.

3. Under Secretary of Defense for Acquisition, Technology and Logistics, *Department of Defense Report to Congress on Future Unmanned Aircraft Systems Training, Operations, and Sustainability* (Washington, DC: Department of Defense, 2012), 2.

4. U.S. Army, *U.S. Army Roadmap for UAS, 2010–2035* (Fort Rucker, AL: U.S. Army UAS Center of Excellence, 2009), i, 1, 3.

5. David R. Buchanan, "Joint Doctrine for Unmanned Aircraft Systems: The Air Force and the Army Hold the Keys to Success," Naval War College Department of Joint Military Operations, March 5, 2010, 4, http://www.dtic.mil/dtic/tr/fulltext/u2/a525266.pdf.

6. *Department of Defense Report to Congress on Future Unmanned Aircraft Systems*, 2.

7. Brien Alkire, James G. Kallimani, Peter A. Wilson, and Louis R. Moore, *Applications for Navy Unmanned Aircraft Systems* (Santa Monica, CA: RAND, 2010), 2.

8. *Department of Defense Report to Congress on Future Unmanned Aircraft Systems*, 2.

9. Greg Miller, "Under Obama, an Emerging Global Apparatus for Drone Killing," *Washington Post*, December 27, 2011, http://www.washingtonpost.com/national/national-security/under-obama-an-emerging-global-apparatus-for-drone-killing/2011/12/13/gIQANPdILP_print.html.

10. Jeremy Scahill, "The (Not So) Secret (Anymore) US War in Pakistan," *Nation blog*, December 1, 2010, http://www.thenation.com/blog/156765/not-so-secret-anymore-us-war-pakistan#.

11. Mark Mazzetti, *The Way of the Knife: The CIA, a Secret Army, and a War at the Ends of the Earth* (New York: Penguin, 2013), 66, 228.

12. Marc Ambinder, "5 Truths about the Drone War," *The Week: The Compass*, March 13, 2013, http://theweek.com/article/index/241363/5-truths-about-the-drone-war.

13. Daniel Klaidman, "Exclusive: No More Drones for CIA," *Daily Beast*, March 19, 2013, http://www.thedailybeast.com/articles/2013/03/19/exclusive-no-more-drones-for-cia.html.

14. Micah Zenko, "Transferring CIA Drone Strikes to the Pentagon," *Council of Foreign Relations* (Policy Innovation Memorandum 31), April 2013, http://www.cfr.org/defensehomeland-security/transferring-cia-drone-strikes-pentagon/p30434.

15. Mazzetti, *Way of the Knife*, 25.

16. Brian Bennett and Joel Rubin, "Drones Are Taking to the Skies in the U.S.," *Los Angeles Times*, February 15, 2013, http://articles.latimes.com/2013/feb/15/nation/la-na-domestic-drones-20130216.

17. For example, see "Considerations in Selecting a Small UAV for Police Operations," *Aeryon Labs*, May 15, 2013, http://www.aeryon.com/applications/whitepapers/224-whitepaperpolice.html.

18. Singer, *Wired for War*, 922.

19. David R. Mets, "The Force in US Air Force: Fodder for Your Professional Reading on the Implements of Strategy and Tactics for Conventional Air War," *Aerospace Power Journal*, Fall 2000, http://www.airpower.au.af.mil/airchronicles/apj/apj00/fa100/mets.htm.

20. Murray and Millet, *A War to Be Won,* 599–600.

21. Steeljawscribe, "Oh When the Drone Is Called Up Yonder," *Steeljaw Scribe,* May 14, 2013, http://steeljawscribe.com/2013/05/14/%E2%99%AB%E2% 99%AC-oh-when-the-drone-is-called-up-yonder-%E2%99%AC%E2%99%AB.

22. Thomas P. Ehrhard, *Air Force UAVs: The Secret History* (Ft. Belvoir, VA: Defense Technical Information Center, 2010), 4, 5, 9, 25.

23. Ibid., 13, 35, 40.

24. Ibid., 49, 56.

25. Sue Baker, "Predator Missile Launch Test Totally Successful," *Federation of American Scientists, Aeronautical Systems Center Public Affairs,* February 27, 2001, http://www.fas.org/irp/program/collect/docs/man-ipc-predator-010228 .htm.

26. Thomas H. Kean and Lee H. Hamilton, *The 9/11 Report* (New York: St. Martin's, 2004), 16, 213–14.

27. "RQ-2 Pioneer," *The Warfighter's Encyclopedia,* May 17, 2013, http://web .archive.org/web/20070715081423/https://wrc.navair-rdte.navy.mil/warfighter_ enc/aircraft/UAVs/pioneer.htm.

28. Noah Shachtman, "How to Get a New Air Force, without Going Broke," *Danger Room,* July 15, 2010, http://www.wired.com/dangerroom/2010/07/how-to-get-a-new-air-force-without-going-broke/.

29. *U.S. Air Force Remotely Piloted Aircraft and Unmanned Aerial Vehicle Strategic Vision,* 10.

30. Brian Mockenhaupt, "We've Seen the Future, and It's Unmanned," *Esquire Magazine,* October 14, 2009, http://www.esquire.com/features/unmanned-aircraft-1109.

31. George Tenet, "Written Statement for the Record of the Director of Central Intelligence before the National Commission on Terrorist Attacks upon the United States," 9–11 Commission Hearings, March 24, 2004, http://www.9-11commission.gov/hearings/hearing8/tenet_statement.pdf.

32. William Saletan, "In Defense of Drones," *Slate,* February 19, 2013, http:// www.slate.com/articles/health_and_science/human_nature/2013/02/drones_ war_and_civilian_casualties_how_unmanned_aircraft_reduce_collateral.html.

33. Chris Woods and Alike K. Ross, "Revealed: US and Britain Launched 1200 Drone Strikes in Recent Wars," *Bureau of Investigative Journalism,* December 4, 2012, http://www.thebureauinvestigates.com/2012/12/04/revealed-us-and-britain-launched-1200-drone-strikes-in-recent-wars/.

34. Mazzetti, *Way of the Knife,* 91.

35. Mark Mazzetti, "A Secret Deal on Drones, Sealed in Blood," *New York Times,* April 6, 2013, http://www.nytimes.com/2013/04/07/world/asia/origins-of-cias-not-so-secret-drone-war-in-pakistan.html?pagewanted=all&_r=0.

36. Greg McNeal, "The U.S. Practice of Collateral Damage Estimation and Mitigation" (working paper, Pepperdine University, 2011), 2–3.

37. Miller, "Global Apparatus for Drone Killing."

38. Thomas Harding, "Col Gaddafi Killed: Convoy Bombed by Drone Flown by Pilot in Las Vegas," *Telegraph,* October 20, 2011, http://www.telegraph.co.uk/ news/worldnews/africaandindianocean/libya/8839964/Col-Gaddafi-killed-convoy-bombed-by-drone-flown-by-pilot-in-Las-Vegas.html.

39. Joshua Foust, "Do Drones Work?" *American Prospect,* May 15, 2013, http://prospect.org/article/do-drones-work.

40. John Brennan, "The Ethics and Efficacy of the President's Counterterrorism Strategy" (transcript), Wilson Center, April 30, 2012, http://www.wilsoncenter .org/event/the-efficacy-and-ethics-us-counterterrorism-strategy.

41. Cora Currier, "How Does the U.S. Mark Unidentified Men in Pakistan and Yemen as Drone Targets?" *ProPublica,* March 1, 2013, http://www.propublica .org/article/how-does-the-u.s.-mark-unidentified-men-in-pakistan-and-yemen-as-drone-targ.

42. Foust, "Do Drones Work?"

43. Charli Carpenter, "What We Know, Don't Know, Can't Know and Need to Know about the DOD's Classified Study on Drone Deaths," *Duck of Minerva,* July 15, 2013, http://www.whiteoliphaunt.com/duckofminerva/2013/07/what-we-know-dont-know-cant-know-and-need-to-know-about-the-dods-classified-study-on-drone-deaths.html.

44. Greg Miller, "In Interview, Yemeni President Acknowledges Approving U.S. Drone Strikes," *Washington Post,* September 29, 2012, http://articles .washingtonpost.com/2012-09-29/world/35497110_1_drone-strikes-drone-attacks-aqap; David Axe, "Hidden History: America's Secret Drone War in Africa," *Wired: Danger Room,* August 13, 2012, http://www.wired.com/ dangerroom/2012/08/somalia-drones/all/.

45. Mazzetti, "A Secret Deal on Drones."

46. Adam Entous, Siobhan Gorman, and Evan Perez, "U.S. Unease over Drone Strikes," *Wall Street Journal,* September 26, 2012, http://online.wsj.com/ article/SB10000872396390444100404577641520858011452.html.

47. United Nations Office for the High Commissioner of Human Rights, "Statement of the Special Rapporteur Following Meetings in Pakistan," March 14, 2013, http://www.ohchr.org/EN/NewsEvents/Pages/DisplayNews.aspx? NewsID=13146&LangID=E.

48. Eric Posner, "Obama's Drone Dilemma," *Slate,* October 8, 2012, http:// www.slate.com/articles/news_and_politics/view_from_chicago/2012/10/ obama_s_drone_war_is_probably_illegal_will_it_stop_.single.html.

49. Benjamin Wittes, "Implied Consent in Drone Strikes, Congressional Briefings, Dorm Rooms, and Property Disputes," *Lawfare,* September 28, 2012, http://www.lawfareblog.com/2012/09/implied-consent-in-drone-strikes-congressional-briefings-dorm-rooms-and-property-disputes/.

50. Peter Singer, "Do Drones Undermine Democracy?" *New York Times,*

January 21, 2012, http://www.nytimes.com/2012/01/22/opinion/sunday/do-drones-undermine-democracy.html?_r=2&pagewanted=all.

51. Adam Serwer, "When the US Government Can Kill You, Explained," *Mother Jones,* March 5, 2012, http://www.motherjones.com/mojo/2012/03/eric-holder-targeted-killing.

52. Eric Holder, "Attorney General Eric Holder Speaks at Northwestern University School of Law," United States Department of Justice, March 5, 2012, http://www.justice.gov/iso/opa/ag/speeches/2012/ag-speech-1203051.html. See also Marcy Wheeler, "The AUMF Fallacy," *Emptywheel,* February 18, 2013, http://www.emptywheel.net/2013/02/18/the-aumf-fallacy/, for a critique of the Obama administration's interpretation of the AUMF.

53. Michael W. Lewis, "Drones and the Boundaries of the Battlefield," *Texas International Law Journal* 47, no. 293 (2012).

54. John Yoo, "The Real Problem with Obama's Drone Memo," *Wall Street Journal,* February 7, 2013, http://online.wsj.com/article/SB10001424127887323951904578288380180346300.html.

55. Eric Posner, "The Killer Robot War Is Coming," *Slate,* May 15, 2013, http://www.slate.com/articles/news_and_politics/view_from_chicago/2013/05/drone_warfare_and_spying_we_need_new_laws.html.

56. Barack Obama, "Obama's Speech on Drone Policy," *New York Times,* May 23, 2013, http://www.nytimes.com/2013/05/24/us/politics/transcript-of-obamas-speech-on-drone-policy.html?pagewanted=all&_r=0.

57. Christopher Coker, "The Coming of 'Killer Robots,'" *e-International Relations,* May 16, 2013, http://www.e-ir.info/2013/05/16/the-coming-of-killer-robots/.

58. David Wood, "Drone Strikes: A Candid, Chilling Conversation with Top U.S. Drone Pilot," *Huffington Post,* May 15, 2013, http://www.huffingtonpost.com/2013/05/15/drone-strikes_n_3280023.html?utm_hp_ref=tw.

59. Human Rights Watch, "Losing Humanity: The Case against Killer Robots," *International Human Rights Clinic,* November 2012, 1, 3, 4, 5.

60. Kenneth Anderson and Matthew Waxman, "Human Rights Watch Report on Killer Robots and Our Critique," *Lawfare,* November 26, 2012, http://www.lawfareblog.com/2012/11/human-rights-watch-report-on-killer-robots-and-our-critique/; Benjamin Wittes, "Does Human Rights Watch Prefer Disproportionate and Indiscriminate Humans to Discriminating and Proportionate Robots?" *Lawfare,* December 1, 2012, http://www.lawfareblog.com/2012/12/does-human-rights-watch-prefer-disproportionate-and-indiscriminate-humans-to-discriminating-and-proportionate-robots/.

61. Anderson and Waxman, "Human Rights Watch Report on Killer Robots."

62. Wittes, "Disproportionate and Indiscriminate Humans."

63. Joshua Foust, "A Liberal Case for Drones," *Foreign Policy,* May 14, 2013, http://www.foreignpolicy.com/articles/2013/05/14/a_liberal_case_for_drones.

64. Wood, "Drone Strikes."

65. Connor Friedersdorf, "Let's Make Drone Strikes Safe, Legal, and Rare," *Atlantic*, March 27, 2013, http://www.theatlantic.com/politics/archive/2013/03/lets-make-drone-strikes-safe-legal-and-rare/274399/.

66. Glenn Greenwald, "MLK's Vehement Condemnations of US Militarism Are More Relevant Than Ever," *Guardian*, January 21, 2013, http://www.guardian.co.uk/commentisfree/2013/jan/21/king-obama-drones-militarism-sanctions-iran.

67. Singer, *Wired for War*, 42–43.

68. Taylor Owen, "Drones Don't Just Kill, Their Psychological Effects Are Creating Enemies," *Globe and Mail*, March 14, 2013, http://www.theglobeandmail.com/commentary/drones-dont-just-kill-their-psychological-effects-are-creating-enemies/article9707992/.

69. Mockenhaupt, "We've Seen the Future, and It's Unmanned."

70. James Dao, "Drone Pilots Are Found to Get Stress Disorders Much as Those in Combat Do," *New York Times*, February 22, 2013, http://www.nytimes.com/2013/02/23/us/drone-pilots-found-to-get-stress-disorders-much-as-those-in-combat-do.html.

71. Scott Shane, "Coming Soon: The Drone Arms Race," *New York Times*, October 8, 2011, http://www.nytimes.com/2011/10/09/sunday-review/coming-soon-the-drone-arms-race.html?_r=2.

72. Robert Farley, "Over the Horizon: US Drone Use Sets Global Precedent," *World Politics Review*, October 12, 2011, http://www.worldpoliticsreview.com/articles/10311/over-the-horizon-u-s-drone-use-sets-global-precedent.

73. Mark Bowden, "The Killing Machines," *Atlantic*, August 14, 2013, http://www.theatlantic.com/magazine/archive/2013/09/the-killing-machines-how-to-think-about-drones/309434/.

74. Wood, "Drone Strikes."

75. Thomas Ricks, "Cutting the Pentagon Budget: Get Rid of Officer Pilots, Let Enlisted Fly Drones," *ForeignPolicy.com*, September 15, 2010, http://ricks.foreignpolicy.com/posts/2010/09/15/cutting_the_pentagon_budget_get_rid_of_officer_pilots_let_enlisted_fly_drones.

76. Jeff Schogol, "AF Told to Study Rate of UAV Pilots' Promotions," *Air Force Times*, December 29, 2012, http://www.airforcetimes.com/news/2012/12/air-force-rpa-promotions-122912w/.

77. Lolita C. Baldor, "Pentagon Creating New Medal for Drones, Cyberattacks," *Huffington Post*, February 13, 2013, http://www.huffingtonpost.com/2013/02/13/pentagon-drone-medal_n_2678810.html.

78. Chris Carroll, "Hagel Eliminates 'Drone Medal,' Creates Device for Existing Medals," *Stars and Stripes*, April 15, 2013, http://www.stripes.com/news/hagel-eliminates-drone-medal-creates-device-for-existing-medals-1.216722.

79. "Dogfight between MQ-1 Predator Drone and Mig-25 Foxbat," *Youtube.com*, November 19, 2006, http://www.youtube.com/watch?v=wWUR3sgKUV8.

80. "Russian MIG-29 Fighter Shot Down UAV above Georgia," *Youtube.com*, April 22, 2008, http://www.youtube.com/watch?v=U49n1JuWAmc&feature=related.

81. Lawrence Spinetta and M. L. Cummings, "Unloved Aerial Vehicles," *Armed Forces Journal*, November 2012, http://www.armedforcesjournal.com/2012/11/11752540.

82. Spencer Ackerman, "U.S. Troops Will Soon Get Tiny Kamikaze Drone," *Danger Room*, October 18, 2011, http://www.wired.com/dangerroom/2011/10/tiny-kamikaze-drone.

83. Amir Mizroch, "Nano Drones, Ethical Algorithms: Inside Israel's Secret Plan for its Future Air Force," *Wired: Danger Room*, May 11, 2012, http://www.wired.com/dangerroom/2012/05/israel-secret-air-force-plan; "Pentagon Wants Insect-like Nano-Drones," *RT*, May 29, 2008, http://rt.com/news/pentagon-wants-insect-like-nano-drones/.

84. John Reed, "Predator Drones 'Useless' in Most Wars, Top Air Force General Says," *Foreign Policy*, September 19, 2013, http://killerapps.foreignpolicy.com/posts/2013/09/19/predator_drones_useless_in_most_wars_top_air_force_general_says.

85. Patrick B. Johnston and Anoop K. Sarbahi, "The Impact of US Drone Strikes on Terrorism in Pakistan and Afghanistan" (working paper, RAND, January 3, 2013), http://patrickjohnston.info/materials/drones.pdf.

86. Foust, "Do Drones Work?"

87. Reed, "Predator Drones 'Useless.'"

88. Mazzetti, *Way of the Knife*, 91.

89. Micah Zenko, "How Many Civilians Are Killed by U.S. Drones?" *Council of Foreign Relations: Politics, Power, and Prevention*, June 4, 2012, http://blogs.cfr.org/zenko/2012/06/04/how-many-civilians-are-killed-by-u-s-drones/.

90. Eric Schmitt and David E. Sanger, "Pakistan Shift Could Curtail Drone Strikes," *New York Times*, February 22, 2008, http://www.nytimes.com/2008/02/22/washington/22policy.html?_r=0.

91. CBS News, "Boston Bombings Suspect Dzhokhar Tsarnaev Left Note in Boat He Hid in, Sources Say," *CBS News*, May 16, 2013, http://www.cbsnews.com/8301-505263_162-57584771/boston-bombings-suspect-dzhokhar-tsarnaev-left-note-in-boat-he-hid-in-sources-say/.

9. The Way Forward

1. Overy, *The Bombing War*, 42, 627.

2. Bill Sweetman, "Backfire: The Boogeyman Bomber," *Flight International*, December 17, 1977, 1815.

3. Donald Chirpman, "Admiral Gorshkov and the Soviet Navy," *Air University Review*, July–August 1982, http://www.airpower.maxwell.af.mil/airchronicles/aureview/1982/jul-aug/chipman.html.

4. "Troops of National Air Defense (PVO)," *Federation of American Scientists,* September 7, 2000, http://www.fas.org/nuke/guide/russia/agency/pvo .htm.

5. *History of Strategic Air and Ballistic Missile Defense,* vol. 1, *1945–1955* (U.S. Army, 1975), 151, http://www.history.army.mil/html/books/bmd/BMDV1 .pdf.

6. Ibid., 3994; Dale R. Herspring, *The Soviet High Command, 1967–1989* (Princeton, NJ: Princeton University Press, 1990), 135–36.

7. Scrnu Kainikara, "Soviet-Russian Air Power," in Olsen, *Global Air Power,* 4316.

8. Herspring, *The Soviet High Command,* 133, 136, 135.

9. Kainikaru, "Soviet-Russian Air Power," 4263, 4494.

10. Ibid., 4334.

11. Global Security, "Tu-95 Bear (Tupolev)," *Globalsecurity.org,* July 24, 2011, http://www.globalsecurity.org/wmd/world/russia/tu-95-specs.htm.

12. Global Security, "Bombers," *Globalsecurity.org,* July 24, 2011, http://www .globalsecurity.org/wmd/world/russia/bombers.htm.

13. Kainikara, "Soviet-Russian Air Power," 3871.

14. Federation of American Scientists, "Strategic Missile Troops," *Federation of American Scientists,* October 6, 2000, http://www.fas.org/nuke/guide/russia/ agency/rvsn.htm.

15. Lieutenant General Chaim Laskov, Chief of Staff from 1958 until 1961, was primarily an armor officer before serving as commander of the air force shortly prior to his appointment as Chief of Staff.

16. Brun, "Israeli Air Power," 3133.

17. Adamsky, *The Culture of Military Innovation,* 105, 104.

18. Ibid., 105, 104, 107, 94–95.

19. Brun, "Israeli Air Power," 3709, 3745.

20. Lazar Berman, "Beyond the Basics: Looking beyond the Conventional Wisdom Surrounding the IDF Campaigns against Hizbullah and Hamas," *Small Wars Journal,* April 28, 2011, 4–5, http://smallwarsjournal.com/jrnl/art/beyond-the-basics.

21. "Official English Summary of the Winograd's Panel Interim Report" (press release), *Wall Street Journal,* April 30, 2007, 5–7, http://online.wsj.com/ public/resources/documents/winogradreport-04302007.pdf, 7.

22. Builder, *The Icarus Syndrome,* 284.

23. Johnson, *Learning Large Lessons,* xi, xiv–xv, 2, 193–200.

24. Gray, *Airpower for Strategic Effect,* 303, 17–18.

25. Demchak, *Wars of Disruption and Resilience,* 12–13.

26. Vacca, "Military Culture and Cyber Security," 159–60.

27. U.S. Air Force, *Space Operations: Air Force Doctrine Document 2-2* (Washington, DC: Department of the Air Force, 1998), 2–3, 7.

28. Department of Defense, *Space Operations: Joint Publication 3-14* (Washington, DC : Department of Defense, 2009), III-1.

29. Philip Ewing, "The C-27 Truth Vacuum," *DoD Buzz: Online Defense and Acquisition Journal,* March 20, 2012, http://www.dodbuzz.com/2012/03/20/the-c-27-truth-vacuum/.

30. Axe, "Why the U.S. Wants a New Bomber"; Noah Shachtman, "2,400 Miles in Minutes? No Sweat! Hypersonic Weapon Passes 'Easy' Test," *Danger Room,* November 21, 2011, http://www.wired.com/dangerroom/2011/11/2400-miles-in-minutes-hypersonic-weapon-passes-easy-test.

31. John A. Tirpak, "The Sixth Generation Fighter," *Air Force Magazine,* October 2009, 38.

32. Lowe, "Could the COIN Plan Have Saved Lives?"

33. See Scott D. Sagan, *The Limits of Safety: Organizations, Accidents, and Nuclear Weapons* (Princeton, NJ: Princeton University Press, 1993).

34. Wilson, *Bureaucracy,* 192.

35. Don Nicks, "A History of the Air Services in Canada," *CanMilAir.com,* June 20, 2011, http://www.canmilair.com/rcafhistory.htm.

36. "The History of Canada's Air Force: The Creation," *Canadian Wings,* August 23, 2011, http://www.canadianwings.com/history/creation.php.

37. Ibid.; Brereton Greenhouse and Hugh A. Halliday, *Canada's Air Forces, 1914–1999* (Montreal: Editions Art Global and the Department of National Defence, 1999), 120.

38. "No. 405 Squadron," *Canadian Wings: The History and Heritage of Canada's Air Force,* August 24, 2011, http://www.canadianwings.com/Squadrons/squadronDetail.php?No.-405-Squadron-64.

39. "Canada's Naval History," *Canadian War Museum,* May 4, 2010, http://www.civilization.ca/cwm/exhibitions/navy/galery-e.aspx?section=2-F-4.

40. "Unification," *Canadiansoldiers.com,* November 27, 2010, http://www.canadiansoldiers.com/organization/unification.htm.

41. K. W. Bailey, "Integration and Unification Equals Jointness in 21st Century Canadian Forces," *Canadian Forces College,* May 6, 2002, 2, http://www.cfc.forces.gc.ca/papers/csc/csc28/mds/bailey.pdf.

42. Daniel Gosselin and Craig Stone, "From Minister Hellyer to General Hillier: Understanding the Fundamental Difference between the Unification of the Canadian Forces and Its Present Transformation," *Canadian Military Journal,* Winter 2005–2006, 6.

43. Daniel Gosselin, "Hellyer's Ghosts: Unification of the Canadian Forces Is 40 Years Old," *Canadian Military Journal,* October 30, 2008, http://www.journal.dnd.ca/v09/n02/03-gosselin-eng.asp.

44. "Unification."

45. Canadian Military History Gateway, "Implementing Unification," March 29, 2011, http://www.cmhg.gc.ca/cmh/page-709-eng.asp.

46. David P. Burke, "Hellyer and Landymore: The Unification of the Canadian Armed Forces and an Admiral's Revolt," *American Review of Canadian Studies* 2, no. 8 (1978): 3–4.

47. Devin Conley, "Policies of Change and the Canadian Forces: An Institutional Analysis" (Canadian Forces College, April 21, 2010), 22.

48. Wolf Lund, "Integration and Unification of the Canadian Forces," *CFB Esquimalt Naval and Military Museum*, 2011, http://www.navalandmilitarymuseum.org/resource_pages/controversies/unification.html.

49. J.P.Y.D Gosselin, "Unification and the Strong Service Idea: A 50-Year Tug of War of Concepts at Crossroads" (Canadian Forces College, June 1, 2004), 30.

50. Canadian Military History Gateway, "Naval Resistance," March 29, 2011, http://www.cmhg.gc.ca/cmh/page-710-eng.asp.

51. Nicks, "A History of the Air Services in Canada."

52. Geoffrey D. T. Shaw, "The Canadian Armed Forces and Unification," *Defense Analysis* 17, no. 2 (2000): 164.

53. Canadian Military History Gateway, "Naval Resistance."

54. Ibid.

55. F. M. Boomer, "Joint or Combined Doctrine? The Right Choice for Canada," *Canadian Forces College: Advanced Military Studies Course 1,* November 5, 1998.

56. Gosselin, "Unification and the Strong Service Idea," 4.

57. Gosselin and Stone, "From Minister Hellyer to General Hillier," 8.

58. Bailey, "Integration and Unification Equals Jointness in 21st Century Canadian Forces," 3.

59. J. H. Pocklington, "Professionalism and the Canadian Military," *Air University Review,* March–April 1976, http://www.airpower.au.af.mil/airchronicles/aureview/1976/mar-apr/pocklington.html.

60. Shaw, "The Canadian Armed Forces and Unification," 177.

61. Douglas Bland, "Books Critiques: Damn the Torpedoes; My Fight to Unify Canada's Armed Forces," *Canadian Defence Quarterly,* October 1990, http://centreforforeignpolicystudies.dal.ca/cdq/Bland%200ctober%201990.PDF.

Conclusion

1. Walter Pincus, "Air Force Unit's Nuclear Weapons Security Is 'Unacceptable,'" *Washington Post,* May 31, 2008, http://www.washingtonpost.com/wp-dyn/content/article/2008/05/30/AR2008053003120.html.

2. Chuck Spinney, "The Heritage Foundation, Then and Now," *Time: Battleland,* January 10, 2012, http://battleland.blogs.time.com/2012/01/10/the-heritage-foundation-then-and-now/.

3. David A. Fulgham and Bill Sweetman, "New Bomber Brings ISR Surprises," *Aviationweek.com,* August 29, 2011, http://www.aviationweek.com/aw/generic/

story.jsp?topicName=Ibm&id=news/awst/2011/08/29/AW_08_29_2011_p44–358680.xml&headline=New%20Bomber%20Brings%20ISR%20Surprises&channel=&from=specialreports.

4. Norton A. Schwartz, "The Way Ahead," *CSAF's Vector*, July 4, 2010, http://smallwarsjournal.com/documents/csafvector.pdf.

5. Shachtman, "How the Afghanistan War Got Stuck in the Sky."

6. R. Jordan Prescott, "AirSea Battle as Presently Conceived," *Small Wars Journal*, January 11, 2012, http://smallwarsjournal.com/blog/airsea-battle-as-presently-conceived.

7. Air Force Association, "About Us," January 6, 2012, http://www.afa.org/AboutUs/default.asp#top.

8. Bruce Rolfsen, "$59 Million Sought for Awareness Campaign," *Air Force Times*, February 18, 2008, http://www.airforcetimes.com/news/2008/02/airforce_advertising_budget_080218w/.

9. Gross, *American Military Aviation*, 188–89.

10. "Goldwater-Nichols Department of Defense Reorganization Act of 1986."

11. Dana Priest, *The Mission: Waging War and Keeping Peace with America's Military* (New York: Norton, 2003), 61–77.

12. Robert Farley, "Syria, Iran, and the Enduring Allure of Airpower," *World Politics Review*, January 25, 2012, http://www.worldpoliticsreview.com/articles/11279/over-the-horizon-syria-iran-and-the-enduring-allure-of-airpower.

13. Spencer Ackerman, "While Libya War Grows, Obama Team Denies It's a War," *Danger Room*, March 24, 2011, http://www.wired.com/dangerroom/2011/03/while-libya-war-grows-obama-team-denies-its-a-war/.

Selected Bibliography

Abella, Alex. *Soldiers of Reason: The RAND Corporation and the Rise of the American Empire.* Orlando: Harcourt, 2008.

Adamsky, Dima. *The Culture of Military Innovation.* Stanford, CA: Stanford University Press, 2010.

Biddle, Stephen. "Victory Misunderstood: What the Gulf War Tells Us about the Future of Conflict." *International Security* 21, no. 2 (1996): 139–79.

Biddle, Tami Davis. *Rhetoric and Reality in Air Warfare: The Evolution of British and American Ideas about Strategic Bombing, 1914–1945.* Princeton, NJ: Princeton University Press, 2002.

Boyle, Andrew. *Trenchard.* London: Collins, 1962.

Builder, Carl H. *The Icarus Syndrome: The Role of Air Power Theory in the Evolution and Fate of the U.S. Air Force.* New Brunswick, NJ: Transaction, 1994.

———. *The Masks of War: American Military Styles in Strategy and Analysis.* Baltimore: Johns Hopkins University Press, 1989.

Clodfelter, Mark. *Beneficial Bombing: The Progressive Foundations of American Air Power, 1917–1945.* Lincoln: University of Nebraska Press, 2010.

———. *The Limits of Air Power: The American Bombing of North Vietnam.* New York: Free Press, 1989.

Crane, Conrad. *American Airpower Strategy in Korea, 1950–1953.* Lawrence: University of Kansas Press, 2000.

Douhet, Giulio. *The Command of the Air.* Washington, DC: Air Force History and Museums Program, 1998.

Dunlap, Charles J., Jr. "America's Asymmetric Advantage." *Armed Forces Journal,* September 2006, http://www.armedforcesjournal.com/2006/09/2009013.

———. *Shortchanging the Joint Fight? An Airman's Assessment of FM 3-24 and the Case for Developing Truly Joint COIN Doctrine.* Maxwell AFB, AL: Air University Press, 2008.

Ehrhard, Thomas P. *Air Force UAVs: The Secret History.* Ft. Belvoir, VA: Defense Technical Information Center, 2010.

Fahey, John. "Britain, 1939–1945: The Economic Cost of Strategic Bombing." PhD diss., University of Sydney, 2004.

Futrell, Robert Frank. *Ideas, Concepts, Doctrine: Basic Thinking in the United States Air Force, 1907–1960.* Maxwell AFB, AL: Air University Press, 1989.

Gentile, Gian. *How Effective Is Strategic Bombing? Lessons Learned from World War II and Kosovo* [Kindle edition]. New York: NYU Press, 2001.

Gray, Colin. "Understanding Airpower: Bonfire of the Fallacies." *Strategic Studies Quarterly* 1, no. 2 (2008): 43–83.

Gray, Peter. *The Leadership, Direction, and Legitimacy of the RAF Bomber Offensive from Inception to 1945.* Birmingham War Studies. London: Continuum, 2012.

Grayling, A. C. *Among the Dead Cities: The History and Moral Legacy of the WWII Bombing of Civilians in Germany and Japan.* New York: Walker, 2006.

Greer, Thomas. *The Development of Doctrine in the Army Air Arm, 1917–1941.* Washington, DC: Office of Air Force History, 1985.

Gross, Charles J. *American Military Aviation: The Indispensable Arm.* College Station: Texas A&M University Press, 2002.

Headquarters Department of the Army. *Field Manual 3-24, Counterinsurgency.* December 15, 2006, E-1, http://usacac.leavenworth.army.mil/CAC2/COIN/repository/FM_3-24.pdf.

Higham, Robin, and Mark Parillo, eds. *The Influence of Airpower upon History: Statesmanship, Diplomacy, and Foreign Policy since 1916.* Lexington: University Press of Kentucky, 2013.

Hurley, Alfred F. *Billy Mitchell: Crusader for Air Power.* Bloomington: Indiana University Press, 2006.

Johnston, Alastair Iain. "Thinking about Strategic Culture." *International Security* 19, no. 4 (1995): 32–64.

Keaney, Thomas A., and Eliot A. Cohen. *Gulf War Air Power Survey Summary Report.* Washington, DC: Department of the Air Force, 1993.

Kier, Elizabeth. *Imagining War: French and British Military Doctrine between the Wars.* Princeton, NJ: Princeton University Press, 1997.

Luck, Christopher J. *The Smuts Report: Interpreting and Misinterpreting the Promise of Airpower.* Maxwell AFB, AL: Air University Press, 2007.

Maurer, Maurer. *Aviation in the U.S. Army, 1919–1939.* Washington, DC: Office of Air Force History, 1987.

Mazzetti, Mark. *The Way of the Knife: The CIA, a Secret Army, and a War at the Ends of the Earth.* New York: Penguin, 2013.

Meilinger, Phillip S. "Airpower and Collateral Damage: Theory, Practice, and Challenges." *Air Power Australia Essay on Military Ethics and Culture*, April 15, 2013, http://www.ausairpower.net/APA-EMEAC-2013-02.html.

———. *Airpower: Theory and Practice.* Oxford: Frank & Cass, 2003.

———, ed. *The Paths of Heaven: The Evolution of Airpower Theory.* Maxwell AFB: Air University Press, 1997.

Michel, Marshall L., III. *Clashes: Air Combat over North Vietnam, 1965–1972.* Annapolis, MD: Naval Institute Press, 1997.

Murdock, Clark A., et al. *Beyond Goldwater Nichols: Defense Reform for a New*

Strategic Era, Phase 1 Report. Washington, DC: Center for Strategic and International Studies, 2004.

Murray, Williamson, and Allan R. Millet. *A War to Be Won: Fighting the Second World War*. Cambridge, MA: Belknap Press of Harvard University Press, 2000.

Olsen, John Andreas, ed. *Global Air Power* [Kindle edition]. Washington, DC: Potomac, 2011.

———, ed. *A History of Air Warfare*. Washington, DC: Potomac, 2010.

———. *John Warden and the Renaissance of American Air Power* [Kindle edition]. Washington, DC: Potomac, 2007.

Orange, Vincent. *Slessor: Bomber Champion*. London: Grub Street, 2006.

Overy, Richard. *The Bombing War: Europe, 1939–1945*. London: Allen Lane, 2013.

Pape, Robert A. *Bombing to Win: Air Power and Coercion in War*. Ithaca, NY: Cornell University Press, 1996.

———. "The True Worth of Air Power." *Foreign Affairs* 83, no. 2 (2004): 116–30.

Press, Daryl. "The Myth of Air Power in the Persian Gulf War and the Future of Warfare." *International Security* 26, no. 2 (2001): 5–44.

Rosen, Stephen Peter. *Winning the Next War: Innovation and the Modern Military*. Ithaca, NY: Cornell University Press, 1991.

Schelling, Thomas C. *Arms and Influence*. New Haven, CT: Yale University Press, 1966.

Schoenfeld, Maxwell Philip. *Stalking the U-Boat: USAAF Offensive Antisubmarine Operations in World War II*. Washington, DC: Smithsonian Institution Press, 1995.

Sebald, W. G. *On the Natural History of Destruction*. New York: Random House, 2003.

Shaw, Geoffrey D. T. "The Canadian Armed Forces and Unification." *Defense Analysis* 17, no. 2 (2000): 159–74.

Shultz, Richard H., and Robert L. Pfaltzgraff Jr., eds. *The Future of Air Power in the Aftermath of the Gulf War*. Maxwell AFB, AL: Air University Press, 1992.

Smith, Perry McCoy. *The Air Force Plans for Peace, 1943–1945*. Baltimore: Johns Hopkins University Press, 1970.

Tate, James P. *The Army and Its Air Corps: Army Policy toward Aviation, 1919–1941*. Maxwell AFB, AL: Air University Press, 1998.

Van Crevald, Martin. *Age of Airpower* [Kindle edition]. New York: Public Affairs, 2011.

Walzer, Michael. *Just and Unjust Wars*. New York: Perseus Books Group, 2006.

Warden, John A., III. *The Air Campaign: Planning for Combat*. Washington, DC: National Defense University Press, 1988.

———. "Strategy and Airpower." *Air and Space Power Journal*, Spring 2011, 65–77.

Watts, Barry D. *The Foundations of U.S. Air Doctrine: The Problem of Friction in War.* Maxwell AFB, AL: Air University Press, 1984.

Weinberg, Gerhard L. *A World at Arms: A Global History of World War II.* Cambridge: Cambridge University Press, 1994.

Wolf, Richard Irving, ed. *The United States Air Force: Basic Documents on Roles and Missions.* Washington, DC: Office of Air Force History, 1987.

Index